The Meaning of the Body

MARK JOHNSON

The Meaning of the Body

AESTHETICS OF HUMAN UNDERSTANDING

The University of Chicago Press   Chicago & London

MARK JOHNSON is the Knight Professor of Liberal Arts and Sciences in the Department of Philosophy at the University of Oregon. He is the author of *The Body in the Mind: The Bodily Basis of Meaning, Imagination, and Reason* and *Moral Imagination: Implications of Cognitive Science for Ethics* and coauthor, with George Lakoff, of *Metaphors We Live By* and *Philosophy in the Flesh: The Embodied Mind and Its Challenge to Western Thought.*

The University of Chicago Press, Chicago 60637
The University of Chicago Press, Ltd., London
© 2007 by The University of Chicago
All rights reserved. Published 2007
Printed in the United States of America

16 15 14 13 12 11 10 09 08 07   1 2 3 4 5

ISBN-13: 978-0-226-40192-8   (cloth)
ISBN-10: 0-226-40192-8   (cloth)

Library of Congress Cataloging-in-Publication Data
Johnson, Mark, 1949–
    The meaning of the body : aesthetics of human understanding / Mark Johnson.
       p.   cm.
    Includes bibliographical references and index.
    ISBN-13: 978-0-226-40192-8 (cloth : alk. paper)
    ISBN-10: 0-226-40192-8 (cloth : alk. paper)
    1. Meaning (Philosophy).   2. Body, Human (Philosophy)   3. Aesthetics.   I. Title.
    B105.M4.J65   2007
    121'.68—dc22

                                                                            2006100532

CONTENTS

Color plates follow page 206

The Need for an Aesthetics of Human Meaning

People want their lives to be meaningful. This desire—this *eros*—for meaning is so strong in us that we are sometimes even willing to risk death in our pursuit of meaning and fulfillment. It is our need to make sense of our experience and to inquire into its overall meaning and significance that has kept philosophy alive since the dawn of reflective thinking in our species. When philosophy ceases to further our quest for meaning—when it stops addressing the recurring problems that define the human condition—it loses its relevance to human existence.

Unfortunately, meaning is a big, messy, multidimensional concept that is applied to everything from grandiose notions like the meaning of life all the way down to the specific meanings of single words or even morphemes. This book is about meaning—what it is, where it comes from, and how it is made. The guiding theme is that meaning grows from our visceral connections to life and the bodily conditions of life. We are born into the world as creatures of the flesh, and it is through our bodily perceptions, movements, emotions, and feelings that meaning becomes possible and takes the forms it does. From the day we are brought kicking and screaming into the world, what and how anything is meaningful to us is shaped by our specific form of incarnation.

My work over the past three decades has focused primarily on the bodily sources of meaning, imagination, and reasoning. I drew from phenomenology, linguistics, and the newly emerging cognitive sciences to explain how aspects of our bodily experience give rise to our conceptualization and reasoning. However, I have come to realize that, even though I then regarded these earlier efforts as revealing the very heart of human meaning-making, nevertheless, I had not grasped the deepest and most profound bodily sources of meaning. In retrospect, I now see that the structural aspects of our bodily interactions with our environment upon which I was focusing were themselves dependent on even more submerged dimensions of bodily understanding. It was an important step to probe below concepts, propositions, and sentences into the sensorimotor processes by which we understand our world, but what is now needed is a far deeper exploration into the qualities, feelings, emotions, and bodily processes that make meaning possible.

Once I took the leap into these deep, visceral origins of meaning, I soon realized that I was dealing with aspects of experience traditionally regarded as the purview of aesthetics. If this was true, then aesthetics must not be narrowly construed as the study of art and so-called aesthetic experience. Instead, aesthetics becomes the study of everything that goes into the human capacity to make and experience meaning. This entailed that an aesthetics of human understanding should become the basis for all philosophy, including metaphysics, theory of knowledge, logic, philosophy of mind and language, and value theory.

There is a rich tradition in American philosophy, culminating in the work of the pragmatist philosopher John Dewey, which gives pride of place to aesthetics. Unfortunately, most Anglo-American philosophy in the twentieth century ignored or even rejected this pragmatist tradition. What followed was an analytic philosophy built on the marginalizing of aesthetics and the championing of a narrow view of meaning as conceptual and propositional in character.

I contend that this mainstream, and still dominant, tradition has only the most meager resources for dealing with the deepest sources of human meaning. Consequently, much contemporary philosophy focuses exclusively on abstract conceptual and propositional structure, leaving us with a very superficial and eviscerated view of mind, thought, and language. These philosophers have developed elaborate conceptual schemes for identifying the so-called cognitive, structural, and formal aspects of experience, thought, and language, but they lack adequate philosophical resources to plumb the depths of the qualitative feeling dimensions of experience and meaning. Although some phenomenological traditions do address these affective dimensions, phenomenology has been marginalized within mainstream Anglo-American philosophy and has consequently not had the salutary influence on our conception of human understanding that it deserves.

However, there is good news. In the past few years the cognitive neurosciences have begun to entice even hardcore analytic philosophers of mind and language to pay more attention to the vast, submerged continents of nonconscious thought and feeling that lie at the heart of our ability to make sense of our lives. A major part of what I have to say in this book about the nature of meaning and thinking draws on some of these recent developments in the new sciences of embodied mind. I attempt to blend work from cognitive science with traditional phenomenological description, in order to provide an enriched view of human meaning-making.

I will argue that the chief reason that certain philosophers neglect notions like quality, emotion, and feeling is their mistaken view of these as nothing but subjective mental states that are "merely aesthetic" matters of subjective judgment and taste. There is today still a pervasive cultural misunderstanding of, and consequent prejudice against, aesthetics. When the arts are misconceived as a minor, nonpractical, wholly subjective dimension of human life, aesthetics becomes merely a tertiary enterprise having little perceived relevance to the nature of mind and cognition. This "subjectivization of the aesthetic" (as Hans-Georg Gadamer calls it) has led to a number of unfortunate consequences, both for our lives and for our philosophies of meaning and value. Chief among these harmful misconceptions are that (1) the mind is disembodied, (2) thinking transcends feeling, (3) feelings are not part of meaning and knowledge, (4) aesthetics concerns matters of mere subjective taste, and (5) the arts are a luxury (rather than being conditions of full human flourishing).

Following Dewey, I want to turn these misconceptions on their head by showing that aesthetics must become the basis of any profound understanding of meaning and thought. Aesthetics is properly an investigation of everything that goes into human meaning-making, and its traditional focus on the arts stems primarily from the fact that arts are exemplary cases of consummated meaning. However, any adequate aesthetics of cognition must range far beyond the arts proper to explore how meaning is possible for creatures with our types of bodies, environments, and cultural institutions and practices.

In short, this book is about the bodily depths of human meaning-making through our visceral connection to our world. It will become clear as my account develops that I am using the term "meaning" in its broadest and most profound sense. I am going to argue that meaning is not just a matter of concepts and propositions, but also reaches down into the images, sensorimotor schemas, feelings, qualities, and emotions that constitute our meaningful encounter with our world. Any adequate account of meaning must be built around the aesthetic dimensions that give our experience its distinctive character and significance. A philosophy capable of making a difference for how people ought to live must be grounded on how we make sense of things. What we need, in short, is an aesthetics of human understanding. This is a big, sweeping task, but one well worth the journey for anyone who cares about what it means to be human.

I have organized my exploration into three major sections. Part 1 ("Bodily Meaning and Felt Sense") attempts to provide a thick description of the bodily origins of meaning in sensorimotor processes and in feelings. We have to start deep down in the bodily processes where meaning emerges, lives, and grows. My emphasis is on qualities and structures of embodied meaning in movement, infant and childhood development, emotions, and conceptualization and reasoning. My descriptions of the richness and depth of bodily meaning are intended to remind us how meaning arises before we are even aware of it and how that preconscious meaning underlies our higher-level achievements of thinking and communicating.

Part 2 ("Embodied Meaning and the Sciences of Mind") draws on cognitive science and neuroscience to probe the bodily roots of meaning, concepts, and language. This section is necessarily highly selective and partial. I locate human cognition within a broader evolutionary framework of animal cognition, in which sensorimotor capacities play a key role in how any animal experiences and makes sense of its world. Our connection to nonhuman animals reveals that what is known as the representational theory of mind, according to which the mind supposedly operates on internal mental representations of external states, is highly problematic, if not downright false. If mind and body are not two separate and distinct ontological kinds, then thought must emerge via recruitment of various sensorimotor capacities that do not involve internal representations. I therefore reject the classical representational theory of mind, replacing it with an account of embodied meaning that emerges as structures of organism-environment interactions or transactions. I also propose some plausible neurophysiological structures that might underlie the feelings, emotions, images, concepts, and patterns of reasoning that make up human experience and understanding.

Part 3 ("Embodied Meaning, Aesthetics, and Art") argues that various arts make use of the very same structures and processes that operate in ordinary, everyday meaning-making, including images, image schemas, metaphors, qualities, feelings, and emotions. As John Dewey argued seventy years ago in *Art as Experience,* art is not a distinct type of disinterested, nonpractical experience that requires unique forms of judgment and evaluation. On the contrary, art matters because it provides heightened, intensified, and highly integrated experiences of meaning, using all of our ordinary resources for meaning-making. If this is true, then we can find no better examples of how meaning happens than by attending to the arts. I examine some aspects of meaning in poetry, painting, and music. I am led to embrace Dewey's insistence that the arts are important just insofar as they help us grasp, criticize, and transform meanings and values. I end by summarizing the view of meaning, thought, and language that arises from my exploration of embodied meaning, suggesting that philosophy will matter to people only to the extent that it is built on a visceral connection to our world.

ACKNOWLEDGMENTS

Two decades ago, Tom Alexander introduced me to John Dewey's important insight that it is primarily in the aesthetic dimensions of experience that we encounter consummated human meaning. Tom opened my eyes to the felt qualitative unity of situations, beneath the level of propositional and sentential structure, that gives rise to meaning and thought. This book explores that profound idea, as well as Dewey's nondualistic view of the embodied mind.

I realized that to probe the depths of meaning, no single approach or method alone could tell the whole story. I had to employ a plurality of methods, from classical American pragmatism to phenomenology to cognitive science. From the pragmatist tradition, I have benefited most from the writings of William James and John Dewey, about whom I have learned most of what I know from ongoing conversations with scores of members of the Society for the Advancement of American Philosophy. I value that society because it provides a supportive atmosphere that encourages an open, pluralistic discussion of real-life problems. In phenomenology, I resonate most deeply with the body-based approach of Maurice Merleau-Ponty, and I have learned a great deal about his philosophy from conversation with and reading phenomenologists such as Franciso Varela, Shaun Gallagher, David Levin, Eugene Gendlin, and my University of Oregon colleagues Beata Stawarska, John Lysaker, and Louise Westling. On the side of cognitive science, I am indebted to ongoing dialogue with my dear friend George Lakoff, who first introduced me to the importance of cognitive neuroscience for understanding mind, thought, and language.

I have also benefited immensely from the writings of Antonio Damasio, Gerald Edelman, Paul and Patricia Churchland, Vittorio Gallese, and my colleague Don Tucker, all of whom have created a dialogue between philosophy and the empirical research of the sciences of the mind.

Several people provided crucial feedback on my manuscript, especially Shaun Gallagher, Tim Rohrer, and Steve Larson, each of whom read the entire work and gave detailed criticisms and suggestions for improvement. My gratitude toward them is heartfelt and considerable. Scott Pratt and Don Tucker read and commented on parts of the manuscript, providing many important suggestions. For several years now, Scott has proved himself a most valuable interlocutor in our ongoing explorations of some of the key themes in this book. I have learned much from him about American pragmatism by auditing his seminars and by discussing our mutual interests, especially on our trout-fishing expeditions in the Cascade mountains. I want to express my deep gratitude to Nancy Trotic for her meticulous editorial work on this book. It was my good fortune to have an editor who understood my project and took remarkable care in helping me express myself more clearly, concisely, and elegantly than in my earlier drafts. I found Nancy to be a force of nature. She overwhelmed me with constructive suggestions for improving my arguments and giving proper attention to every detail. I cannot thank her enough.

I have been blessed with many wonderful former and current students who, in both classes and personal conversations, have helped me formulate my central ideas over the past few years. They include Don Morse, Tim Rohrer, Tim Adamson, Arnie Cox, Steven Brown, Gary Wright, Mary Magada-Ward, Jen McWeeny, John Kaag, Eric Olofson, and Diego Fernandez-Duque.

My wife, Sandra McMorris Johnson, is an artist. The beauty of her personality and artworks gives daily witness to the importance of the aesthetic dimensions of experience in our human search for meaning.

★   ★   ★

The account of Gendlin's philosophy in chapter 4 is taken, with only slight revisions, from my longer assessment of Gendlin's work in "Embodied Meaning and Cognitive Science," in *Language beyond Postmodernism: Saying and Thinking in Gendlin's Philosophy,* ed. David Michael Levin, 148–75 (Evanston, IL: Northwestern University Press, 1997).

Parts of chapter 7 are taken, with revisions, from my article "The Philosophical Significance of Image Schemas," in *From Perception to Meaning:*

Image Schemas in Cognitive Linguistics, ed. B. Hampe and J. Grady, 15–33 (Berlin: Mouton de Gruyter, 2005).

Much of chapter 6, substantial parts of chapter 7, and a small part of chapter 9 are based on an article I co-authored with Tim Rohrer, "We Are Live Creatures: Embodiment, American Pragmatism, and the Cognitive Organism," to appear in *Body, Language, and Mind,* ed. R. Frank, R. Dirven, T. Ziemke, and J. Zlater (Berlin: Mouton de Gruyter). This material is used with the permission of Tim Rohrer, René Dirven, and Anke Beck. Much of our jointly written article appears in the chapters here, with some substantial additions and deletions of material. I am indebted to Tim Rohrer especially for the sections on the biology and cognitive science of organisms, from one-celled animals up through primates.

Part of chapter 9 is taken, with minor revisions, from my essay "Philosophy's Debt to Metaphor," in *The Cambridge Handbook of Metaphor and Thought,* ed. R. W. Gibbs (Cambridge: Cambridge University Press, forthcoming). The analysis in chapter 9 of causal concepts, along with their role in shaping philosophy, is adapted (with minor changes) from chapter 11 of George Lakoff and Mark Johnson, *Philosophy in the Flesh: The Embodied Mind and Its Challenge to Western Thought* (New York: Basic Books, 1999).

The analysis in chapter 11 of the three major conceptual metaphors by which we understand musical motion is taken directly, with some revisions and several major deletions, from Mark Johnson and Steve Larson, "'Something in the Way She Moves': Metaphors of Musical Motion," *Metaphor and Symbol* 18, no. 2 (2003): 63–84.

Meaning Is More Than Words and Deeper Than Concepts

The central thesis of this book is that what we call "mind" and what we call "body" are not two things, but rather aspects of one organic process, so that all our meaning, thought, and language emerge from the aesthetic dimensions of this embodied activity. Chief among those aesthetic dimensions are qualities, images, patterns of sensorimotor processes, and emotions. For at least the past three decades, scholars and researchers in many disciplines have piled up arguments and evidence for the embodiment of mind and meaning. However, the implications of this research have not entered public consciousness, and so the denial of mind/body dualism is still a highly provocative claim that most people find objectionable and even threatening. Coming to grips with your embodiment is one of the most profound philosophical tasks you will ever face. Acknowledging that every aspect of human being is grounded in specific forms of bodily engagement with an environment requires a far-reaching rethinking of who and what we are, in a way that is largely at odds with many of our inherited Western philosophical and religious traditions.

To see what this reconceptualization means, consider this: The best biology, psychology, cognitive neuroscience, and phenomenology available today teach us that our human forms of experience, consciousness, thought, and communication would not exist without our brains, operating as an organic part of our functioning bodies, which, in turn, are actively engaged with the specific kinds of physical, social, and cultural environments that humans dwell in. Change your brain, your body, or your environments in nontrivial ways, and you will change how you experience your world, what things are meaningful to you, and even who you are.

THE ILLUSION OF DISEMBODIED MIND

Contrast this embodiment hypothesis with our commonsense view of mind. Although most people never think about it very carefully, they live their lives assuming and acting according to a set of dichotomies that distinguish mind from body, reason from emotion, and thought from feeling. Mind/body dualism is so deeply embedded in our philosophical and religious traditions, in our shared conceptual systems, and in our language that it can seem to be an inescapable fact about human nature. One pervasive manifestation of this dualism in many of our ethical, political, and religious practices is the assumption that we possess a radically free will, which is assumed to exist apart from our bodies and to be capable of controlling them. We postulate a "higher" self (the rational part) that must seek to control the "lower" self (body, desire, emotion). We assume that each of us has an inner core (a "true self" or a "soul") that transcends our bodily, situated self. We buy into the notion of thinking as a pure, conceptual, body-transcending activity, even if we realize that no thinking occurs without a brain.

This pervasive illusion of disembodied mind, thought, and meaning is beautifully explored and criticized by the American poet Billy Collins, who unmasks our dream of pure thought by showing that we can think and imagine only through our bodies.

PURITY

My favorite time to write is in the late afternoon,
weekdays, particularly Wednesdays.
This is how I go about it:
I take a fresh pot of tea into my study and close the door.
Then I remove my clothes and leave them in a pile
as if I had melted to death and my legacy consisted of only
a white shirt, a pair of pants and a pot of cold tea.

Then I remove my flesh and hang it over a chair.
I slide it off my bones like a silken garment.
I do this so that what I write will be pure,
completely rinsed of the carnal,
uncontaminated by the preoccupations of the body.

Finally I remove each of my organs and arrange them
on a small table near the window.
I do not want to hear their ancient rhythms
when I am trying to tap out my own drumbeat.

Now I sit down at the desk, ready to begin.
I am entirely pure: nothing but a skeleton at a typewriter.

I should mention that sometimes I leave my penis on.
I find it difficult to ignore the temptation.
Then I am a skeleton with a penis at a typewriter.
In this condition I write extraordinary love poems,
most of them exploiting the connection between sex and death.

I am concentration itself: I exist in a universe
where there is nothing but sex, death, and typewriting.

After a spell of this I remove my penis too.
Then I am all skull and bones typing into the afternoon.
Just the absolute essentials, no flounces.
Now I write only about death, most classical of themes
in language light as the air between my ribs.

Afterward, I reward myself by going for a drive at sunset.
I replace my organs and slip back into my flesh
and clothes. Then I back the car out of the garage
and speed through woods on winding country roads,
passing stone walls, farmhouses, and frozen ponds,
all perfectly arranged like words in a famous sonnet.

Ah, if only mind could float free of its carnal entanglements, thinking pure thoughts of things certain, eternal, and good. *But that is a dysfunctional dream!* It is our organic flesh and blood, our structural bones, the ancient rhythms of our internal organs, and the pulsing flow of our emotions that give us whatever meaning we can find and that shape our very thinking. Collins humorously reminds us that if we want to write great love poems (or any poems), we had better retain not just our sexual organs, but also our whole fleshy body, with all of its desires, emotions, and moods.

HOW THE BODY HIDES OUT

René Descartes, one of the most famous mind/body dualists in the Western philosophical tradition, argued that just by clear thinking, we can indubitably see that mind and body are two radically different and distinct kinds of thing:

> I have a complete understanding of what a body is when I think that it is merely something having extension, shape and motion, and I deny that it has anything which belongs to the nature of a mind. Conversely, I understand the mind to be a complete thing, which doubts, understands, wills, and so on, even though I deny that it has any of the attributes which are contained in the idea of a body. This would be quite impossible if there were not a real distinction between the mind and the body. (Descartes 1641/1984, 86)

> Simply by knowing that I exist and seeing at the same time that absolutely nothing else belongs to my nature or essence except that I am a thinking thing, I can infer correctly that my essence consists solely in the fact that I am a thinking thing. It is true that I may have (or, to anticipate, that I certainly have) a body that is very closely joined to me. But nevertheless, on the one hand I have a clear and distinct idea of myself, in so far as I am simply a thinking, non-extended thing; and on the other hand I have a distinct idea of body, in so far as this is simply an extended, non-thinking thing. And accordingly, it is certain that I am really distinct from my body, and can exist without it. (Descartes 1641/1984, 54)

Why should it seem so obvious to most people that mind and body are two, not one? One important reason is that our lived experience itself reinforces an apparently inescapable dualistic view of mind versus body. We don't have to work to ignore the working of our bodies. On the contrary, our bodies hide themselves from us in their very acts of making meaning and experience possible. The way we experience things appears to have a dualistic character. Ironically, it is the nature of our bodies and brains that gives rise to this experience of a split (mental plus physical) self.

Drew Leder (1990), following the groundbreaking work of Maurice Merleau-Ponty (1962), has catalogued the many ways in which the successful functioning of our bodies requires that our bodily organs and operations recede and even hide in our acts of experiencing things in the world. One of the chief ways the body hides from our conscious awareness is a result of what Michael Polanyi (1969) called the "from-to" character of perception. All our acts of perception are directed *to* or *at* what is experienced and *away from* the body doing the perceiving. This is what phenomenologists call the *intentionality* of the mind. In Polanyi's words, "Our body is the only assembly of things known almost exclusively by relying on our awareness of them for attending to something else. . . . Every time we make sense of the world, we rely on our tacit knowledge of impacts made by the world on our body and the complex responses of our body to these impacts" (1969, 147–48).

For example, our acts of seeing are directed toward and focused on what we see. Our intentionality seems to be directed "out there" into the world. The mechanisms of our vision are not, and cannot be, the focus of our awareness and attention. We are aware of what we see, but not of our seeing. The bodily processes hide, in order to make possible our fluid, automatic experiencing of the world. As Leder says, "It is thus possible to state a general principle: insofar as I perceive through an organ, it necessarily recedes from the perceptual field it discloses. I do not smell my nasal tissue, hear my ear, or taste my taste buds but perceive with and through such organs" (1990, 14). In a discussion of the "ecstatic body," Leder names this perceptual hiding of the body "focal disappearance" of the specific bodily organs and activities of perception.

In addition to focal disappearance of our perceptual organs, there is also a necessary "background disappearance" of other processes and activities that make perception possible, processes of which we are seldom, if ever, aware. This includes such things as the complex of bodily adjustments and movements that make it possible for a certain perception to occur. I see *with* my eyes (which undergo focal disappearance), but that seeing would be impossible without those eyes' existence in a body that makes a number of fine adjustments, such as holding the head in a certain way, keeping the body erect and pointed in a certain direction, and moving the body in ways that ensure a clear line of sight. When I reach out to pick up a cup, I am not aware of the multitude of fine motor adjustments or the ongoing cooperation of hand and eye that make it possible for me to locate and touch the handle of the cup.

Emphasizing dimensions of nonconscious bodily processes, Shaun Gallagher has usefully distinguished between our *body image,* which involves "a system of perceptions, attitudes, and beliefs pertaining to one's own body," and our *body schema,* which is "a system of sensory-motor capacities that function without awareness or the necessity of perceptual monitoring" (Gallagher 2005, 24). It is our body schema that hides from our view, even while it is what makes possible our perception, bodily movement, and kinesthetic sensibility. Our body schema is "a system of sensory-motor functions that operate below the level of self-referential intentionality. It involves a set of tacit performances—preconscious, subpersonal processes that play a dynamic role in governing posture and movement" (ibid., 26). As Gallagher documents with great care and insight, it is only when some breakdown occurs in our body schema, such as through traumatic bodily injury or a lesion to some sensorimotor area of the brain, that we even become aware that we have a body schema.

Another major type of bodily disappearance is based on the recession of the internal organs and processes throughout nearly all of our experience. Without these visceral processes performed by the respiratory, digestive, cardiovascular, urogenital, and endocrine systems, we would die, and so, in an almost trivial sense, they provide conditions for the very possibility of experience. More significantly, these systems underlie some of our most powerful experiences, even though we are almost never aware of their operations, and some of them are simply inaccessible to conscious awareness. To cite just one salient example, our emotional experience depends on complex neuronal and endocrine processes, although we typically cannot have a felt awareness of those processes. The result is that we feel a feeling, but we never feel our internal organs generating that feeling. Joseph LeDoux (2002) and his colleagues have studied the crucial role of the amygdala in the feeling of fear. The amygdala receives neural information about a certain stimulus and controls the release of hormones that create effects in many organs and systems, such as increased heartbeat, changes in respiration, and the activation of certain defense responses. We are not, of course, ever aware of the operations of our amygdala, but only of the systemic organic effects of those operations.

In short, the body does its marvelous work for the most part behind the scenes, so that we can focus on the objects of our desire and attention. We can be directed out into our world and be about the business of affecting the character of our experience so that we may survive and flourish precisely because our "recessive body" is going about its business.

The principal result of these forms of bodily disappearance is our sense that our thoughts, and even our feelings, go on somehow independent of our bodily processes. Our body-based experience reinforces our belief in disembodied thought. Leder summarizes the bodily basis of our latent Cartesianism:

> It is *the body's own tendency toward self-concealment* that allows for the possibility of its neglect or deprecation. Our organic basis can be easily forgotten due to the reticence of the visceral processes. Intentionality can be attributed to a disembodied mind, given the self-effacement of the ecstatic body. As these disappearances particularly characterize normal and healthy functioning, forgetting about or "freeing oneself" from the body takes on a positive valuation. (Leder 1990, 69)

There are disturbing overtones to the dream of "freeing oneself from the body," as if this would actually be a good thing to strive for! It reinforces the dangerous idea, so deeply rooted in Western culture, that purity of mind entails rising above one's bodily nature. Immanuel Kant famously argued for a "pure reason" that generates formal structures that are supposedly not based on anything empirical and thus are in no way dependent on our embodied, phenomenal selves. Kant also claimed that moral laws could issue only from "pure practical reason," completely free of feeling, emotion, or bodily constraints. A good will, on Kant's view, is a pure will, one that rises above the demands of our bodily desires and answers only to the commands of pure moral reason. Within most Christian traditions, a person's "true" self is not *of* this world of the flesh, even though it must temporally dwell *within* that world. In Kantian terms, this is formulated as the view that we most essentially are rational egos—transcendent sources of judgments, spontaneous free acts, and universally binding moral imperatives.

In short, the idea of a fundamental ontological divide between mind and body—along with the accompanying dichotomies of cognition/emotion, fact/value, knowledge/imagination, and thought/feeling—is so deeply embedded in our Western ways of thinking that we find it almost impossible to avoid framing our understanding of mind and thought dualistically. The tendency of language to treat processes and events as entities reinforces our sense that mind and body must be two different types of thing, supporting two very different types of properties. For example, just asking the question "How are body and mind one, not two?" frames our whole conception of the relation dualistically, since it presupposes that two different kinds of things must somehow come together into one. Consequently, anyone who is trying to find a way to recognize the unity of what Dewey called the "body-mind" will not have the appropriate vocabulary for capturing the primordial, nonconscious unity of the human person. Even our language seems to be against us in our quest for an adequate theory of meaning and the self.

MEANING RUNS DEEPER THAN CONCEPTS AND PROPOSITIONS

In challenging our inherited mind/body dualism, my real target will be the disembodied view of meaning that typically accompanies such a dualism. According to the view of "mind" and "body" as two different substances, structures, or processes, meaning is something that belongs first and foremost to words. Linguistic meaning (the meaning of words and sentences) is taken to be based on concepts and their capacity to be formed into sentence-like thought units that philosophers call propositions. I am going to argue that this notion of meaning, which underlies much mainstream philosophy of mind and language, is far too narrow and too shallow to capture the way things are meaningful to people. Any philosophy based on such an impoverished view of meaning is going to over-intellectualize many aspects of human meaning-making and thinking.

The dominant view of meaning and thought that I will be challenging is what I will call the conceptual-propositional theory of meaning. Here is a capsule summary of its key points:

THE CONCEPTUAL-PROPOSITIONAL THEORY OF MEANING
Sentences or utterances (and the words we use in making them) alone are what have meaning. Sentences get their meaning by expressing propositions, which are the basic units of meaning and thought. Propositions typically have a subject-predicate structure. Our language and thought are thus meaningful to the extent that they express propositions, which allow people to make assertions about the way the world is and to perform other speech acts, such as asking questions, issuing commands, pleading, joking, expressing remorse, and so on. Our capacity to grasp meanings, and our capacity for reasoning, depends on our conscious use of symbolic representations in the mind that somehow can relate to things outside the mind. These symbolic representations (usually thought of as concepts) are organized into meaningful propositional structures via formal rules of syntax, and then the propositions are organized into thoughts and arguments via formal rules of logic. According to this objectivist semantics, neither the syntactic rules, nor the logical relations, nor even the propositions themselves have any intrinsic relation to human bodies.

The key components of disembodied views that I want to challenge are the seriously mistaken claims that meaning and thought are exclusively conceptual and propositional in nature and that the apparatus of meaning, conceptualization, and reasoning is not intrinsically shaped by the body, even if these processes have to occur *in* a body. I will argue in chapter 2 that if babies are learning the meaning of things and events, and if babies are not yet formulating propositions, then meaning and understanding must involve a great deal more than the ability to create and understand propositions and their corresponding linguistic utterances. Obviously, I do not mean to deny the existence of propositional thinking, but I see it as dependent on the nature of our embodied, immanent meaning. In short, contrary to the fundamental claim of Gottlob Frege (1892/1970), the father of modern analytic philosophy, propositions are *not* the basic units of human meaning and thought. Meaning traffics in patterns, images, qualities, feelings, and eventually concepts and propositions.

One popular strategy for acknowledging that there is nonpropositional meaning while still privileging the propositional is to claim a rigid dichotomy between two fundamentally different kinds of meaning: (1) descriptive (cognitive) meaning, and (2) emotive (noncognitive) meaning. Once this illusory demarcation was made, it was easy for philosophers of language like A. J. Ayer (1936) and Charles Stevenson (1944) to retain an exclusive focus on the conceptual/propositional as the only meaning that mattered for our knowledge of the world. So-called emotive meaning had no place in science or any allegedly rigorous, empirically testable modes of knowing.

I am going to argue that the cognitive/emotive dichotomy does more harm than good. It is a mistake to banish emotional aspects of meaning to the nether land of the merely emotive and then to claim that *real* meaning is cognitive meaning of the conceptual/propositional sort. Instead, I will be arguing for the central role of emotion in how we make sense of our world. There is no cognition without emotion, even though we are often unaware of the emotional aspects of our thinking.

The idea that meaning and understanding are based solely on propositional structures is problematic because it excludes (or at least hides) most of what goes into the ways we make sense of our experience. In striking contrast to this conceptual-propositional view of meaning and knowledge, a substantial body of evidence from the cognitive sciences supports the hypothesis that meaning is shaped by the nature of our bodies, especially our sensorimotor capacities and our ability to experience feelings and emotions. If we look at prelinguistic infants and at children who are learning how their world works and what things mean to them, we will find vast stretches of embodied meaning that are not conceptual and propositional in character, even though they will later make propositional thinking possible.

In the account of embodied meaning that I am developing in this book, I am using the term *meaning* in a broader sense than is typical in mainstream Anglo-American philosophy of language and mind. I seek to recover most of the resources for meaning-making that are ignored in the writings of influential philosophers such as Quine, Searle, Davidson, Fodor, Rorty, and many others. In addition to the standard notion that meaning involves the conscious entertaining of concepts and propositions, I am focusing on mostly nonconscious aspects of a person's ability to meaningfully engage their past, present, and future environments. I am proposing what I call

THE EMBODIED THEORY OF MEANING

Human meaning concerns the character and significance of a person's inter-actions with their environments. The meaning of a specific aspect or dimen-sion of some ongoing experience is that aspect's connections to other parts of past, present, or future (possible) experiences. Meaning is relational. It is about how one thing relates to or connects with other things. This prag-matist view of meaning says that the meaning of a thing is its consequences for experience—how it "cashes out" by way of experience, either actual or possible experience. Sometimes our meanings are conceptually and propo-sitionally coded, but that is merely the more conscious, selective dimension of a vast, continuous process of immanent meanings that involve structures, patterns, qualities, feelings, and emotions. An embodied view is naturalis-tic, insofar as it situates meaning within a flow of experience that cannot exist without a biological organism engaging its environment. Meanings emerge "from the bottom up" through increasingly complex levels of organic activity; they are not the constructions of a disembodied mind.

The semantics of embodied meaning that is supported by recent re-search in the cognitive sciences provides a naturalistic perspective, one that makes no explanatory use of any alleged disembodied or "purely ra-tional" capacities. A naturalistic theory of meaning takes as its working hypothesis the idea that all of our so-called higher cognitive faculties (e.g., of conceptualization and reasoning) recruit cognitive resources that oper-ate in our sensorimotor experience and our monitoring of our emotions. The guiding assumption for such a naturalistic semantics is what John Dewey called a "principle of continuity."

DEWEY'S PRINCIPLE OF CONTINUITY

The primary postulate of a naturalistic theory of logic is continuity of the lower (less complex) and the higher (more complex) activities and forms. The idea of continuity is not self-explanatory. But its meaning excludes complete rupture on one side and mere repetition of identities on the other; it pre-cludes reduction of the "higher" to the "lower" just as it precludes complete breaks and gaps. . . . What *is* excluded by the postulate of continuity is the appearance upon the scene of a totally new outside force as a cause of changes that occur. (Dewey 1938/1991, 30–31)

An embodied view of meaning looks for the origins and structures of meaning in the organic activities of embodied creatures in interaction with their changing environments. It sees meaning and all our higher functioning as growing out of and shaped by our abilities to perceive things, manipulate objects, move our bodies in space, and evaluate our situation. Its principle of continuity is that the "higher" develops from the "lower," without introducing from the outside any new metaphysical kinds.

I will be using the terms *embodied meaning* and *immanent meaning* to emphasize those deep-seated bodily sources of human meaning that go beyond the merely conceptual and propositional. Structures and dimensions of this immanent meaning are what make it possible for us to do propositional thinking. But if we reduce meaning to words and sentences (or to concepts and propositions), we miss or leave out where meaning really comes from. We end up intellectualizing human experience, understanding, and thinking, and we turn processes into static entities or properties. I will therefore be suggesting that any philosophy that ignores embodied meaning is going to generate a host of extremely problematic views about mind, thought, and language. I want to suggest, in anticipation of my arguments to come, some of the more important consequences of taking seriously a nondualistic account of mind and personal identity and recognizing the bodily basis of human meaning.

PHILOSOPHICAL IMPLICATIONS OF THE BODY-MIND AND OF BODY-BASED MEANING

This fact of embodied mind has several profound consequences for who you are and how you should live your life: it denies a radical mind/body separation, sees meaning, imagination, and reason as embodied, denies radical freedom, ties reason to emotion, and requires an embodied spirituality. Here are some of the more striking implications of taking our embodiment seriously:

1. *There is no radical mind/body separation.* A person is not a mind *and* a body. There are not two "things" somehow mysteriously yoked together. What we call a "person" is a certain kind of bodily organism that has a brain operating within its body, a body that is continually interacting with aspects of its environments (material and social) in an ever-changing process of experience. As I will explain later, we designate certain dimensions of these ongoing experiential processes "mind" and other dimensions "body," but we do this only reflectively and for very specific purposes that we have in trying to make sense of our experience. In short,

"mind" and "body" are merely abstracted aspects of the flow of organism-environment interactions that constitutes what we call experience. When your "body" ceases to function as a living, organic whole of coordinated activities and processes, you lose your "mind." It doesn't just go away somewhere and hide. Rather, it ceases to exist. If there is life after death, we can't know what it is like, but strong neuroscientific evidence suggests that it could not involve the kind of conscious experience and meaning-making that is so distinctive of humans—unless, of course, this life after death involved the resuscitation of our human brains, bodies, and physical and social environments.

This claim is based on the idea that we are beginning to understand how our consciousness and our experience depend on our brain operating within our body and our body operating within our world, so that when our bodies cease to function, in a global, devastating fashion, we lose the capacity for experience. This realization has led many people to reject the idea of disembodied soul and life after death, and to focus instead on the importance of living rightly and well in the world as we know it.

Of course, no one could ever disprove (or prove, for that matter) the existence of a disembodied soul, which must always remain a possible hypothesis. William James, who was a pioneer in the scientific study of mind and is famous for revealing the workings of the body within our thinking and feeling, always insisted that disembodied soul must remain a real possibility. And so it must. However, such a supposition is clearly at odds with virtually all contemporary biology, neuroscience, and cognitive science. My point is that if such a soul exists, it is hard to see any way in which it could be me, or you, as we exist in our present incarnation.

2. *Meaning is grounded in our bodily experience.* If there is no disembodied mind—no transcendent soul or ego—to be the source of meaning, then what things are meaningful to us and how they are meaningful must be a result of the nature of our brains, our bodies, our environments, and our social interactions, institutions, and practices. This fact gives rise to a major problem: how does meaning emerge from a continuous process of organism-environment interactions, bottom-up, if it can't issue top-down from some alleged pure ego? The answer to this is a story based on recent empirical research in the cognitive sciences concerning the nature of meaning and thought. I will try to tell part of this story in part 2 of this book. The core idea is that our experience of meaning is based, first, on our sensorimotor experience, our feelings, and our visceral connections to our world; and, second, on various imaginative capacities for using sensorimotor processes to understand abstract concepts. Any adequate explana-

tion of meaning must avoid attributing it to either "body" or "mind," for then we simply reproduce the dualism that is the source of the problem in the first place.

3. *Reason is an embodied process.* Our "body" and "mind" are dimensions of the primordial, ongoing organism-environment transactions that are the locus of who and what we are. Consequently, there is no mind entity to serve as the locus of reason. What we call "reason" is neither a concrete nor an abstract *thing,* but only embodied *processes* by which our experience is explored, criticized, and transformed in inquiry. Reason is more an accomplishment of inquiry than a pre-given fact or capacity. If there is no "pure" reason, then it is necessary to explain how reason and logic grow out of our transactions in and with our environment. This, again, is a huge problem for any naturalistic account of mind. I will present evidence from the cognitive sciences that reason is tied to structures of our perceptual and motor capacities and that it is inextricably linked to feeling.

4. *Imagination is tied to our bodily processes and can also be creative and transformative of experience.* Our ability to make new meaning, to enlarge our concepts, and to arrive at new ways of making sense of things must be explained without reference to miracles, irrational leaps of thought, or blind impulse. We have to explain how our experience can grow and how the new can emerge from the old, yet without merely replicating what has gone before.

As it turns out, this may be one of the most difficult problems in all of philosophy, psychology, and science: how is novelty possible? As far as I can see, nobody has yet been able to explain how new experience emerges. The problem is that if we try to give a causal explanation of novel experience or novel thought, these come out looking causally determined, rather than creative and imaginative. An embodied theory of meaning will suggest only that new meaning is not a miracle but rather arises from, and remains connected to, preexisting patterns, qualities, and feelings.

5. *There is no radical freedom.* Most people believe that human will possesses absolute freedom, which is why we think we can hold people responsible for their actions. But if there is no transcendent self, no disembodied ego, to serve as the agent of free choice, then what sense can we make of real choice, or of moral responsibility for our actions? This problem has plagued all naturalistic accounts of mind, from David Hume to William James to Antonio Damasio. We need a view of choice that is consistent with cognitive neuroscience and its insistence on the embodiment of mind and yet which doesn't make a shambles of our notions of moral responsibility.

6. *Reason and emotion are inextricably intertwined.* This claim directly challenges the received wisdom that reason and emotion are separate, independent capacities, one disembodied (i.e., reason) and the other embodied (i.e., emotion). The reason/emotion dichotomy is as basic a metaphysical dualism as you will find anywhere, and it has profound consequences for our view of thought and knowledge. It fosters the illusion of dispassionate reason—reason purified of any bodily contamination by feelings. It is extremely difficult to rethink this pernicious dichotomy, because our own experience appears to tell us that reason and emotion are distinct. I will present empirical evidence that emotions lie at the heart of our capacity to conceptualize, reason, and imagine.

7. *Human spirituality is embodied.* For many people, their sense of spirituality is tied to notions of transcendence—of the soul, of spirit, of value, of God. The traditional notion of transcendence is what I call "vertical transcendence," because it requires rising above one's embodied situation in the world to engage a higher realm that is assumed to have a radically different character from that of the world in which we normally dwell. This other world has to be *radically* other (i.e., nonphysical, infinite, transtemporal), because otherwise it would not solve the basic human problems that stem from the fact of human finiteness—problems that the existentialist theologian Paul Tillich (1957) identified as those of meaninglessness, alienation, injustice, sickness, and ultimately death. If, as the traditional view asserts, our body is the locus of our dwelling in this world and thus the locus of our finiteness, then our body must somehow be transcended if there are to be any satisfactory answers to the human condition of limitation, helplessness, and finiteness.

By contrast, if we are inescapably and gloriously embodied, then our spirituality cannot be grounded in otherworldliness. It must be grounded in our relation to the human and more-than-human world that we inhabit. It must involve a capacity for horizontal (as opposed to vertical) transcendence, namely, our ability both to transform experience and to be transformed ourselves by something that transcends us: the whole ongoing, ever-developing natural process of which we are a part. Such a view of embodied spirituality may well support an environmental, ecological spirituality, but it is hardly likely to satisfy anyone for whom the only acceptable answer to our finiteness is the infinite.

What these seven consequences reveal is that acknowledging the profound truth of our embodiment calls into question several key components of what many people think it means to be a person. It is not surprising, therefore, that once most people really come to understand what an embodied conception of mind entails, they are going to be upset about it. Much of what they hold dear is at stake—their view of mind, meaning, thought, knowledge, science, morality, religion, and politics. That is why it is not easy to work out the details of an alternative view in a way that is existentially satisfying to most people.

In this book, I focus mostly on exploring the aesthetics of the body-mind—how meaning grows out of our organic transactions with our environment. I try to show why disembodiment is *not* purity of thought but would, in fact, amount to the loss of all the means we possess for making sense of things. As the Collins poem suggests, our bodies are the very condition of our meaning-making and creativity. If a man were reduced to only a skeleton with a penis at a typewriter, then he would, of course, write poems only about sex and death. Remove his penis, and the remaining skeleton can imagine only death, like the air passing through its bare ribs. Our task is not to supersede the body but to embrace it, to learn how it allows us to have meaning, and to nurture it as the locus of our world. We need an aesthetics of embodied meaning. We need to face the tough questions about where meaning comes from, how abstract concepts are possible, what mind is, and whether we have free choice. Such questions define our task, which is to plumb the meaning of the body—both how the body means and what embodiment means for our lives.

PART I

Bodily Meaning and Felt Sense

Discovering, making, and communicating meaning is our full-time job. We do it from the moment we are born until the moment we die. Sometimes we do it consciously and intentionally; but mostly, meaning emerges for us beneath the level of our conscious awareness. Meaning is happening without our knowing it. So, to figure out where meaning comes from, we have to look deeply into mostly nonconscious bodily encounters with our world.

I submit that if you want to understand human meaning-making, you should probably *not* start with theories of meaning put forth in contemporary analytic philosophy of mind and language. You will find there treatments of concepts, propositions, and various language-like structures, but you will *not* find any awareness of deep, embodied, vital meaning.

For this immanent or embodied meaning, you must look more deeply into aspects of experience that lie beneath words and sentences. You must look at the felt qualities, images, feelings, and emotions that ground our more abstract structures of meaning. In part I, therefore, I dig down into our meaningful engagement with our world as it comes to us through our bodies. Chapter 1 focuses on the importance of felt bodily movement in how our world reveals itself. Chapter 2 explores the hypothesis that infants are learning the meaning of things and experiences, even though they are prelinguistic and are not little proposition-processing machines. Infant experience reveals the crucial role of patterns of felt experience— not just in the baby's world, but equally in our adult sense of reality and in our ability to grasp the meaning of what is happening. Chapter 3 turns to the importance of emotions as one of our primary ways to monitor the nature and adequacy of our ongoing interactions with our environments. Emotions are not second-rate cognitions; rather, they are affective patterns of our encounter with our world, by which we take the meaning of things at a primordial level. In chapter 4 I argue, following John Dewey, that every situation we dwell in is characterized by a pervasive felt quality that is the starting point for all our perceptual discrimination and conceptual definition. This argument leads, in chapter 5, to evidence for the central role of feeling and emotion in human reasoning, along lines first laid out by William James.

Part 1 thus attempts to describe important dimensions of meaning that are typically overlooked by and excluded from views of meaning available in most Anglo-American analytic philosophy. Our first task is to unearth and describe these primary embodied sources of meaning that have been overlooked. Our second task is to begin formulating the larger philosophical picture of mind, thought, and meaning that goes along with this enriched and expanded conception of meaning. In particular, an embodied view of meaning requires an embodied, nondualistic, naturalistic view of mind and body as one process.

CHAPTER 1

The Movement of Life

Life and movement are inextricably connected. The movement of the fetus within the mother's womb gives her the joyful news of new life. The word "*still*born" strikes horror in a parent's breast. Eternal stillness— absolute absence of motion—is death. Movement is life. We are born into the world as screaming, squirming creatures, and through our movements we get "in touch" with our world, taking its human measure.

Attention to bodily movement is thus one of the keys to understanding how things and experiences become meaningful to organisms like us, via our sensorimotor capacities. It is not the whole story (temporality, for example, is equally primordial), but it is a good place to start our account of meaning-making. Movement is one of the conditions for our sense of what our world is like and who we are. A great deal of our perceptual knowledge comes from movement, both our bodily motions and our interactions with moving objects.

MOVEMENT AND MEANING

In *The Primacy of Movement,* Maxine Sheets-Johnstone (1999, chap. 3) provides a phenomenological analysis of movement that can serve as a starting place for our account of embodied human meaning-making. Her account is phenomenological in the sense that it describes the origins, structures, and experienced qualities of human movement. It focuses on the felt qualities and patterns of our body movements and interactions with objects.

As animate creatures, we are born moving. It is originally through movement that we come to inhabit a world that makes sense to us—that is, a world that has meaning for us. Movement thus gives us knowledge of our world and, at the same time, reveals important insights about our own nature, capacities, and limitations.

> In the beginning, we are simply infused with movement—not merely with a *propensity* to move, but with the real thing. This primal animateness, this original kinetic spontaneity that infuses our being and defines our aliveness, is our point of departure for living in the world and making sense of it. . . . *We literally discover ourselves in movement.* We grow kinetically into our bodies. In particular, we grow into those distinctive ways of moving that come with our being the bodies we are. In our spontaneity of movement, we discover arms that extend, spines that bend, knees that flex, mouths that shut, and so on. We make sense of ourselves in the course of moving. (Sheets-Johnstone 1999, 136)

Movement occurs within an environment and necessarily involves on-going, intimate connection and interaction with aspects of some particular environment. This is a fact of monumental importance that should always be kept in mind in everything we say about the relation of self and world. *From the very beginning of our life, and evermore until we die, movement keeps us in touch with our world in the most intimate and profound way. In our experience of movement, there is no radical separation of self from world.* We move in space through constant contact with the contours of our environment. We are in touch with our world at a visceral level, and it is the quality of our "being in touch" that importantly defines what our world is like and who we are. What philosophers call "subjects" and "objects" (persons and things) are abstractions from the interactive process of our experience of a meaningful self-in-a-world. It is one of the primary facts of our existence that we are not now and never were, either as infants or throughout human history, alienated from things, as subjects over against objects. There is no move-ment without the space we move in, the things we move, and the qualities of movement, which are at the same time both the qualities of the world we experience and the qualities of ourselves as doers and experiencers.[1]

1. Immanuel Kant, in his *Critique of Pure Reason* (1781), is famous for his observation that "subject" and "object" are counterparts inseparable in experience, two sides of the same coin that cannot exist without each other. But Kant was also notorious for positing a transcendental ego that must lie behind, and play a role in constituting, the correlation of subject and object in experience. It is Maurice Merleau-Ponty, in his *Phenomenology*

QUALITATIVE DIMENSIONS OF MOVEMENT

What is it that we experience through our movement? Even though we are seldom consciously aware of the nature of our movement, what we are always experiencing are the qualities of things, spaces, and forceful exertions. We put things into and take things out of containers, and so we learn about containment. We experience linear versus nonlinear paths of motion, whereby we develop our understanding of trajectories. We feel various degrees of exertion and force, and we thus learn what level of exertion is appropriate for moving ourselves from one place to another and for moving objects of various weights. Feeling what it takes to cause an object to move from one place to another is a core part of our basic understanding of physical causation.

Movement is thus one of the principal ways by which we learn the meaning of things and acquire our ever-growing sense of what our world is like. This learning about the possibilities for different types of experience and action that comes from moving within various environments occurs mostly beneath the level of consciousness. It starts in the womb and continues over our life span. We learn an important part of the immanent meaning of things through our bodily motions. We learn what we *can do* in the same motions by which we learn how things *can be* for us.

Movements manifest a broad range of recurring structures and patterns that George Lakoff and I have named *image schemas* (Lakoff 1987; Johnson 1987; Lakoff and Johnson 1999). Typical image schemas of bodily movements include SOURCE-PATH-GOAL, UP-DOWN (verticality), INTO–OUT OF, TOWARD–AWAY FROM, and STRAIGHT-CURVED. Image schemas are discussed more fully in chapter 7. For now, my point is only that movements are not defined merely by the internal structure of image schemas, but also by their distinctive *qualities*. For example, my movement along a forest path is not defined only by the SOURCE-PATH-GOAL structure of my walking. In addition, my movement manifests dynamic qualities—it can be, for example, *explosive, graceful, halting, weak,* or *jerky*. Sheets-Johnstone (1999, 140–51) leads us through a phenomenological experiment designed to reveal the primary qualitative structures or parameters of all movement. For example, perform any simple movement, such

---

of Perception (English trans. 1962), and John Dewey, in *Experience and Nature* (1925), who showed us that subjects and objects are abstractions from the interactive process of experience out of which emerge what we call people and things. There is no split of self and other in the primacy of our experience, and so we are never utterly separated from things.

as sitting down comfortably in a chair and then standing up. Next, vary the performance of this motion in every way you can imagine: do it first fast, then slowly; now with an explosive effort, next with carefully controlled, gradual exertion; first jerkily, then smoothly; with body held taut and stiff, or with flowing grace. What this experiment reveals are four recurring qualitative dimensions of all bodily movements: tension, linearity, amplitude, and projection.

1. *Tension.* Every movement a person makes involves effortful action, and effort requires some level of tension in the musculature. Different movements thus demand different degrees of exertion and energy. We learn to anticipate, usually unconsciously, the amount of tension required to perform various activities. If you go to pick up a medium-sized suitcase, you anticipate the amount of effort needed to lift it. If it is empty when you thought it was full, you will be surprised, and your effort will be inappropriate for the task. If the suitcase is full of heavy books, you will be equally surprised when your exertion is inadequate to the task, and so your planned motor program will be disrupted. When your initial effort to lift the suitcase fails (with that telltale jerk on your whole body as you encounter the unexpected resistance of the heavy books), you automatically recalibrate the exertion required, unconsciously make adjustments in the placement of your feet, lower your center of gravity, and lift again. Knowing your world thus requires exquisitely fine adjustments of muscular tension and exertion, calibrated via the tensive qualities that you feel in your body.

2. *Linearity.* Every move you make creates a path of motion. Those paths, actual and projected, are linear or curved, jagged or smooth, up or down. As we will see in the next chapter, infants learn to imagine possible trajectories of the motion of objects, based on speed, direction of motion, and previous location. They come to understand how a certain trajectory reaches forward into space and engages physical objects, and this understanding allows a person to be gracefully at home in their environment. People who are less successful in learning such projections are less skillful at negotiating space and tracking objects. Along with the tensive quality of motion, then, linear trajectories are an important part of an infant's nascent understanding of causation. We learn the *feeling,* the different *qualities,* of these various types of trajectory.

3. *Amplitude.* Any motion can be performed with various amplitudes, depending on whether our bodies fill and use the space available to us in a tight, contractive fashion or in an expansive way. In her provocative essay "Throwing Like a Girl," Iris Marion Young (1980) provides a phenomenological and sociological analysis of the socialization of girls and young

women with regard to how their bodies should occupy and move within space. Young begins with Erwin Strauss's report on an earlier study of the marked differences in the manner of throwing that is typical of boys on the one hand and girls on the other:

> The girl of five does not make any use of lateral space. She does not stretch her arm sideward; she does not twist her trunk; she does not move her legs, which remain side by side. All she does in preparation for throwing is to lift her right arm forward to the horizontal and to bend the forearm backward in a pronate position. . . . The ball is released without force, speed, or accurate aim. (Strauss 1966, 157)

By contrast, according to Strauss, boys tend to throw a ball with sweeping, forceful motions that occupy more of the full space available to them, both vertically and laterally, and that involve more of their whole body and its potential force. Boys are taught to bring the ball back in a sweeping lateral motion, moving their "throwing" foot back as they twist their entire body in preparation for the throw. They utilize their trunk, legs, and arms in a forward thrust and follow-through. Young describes this striking difference in the amplitude of motion as applying not just to throwing, but to all sorts of forceful motions:

> Not only is there a typical style of throwing like a girl, but there is a more or less typical style of running like a girl, climbing like a girl, swinging like a girl, hitting like a girl. They have in common first that the whole body is not put into fluid and directed motion, but rather, in swinging and hitting, for example, the motion is concentrated in one body part; and second that the woman's motion tends not to reach, extend, lean, stretch, and follow through in the direction of her intention. (Young 1980, 146)

What Young is describing is how culture has often taught girls to confine their movements and their occupancy of space to a certain characteristic, highly restricted amplitude. Girls traditionally were not supposed to take up space, nor were they supposed to inject their entire bodily presence into a situation. That was considered unladylike. Culturally, such self-assertion and exertion of force have been reserved for males.

In the forty years since Strauss described these two gendered styles of throwing, certainly much has changed in the socialization of girls. Especially because of the emergence of training for girls in many sports at all levels, from preschool up through professional sports, and because of gradual changes in how girls are taught to stand, hold their bodies, and move, these amplitudinal differences are beginning to change in significant ways.[2] It is conceivable that the earlier observed socially and culturally imposed differences might someday cease to exist. I cite this analysis only to illustrate the notion of amplitude of bodily motions. Whether based on anatomical differences or on gender, class, or other forms of socialization, these variations in amplitude are very real and significant. They are experienced as *qualitative* differences in motion and bodily comportment. They define some of the ways that a person's world is open to them for specific kinds of forceful actions.

4. *Projection.* In exerting force to stand up from a sitting position, I can vary the projective quality of motion. I can thrust myself upward with a violent initial propulsion, or I can raise myself with carefully monitored, deliberate speed. I can switch from smooth to explosive motion and back again. These different patterns entail quite different qualities of their corresponding bodily experiences; violent propulsion feels markedly different from gradual, continuous exertion of force.

MOVEMENT AS A BASIS FOR MEANING

The point I want to emphasize with Sheets-Johnstone's phenomenological description of the four basic qualitative parameters of movement is that dimensions like these will play a crucial role in how things can be meaningful to creatures who have bodies like ours and move in environments like ours. They are part of what we mean by, and what we experience as, force, effort, manner of motion, and direction of action.

As a phenomenologist, Sheets-Johnstone focuses on how these qualities of movements are *felt* and *experienced* by us. However, even prior to conscious experience, our bodies are inhabiting, and interacting meaningfully with, their environments beneath the level of conscious awareness. I want to suggest that even at this nonconscious level, these characteristics of movement are forming the basis for both the meaning of our movements and, at the same time, the meaning of the world that we move within.

2. It may be that these observed differences between the bodily comportment of boys and girls are almost entirely social and cultural constructions. I have run experiments in my introductory philosophy class in which female and male students throw a tennis ball, and the differences Strauss observed are far less pronounced today than they were forty years ago. I attribute this primarily to the fact that girls are now introduced at an early age to sports in which they learn to make maximal use of their bodily potential for motion.

I am thus using the term *meaning* in a broader sense than is common in most philosophy and linguistics.

In subsequent chapters, I will present a view of embodied meaning that recognizes conscious inquiry and conscious grasping of meaning, but also processes of organism-environment interaction that operate beneath our felt awareness and that make that felt awareness possible. *The key to my entire argument is that meaning is not just what is consciously entertained in acts of feeling and thought; instead, meaning reaches deep down into our corporeal encounter with our environment.* This expanded sense of *meaning* is the only way to preserve continuity between so-called higher and lower cognitive processes. The nonconscious interactive processes make possible and are continuous with our conscious grasp of meaning. At some point, these meanings-in-the-making ("proto-meanings" or "immanent meanings," if you will) can be consciously appropriated, and it is only then that we typically think of something as "meaningful to us." But notice that these meanings cannot just pop into existence (arise in our consciousness) out of nothing and from nowhere. Instead, they must be grounded in our bodily connections with things, and they must be continuously "in the making" via our sensorimotor engagements. There is a continuity of process between these immanent meanings and our reflective understanding and employment of them. For example, *tension* has a meaning grounded in bodily exertion and felt muscular tension. *Linearity* derives its meaning from the spatial, directional qualities of bodily motion. *Amplitude* is meaningful to us first and foremost as a bodily phenomenon of expansion and contraction in the range of a motion. *Projection* is learned first as a vectoral quality of certain forceful bodily actions.

The meaning of these differences is known by the quality of our differing experiences, but that meaning is prepared and developed in our nonconscious bodily perceptions and movements. Subjectively, we would say that we *feel* these qualitative dimensions. However, they are not just subjective qualities. It would be a mistake to subjectivize these experiences of qualities of motion, as if they were locked up within some private inner world of feelings. On the contrary, they are *qualities of organism-environment interactions.* As such, they are not merely "subjective-feeling" responses (not just "inner" experiences). They are qualities in the world as much as they are in us. They are the qualities of different experiences that involve both the structure of the organism and the structure of its environments inextricably woven together, and even attuned to one another. Moreover, they are qualities experienced and shared by other people, who have bodies like ours and who inhabit the same kinds of physical environments that we do.

We must guard against the fallacy of assuming that our knowledge or understanding of specific meanings exhausts those meanings. I will later appropriate Eugene Gendlin's account of the "felt sense" to show that meanings are working and developing for us even prior to our conscious awareness of them. Without this experiential rootedness, meanings would be miracles born ex nihilo as disembodied cogitations.

In another chapter, we will examine how qualitative bodily experiences are part of our abstract conceptualization and reasoning and are also present in logical inference. But even with the minimal phenomenological analysis we have done so far, the importance of movement for our capacity to experience the meaning of things is evident. Consider, for example, how our self-movement creates our sense of spaces with their differing designs and patterns. Sheets-Johnstone observes that

> the predominant shifting linear designs of our moving bodies may be now curved (as when we bend over), now twisted (as when we turn our heads), now diagonal (as when we lean forward), now vertical (as when we walk), and so on; the predominant linear patterns we create in moving may be now zig-zag (as in a game of tag), now straight (as in marching), now circular (as when we walk around an object or literally 'go in circles'), and so on. (Sheets-Johnstone 1999, 144)

Such concepts as *curved, twisted, diagonal, vertical, zig-zag, straight,* and *circular* get their meaning primordially from our bodily postures, our bodily movements, and the logic of those movements. You understand what *twisted* means through your bodily experience of the forceful exertions and kinesthetic sensations accompanying the act of twisting yourself or twisting objects. Furthermore, all of this bodily meaning is appropriated even when *twisted* comes to be used in a psychological or moral sense (as in a "twisted" or "warped" personality that leads to "twisted" misdeeds). To give another example, you know the bodily meaning of *standing straight and tall,* and you appropriate this meaning in your conception of *moral* "uprightness." You learn the corporeal logic of circular motions with your eyes, feet, and hands, and this body knowledge carries over into your understanding of circular arguments, circular processes, and temporal circularity. As we will see in detail later, many of our most fundamental concepts, including those lying at the heart of ethics, politics, and philosophy, have their roots in movement and other bodily experiences at a pre-reflective level.

Let us take stock of the argument so far. Life (animation) is intimately tied to movement. We are born into the world moving, in a way that gives us a great deal of grounded understanding of what our world is like. By moving, we are in continual touch with aspects of our surroundings. Through movement, we learn not only the contours and qualities of our world, but also the sense of ourselves as inhabiting a world with which we can interact to achieve some of our ends and goals. Above all, it is not just the *structures* of movements that matter; it is, even more, the *qualities* of movement that constitute our bodily understanding of motion.

Sheets-Johnstone regards movement as a paradigmatic example of the ways that our capacity to make any sense of our world is rooted in our bodily acts of sense-making: "We make sense of our bodies first and foremost. We make sense of them in and through movement, in and through *animation*. Moreover, we do so without words. This primordial sense-making is the standard upon which our sense-making of the world unfolds" (Sheets-Johnstone 1999, 148).

This statement of the primacy of bodily movement is not meant to exclude other bodily acts that give rise to meaning, such as seeing, touching, and hearing, but it does emphasize the importance of movement for our learning about our own bodies and our world. The bodily basis of meaning and thought is a profound truth about human beings. It cannot, however, be demonstrated solely on the basis of phenomenological analysis of experience, because, as I have said, meaning cannot be reduced only to felt qualities or conscious processes. It must also include nonconscious bodily interactions with the world. Therefore, at this point, we cannot yet explore all the ramifications of this fundamental claim that meaning is embodied. That will have to wait for subsequent chapters, where we will survey some of the empirical evidence for the embodiment of concepts and reason. Sheets-Johnstone is correct, however, in saying that "a phenomenology of the qualitative dynamics of originary self-movement leads us to the origin of concepts foundational to our lives as animate organisms and to our knowledge of ourselves as animate—*moving*—organisms to begin with" (1999, 155). Phenomenology *leads* us to the primacy of movement, but it alone is not enough to prove the case. What is required additionally is empirical research from the cognitive sciences of the embodied mind.

THE MOVEMENT OF TIME

A phenomenological analysis of bodily movement and the perceived motion of objects gives us insight into how we experience and conceptualize time. Sheets-Johnstone suggests that prior even to our experience of *befores*, *nows*, and *afters*, which turn out to be products of reflection, we encounter the qualitative flow of events that makes up the contours of our lived experience. Take any bodily motion, such as opening and closing your mouth, raising and lowering your right arm, standing up and sitting down. As we have seen, any movements like these manifest distinctive qualities, depending on how the act is performed, and those qualities involve tension, linearity, amplitude, and projection, at the very least. There is also a temporal quality to the way any particular action is performed. Marching has a temporal quality very different from that of skipping along or walking on tiptoes. Marching, skipping, and tiptoeing give us three qualitatively different experiences of the passage of time. Time can move resolutely along in measured beats; it can skip along with exaggerated rhythms; or it can pass us with the caution and high tension associated with tiptoeing. Sheets-Johnstone concludes that

> for any particular temporality to be the temporality it is . . . a certain temporal quality is essential to it: an ongoing evenness as when we walk normally or an ongoing unevenness as when we walk with a limp; a jaggedness as when we move in fits and starts, a swiftness as when we punch an oncoming ball; a suddenness as when we duck, a hesitant slowness as when we move warily with apprehension and stealth. (Sheets-Johnstone 1999, 157)

Experiential correlations like these, between motions and the felt passage of time, provide one primary basis for much of our conceptual understanding of time. This correlation of the motion of an object with the passing of time is present in infants and children as well as adults. The principal difference between children and adults regarding this experience is not the existence of the correlation, but rather that adults have acquired the ability to make use of this experiential correlation as a basis for abstract thought. We (adults) conceptualize time via deep, systematic *spatial-movement* metaphors in which the passage of time is understood as relative motion in space. I want to consider briefly two of our most basic metaphorical conceptualizations of time, in order to emphasize their grounding in experienced correlations of motion with the passage of time. This jump to the level of our metaphorical understanding of time may seem a bit premature, since the nature of metaphor and its indispensable role in human understanding are not discussed until a later chapter. However, by way of anticipation, I want to connect our phenomenological account of the qualities of temporal flow with our ability to conceptualize time and temporal relations. For, already in our perception and bodily movement, we experience this intimate correlation of movement and temporal change that is the basis for some of the ways we think more abstractly about time, and it is precisely the various qualities of different movements that permit us to conceptualize different experiences of the passing of time.

Phenomenologically—at the level of felt experience—two of the most important ways in which time comes to be experienced are through the motion of objects and through movement of our bodies. This gives rise to two fundamental metaphorical spatializations in our concepts of temporal change. In *Philosophy in the Flesh,* George Lakoff and I (1999) analyzed in detail these and other metaphorical conceptualizations of time.[3] The first spatialization understands discrete times metaphorically as objects moving toward a stationary observer, first in front of the observer, then passing her, and finally moving further and further away behind her. The metaphor consists of a conceptual mapping of entities, structures, and relations from the domain of moving objects in space onto the conceptual domain of temporal change, as follows:

The MOVING TIME Metaphor

Source domain (spatial motion)		*Target domain (temporal change)*
Location Of Observer	→	The Present
Space In Front Of Observer	→	The Future
Space Behind Observer	→	The Past
Moving Objects	→	Times
Motion Of Objects Past Observer	→	The "Passage" Of Time

Notice that this MOVING TIME metaphor is grounded very naturally in our experience of correlations between objects moving in space and temporal change. Although many linguists and philosophers have argued that such a metaphor can only be based on a set of preexisting literal similarities between objects moving in space and the passing of time, this is clearly not the case. There are no such literal similarities between the source domain (moving objects) and the target domain (temporal change) that would be relevant to the meaning of the expressions based on the metaphor. Instead, it is these experiential correlations that ground the metaphor, because spatial motions are one of the principal ways in which time "moves" or "passes" for us.

Once this initial orientation of stationary observer and moving time is established, the conceptual mapping of structure from source domain

3. The following analysis is based on the more thorough treatment given in chapter 10 of Lakoff and Johnson 1999.

to target domain allows us to use our knowledge of moving objects to construct a metaphorical understanding of the "passage" of time. For example, human perceivers project fronts and backs onto moving objects. Fronts are projected in the canonical direction of motion of the object, so that the front of a bus passes a stationary point before the back of the bus does, given that the bus is moving "forward." Any object upon which we can imaginatively project a front and a back can thus be "in front of" or "behind" another object, depending on their relation to each other and their shared direction of motion. When this knowledge structure is applied to our understanding of time, we construct a corresponding knowledge structure for moving time. We speak of Tuesday *following* (or *coming after*) Monday, of Tuesday *preceding* (or *coming before*) Wednesday. We also experience objects moving past us at various speeds and with various types of motions (creeping, flying by, racing). Correspondingly, times move with various speeds, as in "Tuesday *went by in a flash*," "The hours *crept past*," "Our meeting *dragged along at a snail's pace*," "Time *flies* when you're having fun," and "The lazy days of summer *roll by*." Lastly, at the moment when a particular time "passes" you (the observer), it is conceptualized as located where you are. Thus, we talk about doing something *here and now*.

The second major metaphor system arising from the spatialization of time is based on the moving of our bodies through space. In this second orientation, the observer is not stationary but moves from one location to another over a spatial landscape. This source-domain structure gives rise to a mapping in which times are spatial locations and the motion and speed of the moving observer determine the character of temporal change.

The MOVING OBSERVER Metaphor

Source domain (spatial motion)		*Target domain (temporal change)*
Location Of Observer	→	The Present
Space In Front Of Observer	→	The Future
Space Behind Observer	→	The Past
Locations On Observer's Path Of Motion	→	Times
Distance Moved By Observer	→	Amount Of Time "Passed"

Like the MOVING TIME metaphor, the MOVING OBSERVER metaphor uses our knowledge of the source domain to construct a corresponding knowledge of the target domain. Spatial locations can be of various sizes, and we can measure their length by established units. Correspondingly, times can be of differing lengths, and we can measure their lengths by established units (seconds, minutes, hours, days, etc.). We can visit our relatives for a *short* time or a *long* time. Our stay can *extend* over two weeks, and a conference can *stretch* over four days. One can travel *over* the holidays. As an observer moving along a path, one can approach various places and get nearer to and farther away from them. In the temporal realm, therefore, we speak of *getting closer* to Thanksgiving, *approaching* (or *coming up on*) the weekend, *passing* the deadline, *arriving* in a minute, *leaving* some unhappy event *far behind*, *reaching* Saturday, and being *halfway through* the month.

The crucial point for our purposes is that the metaphor is conceptual, and it is based on experiential correlations between the movement of a person over a landscape and the passing of time. The metaphor is not merely a linguistic entity—a collection of words only. The cross-domain mapping is based on experienced correlations of motion and temporal flow (and not on any supposed after-the-fact similarities between spatial motion and temporal change). The mapping constitutes our conceptual understanding and guides our reasoning about time. And the mapping is, in turn, the basis for the language we use to talk about time. Here is as clear a case as one can find of meaning and concepts being grounded in the qualities and structures of bodily experience.

NONCONSCIOUS BODILY MEANING

I give these two examples of embodied conceptual meaning and thought as an early reminder of where the argument of this book is headed. We need, first, to appreciate the pervasiveness of embodied meaning-making at the corporeal levels of our experience. We must see how our bodies, our brains, and our environments together generate a vastly meaningful milieu out of which all significance emerges for creatures with bodies like ours. We can call this nonconscious dimension *immanent meaning*. Second, we need to see how our "higher" abstract conceptualization and reasoning are grounded in this embodied meaning-making. This requires us to explore the continuity that exists between our mostly nonconscious experience of embodied meaning and our seemingly disembodied acts of thinking and reasoning. Finally, we need to see how recognizing the bodily grounding of meaning leads us to a new understanding of thought, knowledge, and symbolic interaction that challenges many of our most cherished assumptions about the mind.

In this chapter, we began where all life begins—with movement, and with the qualities that lie at the heart of our experience of movement. The next step in plumbing the bodily depths of meaning is to explore some key infant and early-childhood experiences that, even prior to language, provide us with meaningful contact with our world.

CHAPTER 2

Big Babies

Adults are big babies. Keeping this in mind will take us a long way toward understanding how things come to be meaningful to us. This bold claim is an exaggeration; of course there are dimensions of an adult's experience of meaning that are not available to infants, or even to young children. But we can discover a great deal about how people make meaning by studying the ways that infants and children eventually come to experience a world that they share with their adult caregivers. We can see in infant development the coming into existence of structures, qualities, and models that are the basis of adult meaning-making. The key idea of this chapter is that the many bodily ways by which infants and children find and make meaning are not transcended and left behind when children eventually grow into adulthood. On the contrary, these very same sources of meaning are carried forward into, and thus underlie and make possible, our mature acts of understanding, conceptualization, and reasoning. Consequently, if we want to discover how meaning is made, we will do well to begin with the blossoming world of babies.

Now, babies are not proposition-crunchers. They do not lie in their cribs combining subjects and predicates into propositions by which they understand the world. They do not look around thinking "Mom's lips are really red today," "My bottle weighs twelve ounces," or "Oh my! I've misplaced my pacifier." And yet, babies *are* learning how to grasp the meaning of things, people, and events. The world is becoming meaningful to them, even though they lack language and are not engaged in full-blown conceptual, not to mention propositional, thinking. There is meaning here, and we need to figure out what this kind of meaning consists in and how it relates to conceptual-propositional meaning. My thesis is that this immanent, preconceptual, and nonpropositional meaning is the basis for all forms of meaning.

My claim about adults' being big babies is meant polemically, as an antidote to disembodied and overly intellectualized propositional theories of meaning and reason. By looking at some of the ways by which infants and young children learn the meaning of their world, we can understand a great deal about where meaning comes from and how much broader and deeper it is than most contemporary analytic philosophy of mind and language can fathom. If babies aren't little proposition-processing machines but nevertheless manage to be learning what various objects, persons, and occurrences mean, then we must formulate a theory of meaning that is not predicated on the proposition as the basic unit of meaning. What better place to look for such structures of meaning than in the burgeoning activities of infants? I want to survey some of the dimensions of meaning that develop for infants and young children and that continue to play a central role in our experience of meaning as adults. The point is to tie meaning to embodied interactions, rather than to alleged disembodied entities and processes.

WHAT BABIES EXPERIENCE

Even as recently as thirty years ago, psychologists did not have well-tested empirical techniques for figuring out how infants experience their world. Since babies can't speak, they can't tell us what they are experiencing, and therefore the so-called inner lives of infants were shrouded in mystery. But that is changing now, due largely to the development of experimental techniques that allow researchers to test hypotheses about what infants feel and think. The ability to monitor eye movements and to track focusing has made it possible to study infants' preferential looking. We have devices to record the strength and frequency of sucking responses. We can make educated judgments about when babies are expressing alarm, surprise, frustration, anger, and joy.

Such techniques for monitoring sucking, looking, arm and leg movements, and emotional responses have become the basis for what are known as habituation/dishabituation studies. For example, if an infant is repeatedly presented with the same visual image or scene, it will typically begin to lose interest and will spend a rapidly decreasing amount of time looking at or attending to the successive identical images. But when a novel scene or image is presented, the length of time the baby stays focused on the new image will be markedly greater (this is called dishabituation). Such experimental methods have been used to great effect to test hypotheses about how an infant is experiencing something and what it expects to see happen. As every parent knows, babies express surprise and frustration when things do not go as they had expected. Not only can this tendency tell us what changes babies recognize in their experience, but, coupled with judgments about their emotional responses, it can also be used to study babies' expectations about such things as object permanence, inertial motion, and causation.

The starting point for examining how infants experience objects, surroundings, caregivers, and their own bodies is the universally acknowledged commonplace that infants are not born into an adult world; instead, they must *learn* the perceptual and conceptual experiences that adults take for granted. Babies must develop a workable understanding of object permanence (e.g., that objects don't cease to exist when they pass behind an occluding object), causation (e.g., that objects move and are changed by physical forces), and inertial motion (e.g., that objects put forcefully into motion tend to maintain the direction and force of their initial motion unless affected by other forces). In other words, babies and children have to learn the *meaning* of objects and events that will eventually make up their mature, shared experience of a common world. They must learn how to understand what is happening to them—what they are experiencing and what they are doing. What *is* given to infants are their various sensorimotor and conceptual capacities (which must themselves be activated through experience and continually developed, often in certain ordered sequences and within certain time frames) that set constraints on what can be experienced and how it can be meaningful to humans. These mental capacities are extremely plastic and dynamic, and the way they develop depends partly on genetic programs and partly on the specific experiences and developmental history of the individual infant. We thus grow into a meaningful world by learning how to "take the measure" of our ongoing, flowing, continuous experience. We grow into the ability to experience meaning, and we grow into shared, interpersonal meanings and experiences.

In their survey of infant and childhood perceptual development, Eleanor Gibson and Anne Pick (2000) argue that infants must master three major kinds of developmental tasks if they are to function successfully in their physical and social environments. These tasks appear to be taken up sequentially, in the following order, although each stage will overlap with the others.

1. *Communication.* From the moment of birth, infants enter our world with capacities for immediately and directly communicating with other people, especially their caregivers. Even as newborns, they can look at and listen to others, and they quickly learn how to respond in order to get nourishment, care, and affection. As we will see below, babies make these primitive connections via mutual gaze, expressive behavior, joint attention, and other highly nuanced forms of attunement. Because their muscle control is so limited at this stage, they tend to accomplish this essential communication mostly via facial expressions and expressive vocalizations.

2. *Object perception and manipulation.* By about the fourth month, as their perceptual and motor capacities develop more fully, infants begin to learn about the possibilities for interacting with objects through reaching and manipulation. They begin to acquire a sense of a world populated by objects that they can utilize to achieve various desired effects.

3. *Bodily motion.* At six months or later, as the lower limbs become stronger and better coordinated, infants acquire the ability to move around in their environment in a rich, exploratory manner. This capacity for locomotion opens up a vast new world of meaningful objects and possibilities for accomplishing goals and realizing intentions.

These ways of learning the meaning of the world all involve the body—its perceptual capacities, motor functions, posture, expressions, and ability to experience emotions and desires. Such capacities are at once bodily, affective, and social. *They do not require language in any full-blown sense, and yet they are the very means for making meaning and for encountering anything that can be understood and made sense of.* I will argue that when we grow up, we do not somehow magically cast off these modes of meaning-making; rather, these body-based meaning structures underlie our conceptualization and reasoning, including even our most abstract modes of thought.

What follows is a very brief survey of just a few of the more important ways in which this body-based process of meaning-making develops in infants in a way that is carried forward in our adult experience. My primary interest here is to reveal the bodily components of these meaning-constituting experiences, processes, and activities that are so evident in infant development.

INFANT COMMUNICATION AND PRIMARY INTERSUBJECTIVITY

Besides breathing on its own, the very first thing a baby has to do after its tumultuous entrance into the world is to establish communicative contact with its caregivers, those people who will feed and care for it. Failure to do so would be disastrous, even fatal. So it is no surprise that infants exit the womb primed to establish connections to other people. At first, they don't have a vast array of resources to accomplish this essential task, so they use everything they've got—primarily their face, voice, and body movements.

If you were to bend over your baby's crib in order to talk "baby talk" to her, how would you do this? Without thinking, you would automatically align your face with your baby's. You would position yourself alongside her crib and then lean over her, cocking your head to create eye contact and facial alignment. If you picked her up, you would support her with your hands and align her face with yours, thereby establishing mutual gaze. You would go out of your way to engage your baby in this way because you instinctively know that this face-to-face alignment is an optimal way to establish visual, olfactory, and verbal communication. Nobody ever taught you to align your face with the baby's—you just do it, and thereby you are able to connect, intuitively and directly, with her. Moreover, humans have a face-recognition center in their brains and are very good at facial recognition. But if you rotate a face in the vertical plane 180 degrees from the typical alignment for looking at another's face, normal people mostly lose their ability to make a rapid recognition. Getting the face in the proper orientation is thus important, both for identification and for the delicate dance of "dialogue" with an infant.

Mutual gaze is normally present from birth. In addition to this primordial intersubjective connection, other forms of visual coordination develop at later stages. Toward the end of the first year or the beginning of the second, infants can engage in what is known as joint visual attention, wherein the infant can follow the direction of another's gaze and recognize the target of the other person's attention (Collis and Schaffer 1975; Butterworth and Grover 1990). Daddy can make eye contact with Baby and can then get Baby to direct her gaze to a particular toy, just by slowly moving his eyes toward, and then fixing them on, the toy. So from the very beginning of our tenure in the world, we are fitted to make eye contact, and we later learn to identify the direction and even the object of another's gaze. This universal phenomenon is used to great effect in movie thrillers, in scenes in which a terrified character points with her gaze to the location of a threatening creature or person lurking in the shadows.

Mutual gaze is a form of primitive I-Thou relation between humans. It constitutes a very basic level at which we begin to read the intentions

of other people. As such, it is a primordial form of human intersubjectivity, a form of shared meaning and communicative intention. Mutual gaze
and joint attention do not need to be translated into conceptual or propositional knowledge. They are rudimentary forms of interconnectedness
with others by which we share some aspect of our joint world, even without speech or reflective thought.

Because communication is an absolute necessity if an infant is to receive
the sustenance, nurturance, and affection it needs to survive and grow,
evolutionary development has fitted the infant with remarkable physiological and cognitive resources to negotiate meaning and social intercourse with its caregivers. Babies "goo-goo" and "wah-wah" their way
into our hearts. At a bodily level, self and other in the baby-caregiver relationship are directly and intimately bound together. Basic mimetic bodily
relations reveal this primary togetherness. Andrew Meltzoff and M. Keith
Moore (1983, 1989) studied the ability of infants, even those less than an
hour old, to imitate the adult gestures of tongue protrusion, mouth opening, lip protrusion, and finger movement. The babies typically "prac-
ticed" these gestures, with varying degrees of coordination, fluidity, and
correction for mistakes, until they eventually matched those of the adult
they were observing. In order for this remarkable imitative behavior to
occur, infants must be born with "something like an act space or primitive body scheme that allows the infant to unify the visual and motor/
proprioceptive information into one common 'supramodal' framework"
(Meltzoff and Moore 1995, 53).[1] This suggests the intimate connection,
even from birth, of self and other. There appears to be an "intrinsic relat-
edness between the seen bodily acts of others and the internal states of oneself (the sensing and representation of one's own movements)" (ibid., 54).
What we see gesturally enacted in others, we can reproduce in ourselves,
via our ability to make cross-modal connections and to realize patterns in
our proprioception (our felt sense of our bodily posture and our joint and
limb positions).

Bodily connectedness and coordination with others is thus a basic condition for infants to learn the meaning of their world and to interact successfully with other people. Colwyn Trevarthen says of this bodily inter-

---

1. There is currently a controversy about whether the postulation of so-called supramodal representations is required in order to explain infant imitation and learning. For
a criticism of this view, see Stawarska 2003. Developing research on the mirror-neuron
system, discussed below and in chapter 8, will surely shed light on the brain mechanisms
of imitative learning, including whether there are supramodal representations.

subjective coupling, "The core of every human consciousness appears to be an immediate, unrational, unverbalized, conceptless, totally atheoretical potential for rapport of the self with another's mind" (1993, 121). At this primordial level of connection with others, our so-called "knowledge" of them and of their "minds" is not primarily inferential. Instead, it is directly grasped. Following Mary Catherine Bateson (1975), Trevarthen has aptly described this prelinguistic, bodily dance of infant-caregiver communicative sharing of meaning and understanding as a *proto-conversation*. He explains that once the mother has established eye contact and alert responsiveness with her baby, there often ensues a typical "dialogue"—a back-and-forth, highly nuanced, mutual pursuit of shared meaning:

> The next, and crucial, phase is signaled by the infant's making a "statement of feeling" in the form of a movement of the body, a change in hand gesture away from clasping the mother, a smile or a pout, a pleasure sound or a fretful cry. The mother, if she is alert and attentive, reacts in a complementary way. A positive, happy expression of smiling and cooing causes her to make a happy imitation, often complementing or praising the baby in a laughing way, and then the two of them join in a synchronized display that leads the infant to perform a more serious utterance that has a remarkably precocious form. (Trevarthen 1993, 131)

The subsequent "precocious" display that Trevarthen is referring to is some bodily expression or gesture that can be received by the mother as expressing something the baby "knows" and wants to tell her. None of this, of course, is propositional, linguistic, or even necessarily verbal, but it is nonetheless a sharing of meaning and a meaningful coordination of behaviors. When the child later begins to acquire language, these bodily, gestural, expressive displays of intersubjective engagement will sometimes be accompanied by linguistic utterances, though they are typically not dependent on such utterances.

There is growing evidence that the remarkable mimetic intersubjective achievements of the sort revealed in infant imitation experiments are based upon what has come to be known as our mirror-neuron system. Giacomo Rizzolatti, Maurizio Gentilucci, Vittorio Gallese, and other researchers first discovered that when a macaque (a type of monkey) observes a manual operation, such as another monkey or a human grasping a banana, there is neural activation in the motor and premotor cortices, which would be activated if the monkey itself were grasping that object (Rizzolatti and Gentilucci 1988; Gallese and Goldman 1998). Subsequently, this mirroring phenomenon was demonstrated in humans (Fadiga et al. 1995). If I observe you tearing a sheet of paper, there will be a weak and partial activation in my motor cortex, just as if I were tearing the paper myself. As we will discuss in more detail in chapter 8, this mirroring capacity extends even to merely imagining that one is performing an action. My understanding of bodily actions performed by others is based on the activation of my own bodily sense of performing such an action.

Meltzoff and Moore recognize that a baby's capacity for facial and gestural imitation is a momentous fact about human meaning-making: namely, infants see other people as like themselves, and they come to understand themselves and others as similar in their being what we, as adults, would call *human actors*. Moreover, they learn this in a bodily way, by experimenting at imitating the gestures and actions of other people. In addition, what infants experience as human appears to be, for them, different in kind from everything that is other than human. In other words, infants are born with a capacity to discriminate animate expressive gestures of the sort characteristic of humans. Meltzoff and Moore speculate that

> the basic cut infants impose on the world of objects is neither self-initiated movement versus moved by a seen force (trees in the wind are not viewed as special), nor animate versus inanimate (armadillos will not be of much interest), nor even people (as adults know them) versus things. The aboriginal distinction may be something closer to *human acts versus other events*. (Meltzoff and Moore 1995, 54–55)

Notice, once again, that whatever the infant takes to be the most primordial ontological distinction is a question of *affordances*. It is not an absolute ontological fact that the world comes divided into two ultimate categories—human versus other-than-human—any more than that the basic categories are animate versus inanimate. Instead, the basic ontological categories *for embodied, social creatures like us* will depend on the nature of our bodies, our brains, our environment, and our social interactions. In other words, no matter what our ontological categories might be, or turn out in the future to be, they are not built into the nature of some allegedly mind-independent world. Our realism, as Hilary Putnam (1987) has argued, is "realism with a human face"; what we "take" as real depends on how we experience things via the affordances of our world at a given time and place, relative to our bodies, our interests, and our purposes in making conceptual distinctions.

Meltzoff and Moore nicely summarize the key aspects of infant meaning-making regarding both objects and people:

> We are proposing that infants use three criteria for understanding the identity of objects: spatiotemporal, featural, and functional. 'Spatiotemporal' refers to location in space and time, 'featural' refers to perceptual properties; and 'functional' refers to how an object acts or how one can act with it. We are suggesting that for young infants, human behavior—in particular the type of distinctive acts we call gestural signatures—are used to identify individuals. These are the precursors of our everyday adult recognition that individual people have distinctive mannerisms, styles, and modes of behavior that can be expected from them. (Meltzoff and Moore 1995, 58–59)

FELT QUALITIES AND EMOTIONAL PATTERNS

In *The Interpersonal World of the Infant,* Daniel Stern (1985) presents evidence concerning the development of a sense of self in prelinguistic infants. One striking aspect of his account is the role of bodily experience and feeling in this developmental process. In the first couple of months, a baby's experiences are focused largely around basic attempts at social communication related to its need for nourishment and nurturance. With its neuro-muscular systems so poorly developed, what can such a creature possibly be experiencing? Could there be any meaning at all at this prelinguistic stage?

Stern's hypothesis is that "the infant can experience the *process* of emerging organization as well as the result, and it is this experience of emerging organization that I call the *emergent sense of self*" (Stern 1985, 45). The key to understanding this early sense of an emerging self is its tie to bodily states and processes: "The first such organization concerns the body: its coherence, its actions, its inner feeling states, and the memory of all these. That is the experiential organization with which the sense of a core self is concerned" (ibid., 46).

Even before infants learn to experience objects and their generic properties and causal interactions, they are already feeling the patterns of organizing processes that give their experience form and meaning. Stern describes three types of organizing process involved in an infant's emerging sense of a core self: amodal perception, vitality affects, and physiognomic perception. I want to focus especially on the first two, because of the way they reveal the grounding of meaning in bodily experience and feeling.

Cross-Modal Perception and Motor Coordination

Stern cites an experiment by Andrew Meltzoff and R. W. Borton (1979) in which blindfolded three-week-old infants were given one of two pacifiers to suck on. One of the pacifiers was smooth, while the other had protruding nubs. The pacifier was then taken away, and after a period of time the two different pacifiers were shown to the baby. After a cursory visual inspection of both pacifiers, infants tended (approximately 75 percent of the time) to focus their gaze on the one they had been sucking on. This is a remarkable finding, because it reveals that even neonates have an inborn ability to recognize a single identical pattern present in two or more different perceptual modalities (here, the visual and the haptic). Stern also summarizes some of the previously mentioned infant imitation studies by Meltzoff and Moore (1977, 1983) and emphasizes that such behavior requires complex coordination of visual perception, proprioception, and motor control of the mouth and tongue. Stern concludes that

> infants thus appear to have an innate general capacity, which can be called *amodal perception,* to take information received in one sensory modality and somehow translate it into another sensory modality. . . . They can perceive amodal qualities in any modality from any form of human expressive behavior, represent these qualities abstractly, and then transpose them to other modalities. . . . These abstract representations that the infant experiences are not sights and sounds and touches and nameable objects, but rather shapes, intensities, and temporal patterns—the more "global" qualities of experience. (Stern 1985, 51)

Stern's use of the term "amodal" to describe these processes is unfortunate, insofar as it suggests that the representations are not tied to perceptual modalities, such as vision, touch, or hearing.[2] What his evidence actually shows is that such representations are, rather, *intermodal* or *cross-modal,* since the same experiential pattern can appear in, for example, vision *and* hearing. Henceforth, I will use these two latter terms for patterns that do not exist outside or above our perceptual capacities but that are not tied to only one of those modalities.

The key point here is that infants have an ability to correlate structures experienced in one perceptual domain with those in a different perceptual

---

2. I am indebted to Shaun Gallagher for reminding me of the inaptness of Stern's term "amodal," which could mislead us into thinking of an abstract representation that is not intimately related to our human modes of perception and bodily movement.

modality and in various motor programs. Such correlations are what make it possible for a child to see a rolling ball, track its motion, move his or her body in pursuit, and eventually reach out to grab the ball. Stern's use of the term "abstract representations" to name these cross-modal structures should not lead us to think of them as "representing" anything (as though they were images of some external state of affairs). Perhaps it is more accurate to think of such "representations" as flexible, recurring cross-modal patterns of our ongoing interactions that shape the very contours of our experience.

Vitality Affects—Patterns of Feeling

Intermodal perception is about pattern matching and coordination. These patterns are not just skeletal structures of perception and motor activity; rather, they involve our experience of felt qualities and proprioception. There is a way it feels to stick out your tongue, and there is a distinctive quality to the experience of sucking a pacifier with protruding nubs that is different from the quality experienced with a smooth pacifier. Feeling is one of the most notoriously difficult aspects of our experience to describe, and consequently we tend to overlook it in our accounts of meaning and thought. Nevertheless, it lies at the heart of all meaning. This crucial role of quality and feeling in our experience and understanding is one of the central themes of this book.

Stern points to pervasive patterns of feeling that make up an infant's emerging sense of self and world. Human experience has a feeling of flow, and differences of pattern in this flow are the basis for different felt qualities of situations. Stern gives the example of a mother comforting her baby, stroking its back as she purrs, "There, there, there." To the baby, what the mother *says* and what the mother *does* manifest the same contour of feeling. The stress on the initial *th* of each spoken "there" trails off in the remainder of the word, in a manner precisely paralleled by the stronger pressure at the onset of each comforting stroke, which then trails off as the stroke is completed. The baby experiences the same pattern in what it hears and in what it feels through the mother's comforting strokes, and this is what Stern calls a shared *vitality-affect contour.*

Vitality affects are not the classic emotions like fear, anger, surprise, and joy. Rather, they are the patterns of flow and development of our experience: "These elusive qualities are better captured by dynamic, kinetic terms, such as 'surging,' 'fading away,' 'fleeting,' 'explosive,' 'crescendo,' 'decrescendo,' 'bursting,' 'drawn out,' and so on" (Stern 1985, 54). Just like patterns of cross-modal perception, such feeling qualities and patterns cut across all our sensory and motor capacities. They are the different felt qualities that differentiate our experience of time "dragging along" during a boring lecture from the way it "flies by" when we're having fun. They constitute the qualitative difference between the mellow fulfillment of a long-hoped-for event and the abruptness we experience if we are surprised by an unexpected event. Stern explains that the same vitality-affect contour can be present in different sensory experiences, even though each experience will have its distinctive overall quality: "For example, a 'rush' of anger or joy, a perceived flooding of light, an accelerating sequence of thoughts, an unmeasurable wave of feeling evoked by music, and a shot of narcotics can all feel like 'rushes.' They all share similar envelopes of neural firings, although in different parts of the nervous system" (ibid., 55).

Until quite recently, only a handful of philosophers—most notably William James, John Dewey, and Susanne Langer—have recognized the crucial importance of these patterns of feeling for our ability to experience the meaning of a given situation, action, event, or utterance. Their profound insights on these feeling dimensions of meaning and thought have been largely ignored by mainstream philosophers captivated by abstract, formal, and narrowly conceptual and propositional views of meaning, thought, and knowledge. Langer (1967), for instance, spoke of the forms of feeling that constitute the patterns of our sentience, which she tied to our life processes and functions. She recognized the organic basis of such vitality-affect contours in our breathing, eating, sexuality, waking and sleeping, and our feeling of the waxing and waning of emotions. Because Langer was writing at a time when logical empiricism permitted only conceptual and propositional structures to be part of cognitive meaning, she had to coin a new term, "vital import," to identify the kind of significance she was pointing to. She knew, but wasn't then permitted to say, that vital import was just as much a part of human meaning as any abstract "cognitive content" of propositions or sentences.

I will examine what James and Dewey had to say on the qualitative, felt dimensions of experience later. What is important now is to recognize that what Stern identifies as being at the heart of an infant's sense of itself and the meaning of its experience also lies at the heart of meaning in an adult's experience. The vitality-affect contours that make up a large part of an infant's meaningful experience continue to operate pervasively in adults. We never abandon or transcend our early meaning-making ways; we only extend and build upon them. Stern cites the expressive forms of dance and music as exemplars of the way meaning can be tied to patterns of feeling: "Dance reveals to the viewer-listener multiple vitality affects and their variations, without resorting to plot or categorical affect signals from which the vitality affects can be derived. The choreographer is most often trying to express a way of feeling, not a specific content of feeling" (Stern 1985, 56). We know the meanings of various bodily movements and gestures in dance precisely because we know the feeling and meaning of our own bodily gestures. We know how it feels when our bodies sway gracefully and rhythmically versus when we slip and fall, or jump back in fright. We know intuitively what it means to "be up" and happy, just as we know what it means to "feel low" when we are depressed. Our bodily posture and openness to the world is upright and expansive when we are joyful, and it is drooping and contracting when we are sad.

There is a long-standing tradition of music theory that ties the power of music to its imaginative presentation of patterns of feeling. Eduard Hanslick famously and quite controversially argued that the meaning of what he called "musical ideas" stems primarily from "audible changes of strength, motion, and proportion; and consequently they include our ideas of increasing and diminishing, acceleration and deceleration, clever interweavings, simple progressions, and the like" (Hanslick 1854/1986, 10). Music jumps, skips, hops, drags, speeds up, slows, flows, swells, and falls—just like the patterns of all of our experiences, bodily and intellectual alike. There is powerful meaning in the buildup and release of tension, in the speeding up or slowing down of the pace of an event, in moving smoothly in connected steps versus jumping rapidly across wide intervals. This is true of all types of our experience, whether in music, painting, sculpture, dance, lovemaking, having a conversation, or taking a walk.

Vitality affects are meaningful to us at the most primordial levels of our bodily understanding of our world and our experience. They are meaningful because they give our experience motivation, direction, and intensity. They constitute the erotic, desire-full character of a particular situation that makes it matter to us.

OBJECTS AND PHYSICAL FORCES

Infants come to understand the properties and characteristics of objects by interacting with them in a bodily way, long before they acquire language and abstract conceptualization. What objects mean to us is something we have to learn. Infants must learn how to "take" objects; that is, they must learn what counts as an object, how to differentiate things, and how causation works. They must learn how to manipulate and respond to things in order to achieve their goals, satisfy their needs, and realize their intentions. They do this with their bodies.

It is extremely difficult for most people to get over the misleading "objectivist" model of the world, according to which the world is just "out there" waiting to be experienced, consisting of middle-sized objects that possess objective properties and that stand in definite relations to other objects, independent of beings for whom those objects *are* objects. Because infants learn the meaning of their world through their bodily interactions with macroscopic things that appear to move and be moved and that seem to exist independent of people, they naturally acquire just such an objectivist metaphysics of experience. Most people tend to adopt this objectivist metaphysics, because they use their basic-level, body-relative experience of objects and forces as a model for all that exists. They thus come to think that objects have their properties "in themselves," independent of sentient organisms, since as infants they learn object permanence and eventually come to experience properties as inhering in objects.

In challenging objectivism, I do not mean to deny that our world presents itself to us as a world of middle-sized, mind-independent objects with properties that seem to be in the objects themselves. I agree with Hilary Putnam (1981) that this world of perceived objects is *just as valid and real* as the world as it is understood by various sciences. Our world as experienced is quite different from our world as it is described by mathematical physics or perceptual psychology or cognitive neuroscience. These substantially differing versions are each in their own way correct, relative to certain explanatory frameworks that presuppose differing interests, values, and views of what counts as data and adequate explanation. In other words, our different worlds are value-dependent.

What I object to in the objectivist metaphysical picture is not the idea of objects of experience, but rather the failure to recognize that these objects are mind-dependent and individuated relative to our conceptual systems and structures for meaning-making. The world does not come to us prepackaged with determinate objects with their determinate properties. Instead, we have to *learn* the meaning of physical objects, which we do by watching them, handling them, subjecting them to forces, and seeing how they can be used—in short, by forms of interactive inquiry that are at once bodily and reflective. We learn about the meaning of objects by means of what James J. Gibson (1966, 1979) called "affordances," that is, the possibilities for interaction with objects that result from (1) the plastic, ever-developing sensorimotor capacities of the organism, (2) the characteristics of objects, and (3) the nature of the environments inhabited by the organism. The same "object" can thus present different affordances to different organisms, or even to the same organism at different times. A blade of grass, for instance, might afford climb-up-ability for a chigger, but not for a human. A microscopic parasite might find the human skin quite penetrable, while the skin affords impenetrability for a common housefly. For human beings, but not for an earthworm, other human beings afford possibilities for communication and shared meanings. What counts as an *object* is thus determined relative to an organism of a certain size, shape, and functional makeup. The meaning of objects, established via their affordances, is therefore always relative to characteristics of organisms and their environments. Gibson and Pick (2000, 16) argue that "the realization of an affordance requires that animal and environment be adapted for one another" and that the experience of an affordance depends on establishing a reciprocity between the organism's perception and its action: "Perception guides action in accord with the environmental supports or impediments presented, and action in turn yields information for further guidance, resulting in a continuous perception-action cycle."

An object, therefore, should not be thought of as if it were a fixed entity with inherent properties existing entirely independent of creatures who interact with it. Objects, as we experience them, are actually stable affordances for us—stable patterns that our environment presents to creatures like us with our specific capacities for perception and bodily action. Many objects are so stable that for nearly all intents and purposes, they appear to us to have fixed essences and to be observer-independent givens. This picture of mind-independent objects works well for us most of the time. We have languages with grammatical categories such as *noun* that can be used to pick out these supposedly fixed entities. In the following discussion, therefore, I will frequently fall back into our commonsense way of talking about objects (as in "Babies must learn object permanence"); but, to be correct, we should keep in mind that objects are actually stable events, or stable patterns in interactive perceptual and motor processes.

Over the past twenty years, the study of how infants learn about objects has become a cottage industry in developmental psychology. Despite debates concerning the interpretation of various well-known experiments, a growing consensus has emerged about the chief stages of object-knowledge acquisition (see Gibson and Pick 2000 for an excellent survey of recent research). According to experiments reported by Meltzoff and Moore (1995), infants typically learn to recognize object identity in three stages. During their first four months infants learn object identity, but only in cases where the object maintains a steady state, such as remaining at rest in a place or else moving uniformly along a trajectory. From five to eight months infants can also discern the stable identity of things that either begin to move after being at rest or come to a stop after being in motion. Sometime between nine and eighteen months a big leap forward is made, as they recognize object permanence even when objects are occluded, such as when a stationary object is blocked by a screen or a moving toy passes behind an occluding object. This is the period in which "hide the rattle" is not just a game, but a revelation of the persistence of objects.

When you think about everything an infant must learn before it can grasp the "meanings of things" as they are experienced by adults, it is mind-boggling. Among the characteristic affordances of various objects that have to be learned are at least the following basic types of knowledge, as surveyed by Gibson and Pick (2000).

1. *Detachability/segregation.* A. Needham's experiments (1998) suggest that infants younger than four and a half months are typically unable to distinguish separate objects within a visual array solely on the basis of the different features of the objects. One *learns* to experience the world as consisting of separable objects defined by their distinguishing features or properties.

2. *Solidity.* As early as sixteen weeks, babies can perceive the three-dimensional character of objects, but only when those objects are rotated on various axes and are moved around in space (Kellman 1984).

3. *Size.* Size is learned by movement of the object (nearer and farther away), by head-eye movement, and by touch.

4. *Substance.* Whether objects are hard and rigid or soft and malleable is determined primarily by touching and mouthing them. Infants squeeze elastic objects more with their mouths than they do with their hands, whereas they squeeze rigid objects more with their hands than with their mouths (Rochat 1987). By five months, infants can even use visual information to determine how rigid or elastic an object is.

5. *Shape.* Philippe Rochat's experiments (1987) with rotating objects show that three-month-old babies can discern the invariance of an object's shape while the object is moving in a way that results in views from changing perspectives. There is evidence that even newborns may experience constancy of shape in rotating objects (Slater and Morrison 1985).

The chief moral of this developmental summary is that *infants are not born with an objectivist metaphysics of mind-independent objects.* Rather, they learn it by exploring the affordances of things and by gradually acquiring our adult sense of object independence and permanence. They learn through their perceptions, actions, and bodily experiments (which are all forms of primitive inquiry) to grasp the meaning of object identity. Or, to avoid the objectivist interpretation, we might say that they learn how to regard certain kinds of stable regularities in their environment as objects and other regularities as events (Baldwin and Baird 2001). The meaning an object comes to have for an infant at a given point in time will depend on a large number of factors, including stage of development of perceptual capacities (for fine discrimination, depth perception, discernment of hues, etc.), dynamic growth of posture (which permits head turning, reaching, and grasping), capacities for bodily movement, coordination of motor programs, character of prior experiences, and more. It is by coordinating all of these bodily capacities that infants come to experience the regularities and patterns that make up the adult world they will grow up to inhabit. In the words of Gibson and Pick, "Information about object properties and especially about what they afford is actively obtained by *exploring,* and after a few more months by actively using objects. Exploring objects and discovering how they can be used is the way meanings are learned" (2000, 86). Such exploration depends on the massive coordination of a host of bodily capacities that put us in touch with the things (as stable affordances) that populate our world.

LOCOMOTION

In its earliest stages of development, a more or less stationary infant learns by vision, touch, taste, sound, and smell. Since it cannot raise itself up very well, let alone assume an erect posture, its repertoire of experiences is limited. Although the youngest infants cannot learn by moving their bodies around in their environment, they can observe the movement of objects, and they can learn to manipulate and move objects. As a baby's muscles become stronger and better coordinated, so that the child can reach and manipulate objects, its world is vastly expanded and enriched. But that is only the beginning. When the baby's developing posture and muscular coordination allow it to move around, first by rolling and turning, next by crawling, and later by walking, it is as if a new continent—a confusing, wondrous, brave new world—opens before it. The child's world is the world of its bodily and social interactions. It is a world learned by observing, imitating, and acting, often in ways that require much trial and error.

The baby's ability to move things and to move itself gives rise to affordances that did not exist for it in its earlier stages of development. Locomotion adds marvelous opportunities for the infant to acquire mountains of new meaning through its bodily activities. One of these types of information is tied up with the various phenomena of optical flow described by James Gibson (1979). Gibson argued that our ability to determine the movement of objects and the movement of our own bodies depends on information specified within the optic array that is available to us. For example, if you are moving forward in a linear fashion, you experience a visual "flow" that emerges from a horizontal focal point in front of you, expands out from that point and streams toward you, and then envelops and flows past you. This "streaming-past" flow tells you that you are moving in a specific fashion and direction. D. N. Lee and E. Aronson (1974) conducted the now-famous "moving room" experiments, in which a subject stands on a floor in a room that is constructed so that the walls can be moved independently of the floor. Even a slight movement of the walls can cause a one-year-old to fall down, because he will lean or step forward or backward (depending on the direction the walls are moved) to adjust for what he perceives as his own forward or backward motion. Adults do not typically fall down, but they often wobble in response to this illusion of motion. We are attuned to the optic flow, and we automatically and unconsciously make appropriate bodily responses to it. When you are sitting in a stationary train and the train on the adjacent track begins to move, your sense that *you* are moving results from the information you are receiving from optical flow. By contrast, a different kind of optical experience, such as when an object looms up in your visual field, tells you that something is moving toward you, rather than you moving toward it.

BODY-ENVIRONMENT COUPLING

Optic flow as a basis for our perception of relative motion is just one of many indications we have for the primary phenomenon that Lee (1993) calls "body-environment coupling." In addition to optic flow, Lee describes patterns of acoustic and haptic flow that give us our fundamental experience of our relation to our environment. Babies learn these patterns of body-environment coupling, which remain foundational for orientation and information-gathering in adulthood. Gibson and many subsequent researchers have insisted that the basic information we receive from these experiential flow patterns reveals how we are directly in touch with our surroundings at the most basic bodily level. The fact that perceptual illusions (such as the moving room) can fool us into thinking that we are moving does not undermine the claim that we are ordinarily intimately connected to our surroundings in a knowing way and that this is the result of a long history of evolutionary development. The experimental illusions are possible only because of the stability and reliability of the information we routinely receive from our bodily interactions with our environment. Lee summarizes the profound importance of this ongoing interaction:

> Like all animals, we exist by virtue of coupling our bodies to the environment through action. Inadequate coupling, whether it be on the perceptual side, as when driving in a fog, or on the movement side, as caused by muscular dysfunction, can be a prescription for disaster. Perception is necessary for controlling movement just as movement is necessary for obtaining perceptual information. Perception and movement compose a cycle that is action.
>
> Action in the environment is the root of the ecological self. . . . We are what we do. Therefore, to understand the self, we need to understand how actions can be geared to the environment. (Lee 1993, 43)

BIG BABIES

The purpose of my exaggerated claim that adults are just big babies has been twofold. First, I have been reminding us of some of the many ways that we learn to understand our world not with conceptual and propositional knowledge, but more fundamentally, via bodily interactions and feelings. I have been using infant-development studies to sketch the vast extent of this body-based meaning-making. I have called such meaning *embodied* or *immanent* meaning. When we grow up, we do not shed these embodied meanings or our bodily ways of meaning-making. Instead, we appropriate and recruit them in what we might think of as our more refined, abstractive modes of understanding and thinking. I will develop this crucial theme more fully in subsequent chapters.

My second point has been that from the very beginning of human life, we acquire our burgeoning understanding of our world intersubjectively. We are not solitary, autonomous creatures who individually and singly construct models of our world in our head. On the contrary, we learn about our world in and through others. We inhabit a shared world, and we share meaning from the start, even if we are completely unaware of this while we are infants. In other words, *body-based intersubjectivity*—our being with others via bodily expression, gesture, imitation, and interaction—is constitutive of our very identity from our earliest days, and it is the birthplace of meaning.

CHAPTER 3

"Since Feeling Is First"

Emotional Dimensions of Meaning

Before there is abstract thinking, before there is reasoning, before there is speech, there is emotion. The poet E. E. Cummings understood this:

since feeling is first
who pays any attention
to the syntax of things
will never wholly kiss you;

wholly to be a fool
while Spring is in the world

my blood approves,
and kisses are a better fate
than wisdom
lady i swear by all flowers. Don't cry
—the best gesture of my brain is less than
your eyelids' flutter which says

we are for each other: then
laugh, leaning back in my arms
for life's not a paragraph

And death i think is no parenthesis

FEELING AND MEANING

Emotion and feeling lie at the heart of our capacity to experience meaning. And yet, you can examine a hundred different accounts of meaning, especially in analytic philosophy of mind and language, without finding any serious treatment of emotions or feelings. The reason for this blindness to the crucial role of emotion in meaning is that philosophers are notoriously incapable of explaining what they regard as evanescent, subjective, private feelings. Insofar as they think of feelings as noncognitive, they see no role for them in meaning. When it comes to their theories of meaning, therefore, they talk of concepts, propositions, and sometimes even images, but they have no resources for exploring the workings of either feelings or emotions as part of conceptual meaning. Consequently, most theories of meaning focus exclusively on the conceptual-propositional skeletal structures of meaning, while entirely overlooking the emotional flesh and blood of actual human meaning. Even today, we still succumb to the old logical empiricist ploy of claiming a rigid distinction between "descriptive" or "cognitive" meaning (or uses of language) on the one hand, and "emotive" meaning (or uses of language) on the other. This overly rigid dichotomy, articulated in C. K. Ogden and I. A. Richards's *The Meaning of Meaning* (1923) and later championed by A. J. Ayer in his highly influential *Language, Truth, and Logic* (1936), was viewed as a matter of different *kinds* of meaning, or else different associated functions of language. The cognitive/emotive dichotomy effectively excluded emotion and feeling from the privileged domain of cognitive meaning and descriptive uses of language, thereby absolving philosophers of language from having to give any serious consideration to feeling within their theories of meaning.

If you are skeptical about the claim that emotion is an essential aspect of meaning, just consider this: ask yourself what your experience of "being skeptical about Johnson's claim for the central role of emotions in meaning" really amounts to. As William James pointed out long ago, and Charles Sanders Peirce before him, one's experience of *doubt* is a fully embodied experience of hesitation, withholding of assent, felt bodily tension, and general bodily restriction. Such felt bodily experiences are not merely accompaniments of doubt; rather, they *are* your doubt. The whole meaning of the situation you find yourself in is doubtful. Doubt retards or stops the harmonious flow of experience that preceded the doubt. You *feel* the restriction and tension in your diaphragm, your breathing, and perhaps in your gut. *The meaning of doubt is precisely this bodily experience of holding back assent and feeling a blockage of the free flow of experience toward new thoughts, feelings, and experiences.*

The two philosophical traditions that have given us the most insight into the emotions have been phenomenology, with its rich descriptions of lived experience, and American pragmatism, with its focus on the felt dimensions of the flow of experience.[1] I will give more attention to both of these traditions in the next two chapters, but now I want to survey some of the most promising research on emotion that is coming out of empirical studies in cognitive neuroscience. The best way I know to counteract our traditional prejudice against emotion as a key component of meaning is to turn to the cognitive neuroscience of the emotions. What I find especially important in this research is the way it shows how emotion and feeling are the means by which we are most primordially in touch with our world, are able to make sense of it, and are able to function within it.

THE COGNITIVE NEUROSCIENCE OF THE EMOTIONS

Over the past two decades, there have been stunning advances in our knowledge of what emotions and feelings are and how they contribute to human meaning-making. This research shows that emotions are crucial to our ability to evaluate situations and to assess, both moment to moment and over the long run of our extended lives, the meaning of our experience. Although there is still considerable disagreement about the precise neurochemical bases for specific emotions and feelings, there is now widespread agreement about the basic outlines of a theory of the emotions. For my purposes, therefore, I can sidestep most of the arguments over the specific mechanisms of various emotions, because the major neuroscientists agree that emotions play a central role in an organism's assessment of its internal milieu—its bodily states and processes that are tied to its ongoing interactions with its environment, thereby motivating both internal body-state adjustments and outwardly directed actions in the world.

I am going to base my summary account chiefly on the celebrated work of Antonio Damasio and Joseph LeDoux, two of the most distinguished researchers in the field of cognitive neuroscience today. In a series of three

---

1. Besides these two traditions, I cannot help but mention the brilliant early work of David Hume, who appreciated the central role of feeling in human understanding. His perspective has not, unfortunately, defined an entire tradition, although the history of Hume scholarship has culminated recently in an increasing emphasis of his account of feeling, emotion, and passions.

groundbreaking books—*Descartes' Error: Emotion, Reason, and the Human Brain* (1994); *The Feeling of What Happens: Body and Emotion in the Making of Consciousness* (1999); and *Looking for Spinoza: Joy, Sorrow, and the Feeling Brain* (2003)—Damasio has brought new attention to the role of emotions and feelings in consciousness, judgment, and reasoning. Damasio's work is grounded in clinical observations of his patients with brain lesions and in the experiments he and his colleagues perform both with these patients and with normal subjects. I am attracted to Damasio's work partly because of his humane concern for his patients, even as he runs experiments and uses all of the most current neuroimaging technologies, such as fMRI (functional magnetic resonance imaging) and PET (positron-emission tomography), to build a theory of emotion and feeling. He understands the existential meaning of his patients' dysfunction—their suffering, frustration, life disruption, and anguish. He never allows us to overlook the human cost for those whose lives have been radically altered by disease, accident, or genetic conditions. He feels the social, moral, and existential implications of their dysfunction, including how it affects their ability to grasp the meaning of things. But beyond his humanity, I am attracted by his philosophical turn of mind, as he grapples with problems of how emotion and feeling shape the nature of mind, thought, consciousness, and communication. It is rare for a neuroscientist to be philosophically sophisticated, just as it is rare for philosophers to understand the intricacies of cognitive neuroscience—let alone to *do* the science. Damasio stands out for his philosophical engagement with his science and with the implications of his research for human existence.

Damasio's account of the emotions begins with a foundational evolutionary and ecological claim about the life-sustaining role of emotions for certain sentient organisms. The primary task for any organism—the task that must be accomplished before all others—is the preservation of life and the furtherance of conditions for the organism's growth. Damasio begins by observing, in *Looking for Spinoza,* that over our evolutionary history we humans have developed a large ensemble of interrelated systems (many of which we share with other animals) geared toward our continued existence, growth, and flourishing. These systems include:

1. *Metabolism.* Complex chemical and neural processes work to preserve the proper chemical balance within the organism in order to maintain its most basic, life-sustaining bodily functions, such as heart rate, respiration, temperature control, and digestion.

2. *Basic reflexes.* Reflex responses, such as closing the eyes and turning away from an oncoming projectile, operate automatically to protect us from physical harm.

3. *Immune system.* We have immune reactions that ward off threats from external and internal agents (such as bacteria, viruses, and toxins) that may be harmful to us.

4. *Pain and pleasure behaviors.* Evolutionarily, we have developed in such a way that we often experience pleasure in situations that are conducive to our well-being. Many harmful conditions are felt as painful. Although this correlation between pleasure and well-being does not always hold (e.g., addictive use of methamphetamines is harmful), pleasure and pain have generally served our functional success.

5. *Basic drives and motivations.* Over most of our evolutionary history, our appetites and aversions have inclined us toward things that are typically, though not unerringly, helpful to us and directed us away from what is not conducive to our flourishing. Obviously, these drives can also occasionally lead us to harmful things—such as addictive psychopharmaceuticals or risky sexual behavior, which were not present in our earlier environments.

6. *Emotions.* Emotions are complex neural, chemical, and behavioral responses to various types of stimuli that typically have positive or negative value for us. They are part of the process by which our bodies assess their state and make adjustments to maintain a homeostasis within our internal milieu. They include background emotions (e.g., energy or malaise, edginess or calmness), primary emotions (e.g., fear, joy, anger, sadness), and social emotions (e.g., shame, honor, pride, jealousy).

7. *Feelings.* Under certain specifiable conditions, we have a qualitative awareness of our sensations and emotional responses. Such awareness is called a feeling.

All of these systems together make up a vast, interconnected system of monitoring and response processes, developed over our long evolutionary history, that are geared toward keeping us alive and functioning more or less smoothly within the kinds of environments (physical, social, moral, and cultural) that we inhabit. Each "higher-level" system (e.g., feelings or emotions) depends on and makes use of processes at "lower" levels (e.g., metabolism). Even though we are seldom conscious of occurrences at most of these levels, their life-sustaining activities are as significant and meaningful to us as anything could possibly be. Without them, we would cease to exist and would have no possibility for enhancing the quality of our experience.

I am going to argue that mostly nonconscious processes like these make meaningful experience possible for creatures like us, and they play a crucial role in shaping our values. *What* is meaningful to us, and *how* it is meaningful, depends fundamentally on our ongoing monitoring of our bodily states as we experience and act within our world.

Once again, as we proceed, it should become clear that the "meaning" I am discussing involves bodily processes that are mostly automatic and nonconscious but that help make possible our more conscious acts of meaning-making, such as our use of language. I am going to end up suggesting that meaning at this level is intimately tied to emotions, only some of which rise to the level where there is a conscious feeling of the emotion as having a meaning.

Damasio argues that the above-mentioned systems of body-state monitoring evolved to preserve a global homeostasis, or balanced equilibrium, within the organism:

> All living organisms from the humble amoeba to the human are born with devices designed to solve *automatically,* no proper reasoning required, the basic problems of life. Those problems are: finding sources of energy; incorporating and transforming energy; maintaining a chemical balance of the interior compatible with the life process; maintaining the organism's structure by repairing its wear and tear; and fending off external agents of disease and physical injury. The single word homeostasis is convenient shorthand for the ensemble of regulations and the resulting state of regulated life. (Damasio 2003, 30)

In short, whatever else a living organism does, it must at all costs continually monitor its own internal bodily states. If it fails to do so, it can risk losing the homeostasis necessary for life or, less dramatically, for smooth functioning. It is especially important to know when there are changes in internal bodily states and then to develop ways of modulating the internal milieu so as to either preserve or reestablish a relative homeostasis for the whole system. Otherwise, the organism will fall out of harmony with its environment and cease to function adequately within its current situation, and in extreme cases it may even die.

Because most of this homeostasis-oriented processing occurs beneath the level of conscious awareness, it happens "before you know it." It must be more or less automatic, for if we had to consciously control all of this monitoring and adjustment, we would have to devote all our energy to controlling even the most elementary bodily operations. This would quickly exhaust our cognitive resources and would make it impossible for us to carry out the multitude of coordinated functions required for life.

However, although most animals function via such nonconscious operations, human life is so complex that either automatic processing alone
cannot handle the homeostasis challenge, or else our flourishing is better
served by the addition of conscious experience and reflection on it. This
need for additional checking on how things are going for us, and the need
for appropriate changes within our bodies, gives rise to conscious awareness and even deliberation. For now, however, I want to focus exclusively
on the mostly nonconscious processes of meaning.

A cautionary word is in order concerning the ambiguous language of
"monitoring" of bodily states. When I speak of an organism's "monitoring changes in its state," I do not mean to imply that there is any conscious
or reflective process required. There is no "I," no single, unified execu-
tive system that coordinates all of the necessary bodily changes. Instead,
there are numerous systems simultaneously "communicating" with one
another in a vast dance of ongoing coordination and readjustment. Therefore, instead of saying that "I" monitor my bodily states, it would be more
accurate to say that "my body" (or bodily systems) monitors the ongoing
processes within the body, as it interacts with its environment. However,
since there is no "I" without my concrete embodiment, it is easy to fall
into the locution "*I* monitor *my* bodily states," even though there clearly is
no phenomenological awareness of *my* doing so.

It is in the monitoring and modulating of body states that emotions
come into the picture. According to Damasio, emotions—or what might
more appropriately be called *emotional responses*—are processes arising from
the perception of ongoing changes within an organism that require some
transforming activity, either to continue the harmonious flow of experience or to help reestablish equilibrium in response to a perceived imbal-
ance or disruption within the organism. Functionally, emotions evolved
to evoke changes within the organism and motivate it to act in ways that
tend to be conducive to its welfare.[2]

In order to explain the crucial role of emotions in human meaning,
we must have a definition of emotion that is consonant with our commonsense use of emotion-related terms and at the same time in line with
current cognitive neuroscience of the emotions. This turns out to be far

2. Quite obviously, emotions are not always conducive to the organism's flourishing. In humans especially, emotional responses can be inappropriate and misplaced (e.g.,
agoraphobia, jealous rage, and anger may lead to self-destructive behavior). However, it
appears that emotions tend to preserve the flourishing of the organism, in spite of cases
where they occasionally "run wild."

more difficult than one might at first imagine, for there are nearly as many different definitions as there are emotion researchers. Because I intend to develop the implications of Damasio's account, I want to cite in full his summary definition of emotion:

1. An emotion-proper, such as happiness, sadness, embarrassment, or sympathy, is a complex collection of chemical and neural responses forming a distinctive pattern.
2. The responses are produced by the normal brain when it detects an emotionally competent stimulus (an ECS), the object or event whose presence, actual or in mental recall, triggers the emotion. The responses are automatic.
3. The brain is prepared by evolution to respond to certain ECSs with specific repertoires of action. However, the list of ECSs is not confined to those prescribed by evolution. It includes many others learned in a lifetime of experience.
4. The immediate result of these responses is a temporary change in the state of the body proper, and in the state of the brain structures that map the body and support thinking.
5. The ultimate result of the responses, directly or indirectly, is the placement of the organism in circumstances conducive to survival and well-being. (Damasio 2003, 53)

Several key points of this definition must be kept in mind as we develop our explanation of the role of emotions in meaning. First, there is nothing in this account, so far, about feeling. Emotional responses can occur long before we become aware that we are *feeling* an emotion. Since feelings are consciously experienced bodily processes, while emotional responses can operate beneath the level of consciousness, feeling cannot be a necessary condition for an emotional response, even though feeling typically, and importantly, does accompany the emotional response. Moreover, awareness of feeling falls along a continuum that runs from powerful passions that shake us to our core all the way to faint feelings of which we are only marginally, or even subliminally, aware. The whole neural, chemical, and behavioral arc of emotional response runs more or less automatically most of the time, and this is usually a very good thing. When someone steps out of the shadows with a knife and threatens us, we want fear to rise up within us *immediately and without a thought,* preparing us for flight or fight before it's too late. We need our body to marshal its resources and to take action, even before we become consciously aware that we are fearful. The changes in body posture, facial expression, and preparedness for action that often accompany different emotions result from internal neural and chemical processes that are a response to the perceived situation. That is why we can read another's emotional state in their facial expression, gestures, posture, and bodily movements even though the person might not be consciously aware of the emotion. That is why it sometimes happens that we don't know we are angry until someone says to us, "Why are *you* so mad today?"

Second, emotions serve a crucial function in our lives. They emerged over our evolutionary history precisely because they are mostly conducive to our survival and our ability to function harmoniously with our environment and with other people. Emotional responses, such as fear, joy, and disgust, are enacted more or less automatically on the basis of the general tendencies of various emotionally competent stimuli to affect our well-being in certain routine ways. Projectiles speeding toward our heads, large carnivorous predators, screaming knife-wielding assailants, and foul-smelling (rotten) food tend not to be good for our well-being, and we had better be safe than sorry when we encounter such things. We need automatic emotional responses that take us out of harm's way. The fact that certain evolutionarily inscribed emotional responses may today no longer serve our well-being as they once did (e.g., fear of strangers) is a problem for us to solve in specific circumstances, but it does not change the fact that our emotional responses for the most part evolved to help us function successfully. Thus, fear of someone outside your clan might once have been highly adaptive, whereas in today's world it contributes counterproductively to failure of the communication and cooperation that are necessary in our global community. The problem is how to transform these deeply rooted emotional responses into more cooperative habits of personal and communal intercourse, but it does not falsify the claim that emotions exist for the well-being of the organism.

Third, every emotional response is part of a process in which there is some *appraisal* of how a given emotionally competent stimulus stands in relation to the potential well-being of the organism. Our emotional responses are based on both our nonconscious and conscious assessments of the possible harm, nurturance, or enhancement that a given situation may bring to our lives. As Damasio puts it, "Emotions provide a natural means for the brain and mind to evaluate the environment within and around the organism, and respond accordingly and adaptively" (2003, 54). This evaluative dimension is absolutely crucial, and its implications are monumental. Emotional responses are not merely bodily, after-the-fact feeling reactions. Rather, they are bodily processes (with neural and chemical components) that result from our appraisal of the meaning and significance of our situation and consequent changes in our body state, often initiating actions geared to our fluid functioning within our environment. It is in this sense that emotional responses can be said to move us to action. Joseph LeDoux summarizes this point as follows:

> Information received by sensory systems activates emotional-processing circuits, which evaluate the meaning of the stimulus input and initiate specific emotional responses by triggering output circuits. Defense, food-seeking, and sex circuits receive inputs from the same sensory systems, and thus receive similar information, but a given circuit is only activated when the sensory influx contains stimulus information relevant to its operation. . . . These detection and reaction processes take place automatically, independent of conscious awareness of the stimulus and feelings about it. (LeDoux 2002, 206–7)

Fourth, the appraisal dimension reveals a primary sense in which we may say that emotions are an important part of meaning. Insofar as we are assessing how things are going for us in our continually changing interactions with our surroundings, we are taking the measure of our situation. This is, in part, a determination of what that situation *means* for us, here and now. Most of the time we do not need language, nor even elaborate conceptual schemes, to grasp the felt meaning of our current situation as it is unfolding, moment to moment. Philosophers of language are notoriously reluctant to grant any cognitive function to emotions, and they bristle at the idea that emotions are part of cognitive meaning. Because we are often not consciously aware of our emotional responses, they seem to most philosophers of language and mind to be very poor candidates for thought, which they insist must be conscious and propositional. It is one of the central aims of this book to show up this claim for what it is, namely, a very unfortunate prejudice grounded in inadequate, overly narrow views of thought that have made it impossible for us to appreciate the way meaning emerges in our experience. Emotions have meaning for us insofar as they lie at the heart of our ability to appraise the situations we find ourselves in and to act appropriately. When we feel them, they can enter into our more conscious deliberations about how we should respond to our situation.

NEURAL, CHEMICAL, AND PHYSIOLOGICAL BASES OF EMOTIONS

According to current emotion research, emotions are not merely cognitive structures, they are not merely brain processes, and they are not merely bodily responses. Rather, emotions encompass all of these dimensions, and more. The failure to appreciate this multidimensional character of emotions has engendered, on the one side, cognitivist and intellectualist theories that overlook the bodily basis of emotions and, on the other side, purely mechanistic theories that ignore the cognitive and social dimensions. Both of these extremes are equally one-dimensional and impoverished. A brief exploration of the neurophysiology of the emotions is thus necessary if we are to understand how emotion and feeling come to play a central role in meaning. An adequate theory of the emotions must include the role of the brain and the body, even though that will not be the whole story. The summary account I am going to give will necessarily be general and brief; it is meant to emphasize the bodily basis of emotion.

The prevailing consensus in contemporary neurophysiology is that there is no single, unique set of functional brain regions that are activated in exactly the same manner for all emotions. The sets of neural connections and regions that are activated in fear are not precisely identical to those that are activated in joy. However, there are specific parts of the brain that appear to play a key role in emotional responses in general. For example, the amygdala, hypothalamus, and ventromedial prefrontal cortex tend to be implicated as the usual suspects over and over again in explanations of emotions.

Also, there appears to be a series of stages for the incitement, development, and expression of emotions. According to both Damasio (2003) and LeDoux (2002), the first stage in an emotional process is the organism's perception and appraisal of what Damasio calls an emotionally competent stimulus, such as seeing a serpentine form in one's path while walking in the mountains. This leads to a second stage as the perception triggers a series of automatic neural and chemical changes in the body. In the third stage, these neurochemical changes affect the whole body and its musculature, often resulting in observable bodily behaviors and feelings. For example, the hypothalamus might release chemical molecules (such as peptides) into the bloodstream that alter the functioning of the viscera and the central nervous system. Damasio explains, "In all emotions, multiple volleys of neural and chemical responses change the internal milieu, the viscera, and the musculoskeletal system for a certain period and in a particular pattern. Facial expressions, vocalizations, body postures, and specific patterns of behavior (running, freezing, courting, or parenting) are thus enacted" (2003, 63).

LeDoux, who is particularly well known for his studies of fear, argues that there must be an input system (which perceives and evaluates a stimulus) plus an output system that both affects the internal milieu and generates bodily changes and movements. In the case of fear, the amygdalae (two almond-shaped structures deep in the temporal lobe in front of the brain stem nuclei) appear to be the sites that combine the input and output functions. LeDoux's research suggests that

> the amygdala contains a dozen or so distinct divisions or areas, of which only two are necessary for fear conditioning. Information about the outside world is transmitted to the lateral nucleus from sensory-processing regions in the thalamus and cortex, allowing the amygdala to monitor the outside world for signs of danger. If the lateral nucleus detects danger, it activates the central nucleus, which initiates the expression of behavioral responses and changes in body physiology that characterize states of fear. (LeDoux 2003, 214)

At the input level, there is no single pathway by which information is interpreted in a way that engenders fear. Tone conditioning (e.g., hearing a tone that is followed by an electrical shock) is processed mostly within the amygdala, whereas contextual conditioning (e.g., perceiving another person as threatening in a particular situation) requires, in addition, input from the hippocampus, which is involved in relational, configurational, and spatial processing: "While the lateral nucleus is involved in the tone-shock integration, it is not necessary for context-shock integration. The basal nucleus (basal amygdala), which receives the connections from the hippocampus, is critical instead" (LeDoux 2003, 216).

The medial prefrontal cortex also plays a key role in regulating the amygdala. It appears to be an interface between "higher" cognitive systems and systems that regulate the emotions. Studies by Quirk et al. (2000) indicate that when the amygdala is active in creating a fear response, the medial prefrontal cortex must be inhibited, and, conversely, when the medial prefrontal cortex is active, there is inhibition to the amygdala. This suggests channels by which fear reactions can be somewhat controlled and even suppressed.

The bodily expressions and movements that I have called the third stage of the process are thus the direct result of brain regions' signaling the release of various chemicals that change metabolism, muscle tone, posture, and readiness for action. In the case of fear, such as upon seeing the snake in one's path, typical bodily responses would include being rigidly "frozen," increased heartbeat, and preparation of the body for flight or fight. The freezing of the body is part of the execution of the emotional response we know as fear. It is in this execution stage that we manifest the facial expressions, postures, and bodily comportments that are deemed appropriate to various emotions.

Finally, our *feeling* of fear emerges—if it does emerge—after all of these earlier activities have run their course. Damasio's well-known hypothesis is that what we feel are our body states. The feeling of an emotion is the principal way that a person becomes aware of changes in his or her body:

> In brief, the essential content of feelings is the mapping of a particular body state; the substrate of feelings is the set of neural patterns that map the body state and from which a mental image of the body state can emerge. A feeling in essence is an idea—an idea of the body and, even more particularly, an idea of a certain aspect of the body, its interior, in certain circumstances. A feeling of emotion is an idea of the body when it is perturbed by the emoting process. (Damasio 2003, 88)

I regard Damasio's talk of a "mental image" of the body and of feelings as "ideas" as unfortunate and potentially misleading, because I do not think he is using those terms in their usual senses. First, we do not have a *mental* image—in the way that most people mean it—of the current state of our body at a given time. Second, feelings are not *ideas* in the sense that an idea is a conceptual "thought" of our body or its state. Elsewhere, Damasio makes it clear that he is using "image" in a sense different from the ordinary use of the term:

> By the term images I mean mental patterns with a structure built with the tokens of each of the sensory modalities—visual, auditory, olfactory, gustatory, and somatosensory. The somatosensory modality . . . includes varied forms of sense: touch, muscular, temperature, pain, visceral, and vestibular. . . . In short, the process we come to know as mind when mental images become ours as a result of consciousness is a continuous flow of images many of which turn out to be logically interrelated. . . . *Thought* is an acceptable word to denote such a flow of images. (Damasio 1999, 318)

A mental image, as Damasio is using that term, is not an inner representation or model of some nonmental reality, such as a state of the body. Rather, the image is just our awareness of certain aspects of our current body state. Damasio explicitly rejects any classic representational theory of mind when he says, "The problem with the term representation is . . .

the implication that, somehow, the mental image or the neural pattern *represents,* in mind and in brain, with some degree of fidelity, the object to which the representation refers, as if the structure of the object were replicated in the representation" (1999, 320). Consequently, when Damasio says that a feeling is an idea of the body, he is not saying that it is some abstract inner mental picture of the state of the body. Rather, the feeling is our felt awareness of something going on in our body.

Using neuroimaging to search for evidence for their hypothesis about the nature and basis of feelings, Damasio and his colleagues (2000) had their subjects recall an emotional, image-rich experience from their lives that evoked in them fear, anger, sadness, or happiness. Recalling certain emotionally charged situations and experiences did indeed evoke the appropriate emotions. At the moment when the subjects signaled that they were beginning to feel an emotion, a PET scan indicated high brain activity in areas responsible for mapping the body state:

> All the body-sensing areas under scrutiny—the cingulate cortex, the somatosensory cortices of insula and SII, the nuclei in the brain stem tegmentum—showed a statistically significant pattern of activation or deactivation. This indicated that the mapping of body states had been significantly modified during the process of feeling. Moreover, as we expected, these patterns of activation or deactivation varied among the emotions. In the same way that one can sense that our bodies are differently conformed during the feeling of joy or sadness, we were able to show that the brain maps corresponding to those body states were different as well. (Damasio 2003, 99–100)

Damasio's description above is also misleading, if it seems to suggest that emotions are only about a person's internal milieu, or body state. Emotions are not just feelings of our present body state, although they are at least that. The body state itself is always already a measure of how things are going for the organism in its setting, and so emotions arise from and are directed out into the world. A threat is a threat from some situation, whether it be internal to the body (such as a germ or an infection) or external (such as a snake or a sarcastic person). In short, the aspects of the environment are present in a person's body state, which is what it is only in and through the body's ongoing interaction with its environment. In this way, emotions are a primary means for our being in touch with our world. They are a crucial part of the meaning of what is happening.

EMOTION AND MEANING

Damasio's claim is that feeling an emotion is our principal way of becoming aware of changes in our body state, as our bodies respond to changes in their situation (both their internal and external situation). Emotions are key components of complex processes of bodily perception, assessment, internal monitoring, self-transformation, motivation, and action. They are the result of the organism's need to continually monitor how things are going and to initiate changes within itself in response to possibilities for perceived harm and benefit to the organism. It is hard to imagine anything more important than such an emotional process for our self-preservation and our ability to improve our situation in life. What could be more meaningful or significant to us? Importantly, most of this is carried on *beneath the level of conscious awareness,* so that by the time we actually *feel* an emotion, much of the essential, life-sustaining bodily adjustment has already occurred.

Another way of putting this central point is that by the time we feel an emotion, a mostly unconscious assessment has occurred of the situation we find ourselves in, and in cases where we are functioning optimally, we have frequently already taken steps to transform the situation in order to restore homeostasis and enrich the quality of our experience. We have *perceived and understood* our situation in a certain light, although with little or no conscious reflection. This is a way of saying that our world (our situation) stands forth meaningfully to us at every waking instant, due primarily to processes of emotion and feeling over which we have little control. *And yet the situation is meaningful to us in the most important, primordial, and basic way that it can be meaningful—it shapes the basic contours of our experience. The situation specifies what will be significant to us and what objects, events, and persons mean to us at a pre-reflective level.*

Although the assessment portion of this process is seldom conscious, I do not see why we should not include the entire arc of emotional response and experience as a foundational part of meaning, just as William James and John Dewey did a century ago. Dewey has long been ridiculed, quite unfairly, for claiming that emotions are not internal subjective states of feeling and that the entire situation itself has an emotional character. Dewey claimed that it is properly *situations* that are characterized by emotionality, rather than merely a person's mind or psychic state. Framed relative to Damasio's account of feeling, Dewey's view loses its oddness and comes to seem almost obvious: emotions are processes of organism-environment interactions. They involve perceptions and assessments of situations in the continual process of transforming those situations. The body states connected with feelings are states of both response to and re-making of experience. I say, "I am fearful," but this really means "The *situation* is fearful"; fearfulness might appropriately be described as an objective aspect of the situation *for me at this moment*. However much the feeling of fear is "in *me*," it is just as much "in the *situation* as I encounter it." Whenever I say that I am fearful "of the situation" or "of what is happening," *I* am not an agent utterly independent of my situation. I am what I am in and through my changing situation. There wouldn't be an emotion without a brain, a body, and flesh and blood, but neither would there be an emotion if there were not a situation (or at least an image or idea of a situation) that afforded specific threats, enticements, and possibilities for my experience.

Dewey (1925/1981) thus insisted that *situations* were the locus of emotions, not *minds* or *brains*. He did this to counteract our tendency to subjectivize and interiorize our emotions and mental life, for he saw that locking up emotions in the mind led to their expulsion from the realm of meaning and knowledge. If emotions are merely private, interior, subjective responses, then they tell us nothing objective about our world. However, once we see that emotions exist precisely because of the ways they are connected to our shared world and permit us to function within it, then it becomes possible to recognize their crucial role in our communal well-being.

There are two major morals I wish to draw from this brief glimpse at some of the neurophysiological bases for emotions. First, emotions are not merely subjective, private feelings. Those who insist on thinking of the world as composed of subjects and objects should at least recognize that emotions are both subjective and objective at the same time. However, if we understood that what we call subjects and objects are really just abstractions from the interactive flow of organism-environment transactions (or what Varela, Thompson, and Rosch [1991] call "enactions"), then we would find the locus of emotions in a complex arc of neural activations, chemical releases, changes in the viscera and musculoskeletal state (most notably changes of expression and bodily posture), marshaling of resources for action, and sometimes the feeling of these changes in the internal milieu. And all of this activity and processing would be specified in relation to our physical and social environments. In short, emotions are both *in us* and *in the world* at the same time. They are, in fact, one of the most pervasive ways that we are continually in touch with our environment.

The second important moral I want to draw is that emotions are a fundamental part of human meaning. They are part of our cognitive engagement with the world, and they are not merely noncognitive approvals or disapprovals, as the logical empiricists and emotivists asserted. Emotions are key components of complex processes of assessment, evaluation, and transformation. As such, they are integral to our ability to grasp the meaning of a situation and to act appropriately in response to it. Most of this ongoing processing and action is never consciously entertained, but it is nonetheless *meaningful* to us, insofar as it constitutes an important part of our maintaining a workable relation to our surroundings.

The long-standing prejudice in Western philosophy against granting cognitive meaning to emotional experience is due primarily to the widespread belief that emotions are not conceptual. However, once we stop thinking of concepts as abstract, disembodied entities and see them rather as bodily processes of discrimination and relation, we can recognize the crucial role of emotions in the meaning of situations, persons, objects, and events. The fact that our current vocabulary is notoriously inadequate to the complexities and nuances of emotional life is not a sufficient reason for denying that emotions give us meaning. As we will see in chapter 5, emotions even play a crucial role in our reasoning.

CHAPTER 4

The Grounding of Meaning in the Qualities of Life

Our world is a world of qualities—qualities of things, people, situations, and relationships. Before and beneath reflective thinking and inquiry, our world stands forth qualitatively. I know my world by the distinctive light, warmth, and fragrant breeze of a spring day, just as much as I know it by the driving rain, cold winds, and pervading darkness of a stormy winter afternoon. I know you by the qualities of your distinctive eyes, your mouth, your voice, your smell, the character of your walk, and how you hold yourself. All of my thinking emerges within this qualitative world, to which it must return if it is to have any effect on my life.

The first stanza of William Stafford's poem "You Reading This, Be Ready" calls us to an awareness of the qualities that constitute our world:

Starting here, what do you want to remember?
How sunlight creeps along a shining floor?
What scent of old wood hovers, what softened
sound from outside fills the air? [1]

Can you smell the scent of old wood or see (and feel) the sunlight creeping along the floor? Qualities like these make up the fabric of our everyday experience. Unfortunately, most of us are notoriously bad at thinking about, and thinking by means of, these qualities. We have hundreds of

1. I am indebted to Vincent Colapietro for bringing this beautiful poem to my attention.

words for them, such as *blue, warm, silky, abrupt, tense, fearful, flowing,* and *bright,* and we have many metaphorical extensions of these terms, such as *sharp* cheese, a *high* note, and a *murky* argument. But if someone asked us what such terms really mean, we probably couldn't tell them in any clear manner. How is a "sharp" note sharp? What makes a "bright" trumpet blare sound bright? Most of us don't have a clue how to answer such a question, and yet we more or less successfully manage to communicate with others and to interact cooperatively with them using a vast vocabulary of such quality terms.

The problem with qualities is that they are about how something shows itself to us, about how something *feels* to us, and they seem to involve more than can be structurally discriminated by concepts. Qualities are not reducible to the abstractions by which we try to distinguish them. Consequently, to the extent that philosophies of mind and language focus only on conceptual and propositional structures and the inferences supported by those structures, they lack an adequate way to investigate the role of qualities in meaning and thought. It is no surprise, therefore, that qualities, just like emotions, are typically underappreciated in philosophical theories of meaning. Because we cannot capture qualitative experience in propositions with subject-predicate structure, we tend to downplay the importance of qualities as part of meaning. We mistakenly regard something that is only a conceptual limitation (i.e., our inability to adequately conceptualize qualities) as though it were actually a limitation on our experience of meaning itself. Many recent philosophical discussions of cognitive science make reference to the problem of *qualia,* which are felt qualities, like the blueness of a blue sky or the silkiness of a silk dress or the smell of summer lilacs. The problem is that qualia cannot be reduced to conceptual structures or to functional states of an organism. This fact is supposed to be a showstopper for any attempt to give a naturalistic account of concepts, meaning, and experience.

According to the view I am developing, meaning is grounded in bodily experience; it arises from our feeling of qualities, sensory patterns, movements, changes, and emotional contours. Meaning is not limited only to those bodily engagements, but it always starts with and leads back to them. Meaning depends on our experiencing and assessing the qualities of situations.

It is frustrating, therefore, that we have almost no adequate way to describe and explain what qualities are or how they shape our lives. Phenomenology sought to remedy this grave defect by taking as its chief task the articulation of the character of so-called lived experience. But even phenomenology has a hard time with the qualitative dimension, for it is easier to describe the *structural* aspects of experience than it is to describe felt qualities. The tendency is thus always to look for the constituting structures of experience, at the expense of the actual experience of qualities. After all, what can you possibly *say* philosophically about the quality of a red wheelbarrow covered with rain?

so much depends
upon

a red wheel
barrow

glazed with rain
water

beside the white
chickens.

Any experience will be an ongoing flow of qualities and qualitative changes. In this chapter, I want to focus on the nature of qualities and how they situate, give meaning to, and guide the development of our experience and thought.

THE "OH" OF WONDER AND THE "GOOD" OF ORGANIZATION: DEWEY'S PERVASIVE QUALITIES OF EXPERIENCES

Two of the greatest monuments to a philosophical appreciation of felt qualities are William James's *Principles of Psychology* (1890/1950) and John Dewey's several treatments in various books and articles of what he called the "pervasive" or "tertiary" qualities of situations. Even though James's work preceded Dewey's, and even though Dewey saw himself as building on James, I want to begin with Dewey in this chapter and then, in the next chapter, work back to parts of James's view that lead us to the emergence of thought in felt qualities. I do this in pursuit of resources for developing a deeper appreciation of how felt qualities lie at the core of our meaning, conceptualization, and reasoning.

Dewey opens his profound 1930 article "Qualitative Thought" with the bold thesis that quality lies at the heart of human experience: "The world in which we immediately live, that in which we strive, succeed, and are defeated is preeminently a qualitative world. What we act for, suffer, and enjoy are things in their qualitative determinations. This world forms the field of characteristic modes of thinking, characteristic in that thought is definitely regulated by qualitative considerations" (Dewey 1930/1988, 243). The truth of this thesis is so obvious that were it not for the fact that philosophers have notoriously overlooked and even denied it, it would hardly seem necessary to elaborate and defend it. But you would be extremely hard put to cite any treatment of mind, thought, logic, or reasoning that is founded on an account of qualities. Traditional logic treats of concepts (i.e., concepts of objects, properties, and relations), propositions, and formal relations. Qualities, if they are mentioned at all, are represented by symbolic placeholders, such as $F(x)$, which is read as "object x has property (here a quality) F." Even worse, properties are often regarded as fixed structures "possessed" by objects, independent of thought.

Dewey takes great pains to remind us that the primary locus of human experience is not atomistic sense impressions, but rather what he called a "situation." By this he meant not just our physical setting, but the whole complex of physical, biological, social, and cultural conditions that constitute any given experience—experience taken in its fullest, deepest, richest, broadest sense: "By the term situation in this connection is signified the fact that the subject-matter ultimately referred to in existential propositions is a complex existence that is held together in spite of its internal complexity by the fact that it is dominated and characterized throughout by a single quality" (Dewey 1930/1988, 246).

When I look out my office window, I have the gift of experiencing an oak tree, massive almost beyond imagination, whose branches overwhelm my entire visual expanse. In spring and summer, I see virtually nothing but literally hundreds of branches covered in an explosion of leaves, through which I occasionally glimpse a campus sidewalk flanked by grass, with students hustling along to classes or strolling hand in hand. In this moment there is only the situation, not as a mere visual scene, but as an experience with a pervasive unifying quality that is at once visual, auditory, tactile, social, and cultural. The pervasive quality changes as the day passes, and it changes also from day to day and season to season.

Dewey emphasizes that *pervasive qualities are not properties of objects*. Instead, entire situations are characterized by pervasive qualities, and we pick out particular qualities for discrimination within this unified situational whole. Dewey often used artworks as a way of elaborating his conception of a pervasive quality. Artworks are physical objects, in one sense of that term; but when Dewey speaks about their unifying qualities, he is treating them not as objects, but rather as experiences that define the whole situation of our being absorbed in the world of the painting. Consider, for example, how the pervasive quality of a painting by Picasso (say, his *Guernica*) is different from that of a sunset by Emil Nolde or an interior scene by Vermeer. Nobody could mistake a Nolde for a Picasso or a Vermeer. There is no single property or set of properties that makes something a Picasso, but rather "the quality of the whole [that] permeates, affects, and controls every detail" (Dewey 1930/1988, 247). One of the things that first alerts an art expert to the possibility that some painting publicized as a newly discovered Vermeer, for example, might be a forgery is her dim awareness that the painting lacks the pervasive "Vermeer" quality that she has encountered in his authenticated works.

The idea of a pervasive quality of a situation is not a commonplace in our ordinary understanding of experience. We learn to understand and to experience our world as consisting of pre-given, mind-independent objects that have discrete properties and that stand in various external relations to each other. Or, even worse, if we have been infected by an associationist philosophical virus, we think that our world is given to us as a massive set of discrete perceptual inputs (sensations or percepts) that we then have to put together or synthesize into the objects that populate our perceptual world.

Dewey showed why this was all wrong. If you pay attention to how your world shows itself, you will indeed see that the flow of experience comes to us as unified wholes (gestalts) that are pervaded by an all-encompassing quality that makes the present situation what and how it is. My wife, an artist, recently remarked how much she loves a certain kind of April light that pervades the forested valley near our home in Oregon. Toward sunset on what has typically been an overcast spring day, perhaps one punctuated by rain showers, it often happens that the late-day sun breaks through the low clouds and bathes the valley with an indescribable light. Before you perceive *this* or *that* tree, bush, rock, pond, stream, tree trunk, or deer path, you are caught up in the pervading spring-light-bathing-the-valley quality of the *entire situation*. Before you take note of those unique shades of green of the new spring leaves (as opposed to the hard greens of summer, or the tired greens progressing into yellows and browns of early fall), you encounter the whole felt expanse of April greens together. It is out of this pervasive quality of the early-evening situation, here and now, that we *then* begin to discriminate the compressed, intense green of the newly leafed oak from the translucent pale green of the vine maple or the rain-rejuvenated, shiny-tough green of the rhododendron.

In his later book *Art as Experience* (1934), Dewey describes the qualitative unity that marks off "an experience" from encounters that are disjointed, slack, undirected, or overly restricted: "An experience has a unity that gives it its name, *that* meal, that storm, that rupture of friendship. The existence of this unity is constituted by a single *quality* that pervades the entire experience in spite of the variation of its constituent parts. This unity is neither emotional, practical, nor intellectual, for these terms name distinctions that reflection can make within it" (Dewey 1934/1987, 37). An identifiable, meaningful experience is neither *merely* emotional, nor *merely* practical, nor *merely* intellectual. Rather, it is all of these at once and together. We call it *emotional,* after the fact, when we wish to stress the felt quality of its emotional valence. We call it *practical* when we wish to profile its outcome and the interests it might serve. We call it *intellectual* when we are interested primarily in the distinctions, associations, and connections of thoughts that arise through the course of the experience.

Our tendency to separate experiences and judgments into kinds—scientific, technical, moral, aesthetic—has its roots deep in Enlightenment views of mind and knowledge. For example, we have learned to think of art as the basis for an "aesthetic" experience, and theorists from Immanuel Kant through Edward Bullough and Clive Bell have insisted that in experiencing and judging art, one must always abstract from any practical engagement the work has with our everyday lives. They believed that only this kind of "disinterested" apprehension of an object would permit that object to shine forth with its distinctive character and beauty.

However, as Dewey argued, such an abstractive, disengaging move is entirely artificial from the point of view of the qualitative situation we encounter. The fact that we can try to suspend our practical concerns just means that we will grasp only part of the meaning of the artwork—indeed, the part that may be least connected to what matters in our lives. This is a disservice to art and to ourselves, for it impoverishes art's potential to transform our experience and understanding. It is one thing to try to forget that the van Gogh you are seeing is worth $24 million, but quite another to think that the aesthetic value of the painting shows itself only if the painting is divorced from the human concerns of our everyday lives. The former idea—distancing ourselves from the objectification of the artwork as a commodity—actually lets the work reveal its depth and significance, but the latter idea—that in order to fully experience the artwork we should suspend our practical concerns—is just nonsense. The extent to which we do suspend those practical engagements is directly proportional to the extent to which the artwork will cease to speak to our human situation—to who we are, how our world shows itself, and how we might grow and be transformed.

The point I am making is that experiences come whole, pervaded by unifying qualities that demarcate them within the flux of our lives. If we want to find meaning, or the basis for meaning, we must therefore start with the qualitative unity that Dewey describes. The demarcating pervasive quality is, at first, unanalyzed, but it is the basis for subsequent analysis, thought, and development. Thought *starts* from this experienced whole, and only then does it introduce distinctions that carry it forward as inquiry: "All thought in every subject begins with just such an unanalyzed whole. When the subject-matter is reasonably familiar, relevant distinctions speedily offer themselves, and sheer qualitativeness may not remain long enough to be readily recalled" (Dewey 1934/1987, 249).

It is not wrong to say that we experience objects, properties, and relations, but it *is* wrong to say that these are primary in experience. What *are* primary are pervasive qualities of situations, within which we subsequently discriminate objects, properties, and relations: "The total overwhelming impression comes first, perhaps in a seizure by a sudden glory of the landscape, or by the effect upon us of entrance into a cathedral when dim light, incense, stained glass and majestic proportions fuse in one indistinguishable whole. We say with truth that a painting strikes us. There is an impact that precedes all definite recognition of what it is about" (Dewey 1934/1987, 150).

Once we are struck, caught up, seized, only then can we discriminate elements within our present situation. At this point, we may not always understand those April greens as the greens of spring oaks versus vine maples versus rhododendrons, though we understand that they are green leaves. Rather, we are simply able to differentiate colors, forms, and structures. When we see the oak-leaf green, as distinguished from the vine-maple green, we are *not* engaging in acts of synthesizing atomistic sense impressions into complex sensations, or even objects. No! We are *discriminating* within a situation that was given to us whole. All of those qualities were potentially available in the situation together, and we selectively grasp some of them as salient, focal, differentiated. We are not *making* our world of objects, but we are instead *taking up* these objects in experience. In other words, objects are not so much *givens* as they are *takings*.

Dewey claims that objects emerge in an experience out of the background of a pervasive qualitative whole. Objects emerge because of our perceptual and motor capacities, our interests, our history, and our values. Those objects are saturated with the meaning present in the whole situation. Dewey explains that an "object" is "some element in the complex whole that is defined in abstraction from the whole of which it is a distinction. The special point made is that the selective determination and relation of objects in thought is controlled by reference to a situation—to that which is constituted by a pervasive and internally integrating quality" (Dewey 1930/1988, 246). So, yes, I do see trees, but I see them as focal objects within the horizon of my current situation. It is by virtue of everything my situation affords me, emerging out of its pervasive unity, that I encounter objects, people, and events: "Things, objects, are only focal points of a here and now in a whole that stretches out indefinitely. This is the qualitative 'background' which is defined and made definitely conscious in particular objects and specified properties and qualities" (Dewey 1934/1987, 197).

Now, the problem for this kind of naturalistic, holistic account is how to avoid having to postulate a homunculus or a disembodied ego that does the "selecting" or "discriminating" of objects, properties, and relations. There is no single mental entity or agent that somehow picks and chooses what it wants from experience, any more than it synthesizes experience into unified wholes. Objects simply stand forth in our experience—are disclosed—because creatures like us are able to perceive certain light-wave frequencies, can move our bodies and hands within a certain range of motions, and need certain things to survive and flourish. Our brains and bodies have specific neural networks whose function is edge detection. Other neural assemblies compute orientation, such as whether a particular edge is oriented vertically, horizontally, or at a forty-five-degree angle; still others detect motion or play a role in color perception. These various functional neural assemblies determine what stands out, for us, from a situation or scene. Therefore, how we "take" objects would change if our bodies, brains, or environments changed in some radical way. So, saying that "we" select objects is just shorthand for the focal emergence of objects within a horizon of possible experience. I will attempt later to explain how we can avoid letting the homunculus creep back in, but for now let us just remember that the emergence of objects, properties, and relations is not an act of pure thought, will, reason, or understanding. Mind, on this view, is neither a willful creator of experience nor a mere window to an objective, mind-independent reality. Mind is a functional aspect of experience that emerges when it becomes possible for us to share meanings, to inquire into the meaning of a situation, and to initiate action that transforms, or remakes, that situation.

Robert Innis has highlighted Dewey's emphasis on the aesthetic dimensions of human meaning-making as being the key to an adequate understanding of experience, which is neither merely given nor merely made:

> Integral experience, in Dewey's sense of the term, obtains form through dynamic organization (1934:62) in as much as the perceiver is caught up in and solicited by the emerging experiential whole. Even while experiencing the perceptual whole as an *outcome* over which it has no explicit control, the perceiver is *creating* its own experience through continuous participation (1934:60). . . .
>
> The philosophical pivot of Dewey's pragmatist aesthetic is likewise, as in his epistemology as a whole, the picture of the organism as a force rather than a transparency (1934:246). This is certainly a counterpole to all 'mirror' epistemologies with their attendant desire to become a pure 'reflection' of the world already in existence. With a Deweyan perspective we are neither mirror, nor carbon paper, nor Kodak fixation. We are systems of mediations of immediacy, fusions of actions, feeling, and meaning (1934:22). (Innis 1994, 62)

In sum, Dewey is trying to remind us that experienced situations are the soil from which the objects, properties, and relations of our world grow. Moreover, the properties or definite qualities that we experience in objects are richly cross-modal. The red of a ripe bing cherry is not just the result of visual processing. It is not a single-channel visual percept. Rather, our various sensory and motor modalities interfuse, via cross-domain neural connections, to produce the qualities that objects manifest for us.[2] Dewey describes this interfusing of perceptions:

> When we perceive, by means of the eyes as causal aids, the liquidity of water, the coldness of ice, the solidity of rocks, the bareness of trees in winter, it is certain that other qualities than those of the eye are conspicuous and controlling in perception. And it is as certain as anything can be that optical qualities do not stand out by themselves with tactual and emotive qualities clinging to their skirts. (Dewey 1934/1987, 129)

---

2. The neural basis of these cross-modal co-activations is briefly discussed in chapter 8, under the topic of canonical neurons.

The pervasive quality of a situation is not limited merely to sensible perception or motor interactions. Thinking is action, and so "acts of thought" also constitute situations that must have pervasive qualities. Even our best scientific thinking stems from the grasp of qualities. It arises from the feeling that a situation is problematic or that it calls out for interpretation and explanation. This initiates a process of intellectual inquiry in search of generalizations that help us understand the phenomena—phenomena that are identified and known *only* in the context of the inquiry itself, which introduces distinctions, carves out objects and their properties, and seeks a way to explain their behavior. About scientific investigations, Dewey says: "These open with the 'Oh' of wonder and terminate with the 'Good' of a rounded-out and organized situation. Neither the 'Oh' nor the 'Good' expresses a mere state of personal feeling. Each characterizes a subject-matter" (Dewey 1930/1988, 250). The "Oh" and the "Good" are not subjective feelings, nor are they mere properties of things. Rather, they are qualities that characterize the situation as it moves from the start of scientific investigation to its temporary completion in some theory, explanation, or experiment. The "Good" is merely our way of recognizing that something has been more or less satisfactorily resolved through our inquiry, at least for the time being.

The crux of Dewey's entire argument is that what we call thinking, or reasoning, or logical inference, *could not even exist* without the felt qualities of situations: "The underlying unity of qualitativeness regulates pertinence or relevancy and force of every distinction and relation; it guides selection and rejection and the manner of utilization of all explicit terms" (Dewey 1934, 247–48). This is a startling claim: *Insofar as logic pertains to real human inquiry, logic can't do anything without feeling.* Logic alone—pure formal logic—cannot circumscribe the phenomena under discussion. Logic alone cannot define the problem you are trying to solve by inquiry. Logic cannot tell you what should count as relevant to your argument. Logic can only work because we take for granted the prior working of qualities in experienced situations.

We are thus confronted with the question of how thought and symbolic interaction can arise in experience. How, out of the encompassing qualitative horizon of a situation, does thinking emerge, with all of its symbolic structures, forms, and principles? I will take up this deep issue of the nature of logic and rational thought in the next chapter, but first I want to examine more closely the intimate blending of structural and qualitative aspects of experience. This question has been a pivotal focus of the work of the psychotherapist and phenomenologist Eugene Gendlin.

GENDLIN'S FELT SITUATIONS AS A KEY TO MEANING

Ask yourself how it is possible for you to write a letter and know what to say next; or how you can start a sentence in anything you are uttering or writing and suddenly realize that what you've just said or written wasn't what you wanted to say, or should have said. What tells you how to go on with your thoughts? What stops you in the middle of writing a sentence and tells you to try again with different words?

The answer is that your flow of thought just stops, or else when you try to say what you meant, it doesn't feel right. You feel a sort of frustration, tension, and disruption that is stressful. The words were flowing out just fine, and then all of a sudden they stumble or stop. The "stopping" feels a certain way, and it feels very different from the flow of thought that went before. The arrested motion of your thought, or the tension that pervades your thinking, is an unpleasant perturbation within you. Only if you find words that carry forward the meaning you are trying to articulate will you feel the relief that results when you overcome the obstruction and your streaming thought moves along with a renewed flow of meaning. You will then feel the changed and changing quality of your experience as it moves from frustration and blockage to a more harmonious, flowing state. You will have a sense that somehow, you are "getting things right," more or less.

But again, *where* exactly is this so-called meaning that you are trying to express? It is not merely in the words themselves, although it is not wholly independent of them, either. The words help carry it forward, and make it present.[3] But the meaning is in what you think and feel and do, and it lies in recurring qualities, patterns, and structures of experience that are, for the most part, unconsciously and automatically shaping how you understand, how you choose, and how you express yourself. You *have* meaning, or are *caught up* in meaning, before you actually experience meaning reflectively.

Eugene Gendlin has devoted much of his career to helping us recover this vast lost continent of feeling that underlies all our meaning, thought,

---

3. What Maurice Merleau-Ponty says about how an artwork makes meaning real and present holds also for language: "Aesthetic expression confers on what it expresses an existence in itself, installs it in nature as a thing perceived and accessible to all. . . . No one will deny that here the process of expression brings the meaning into being or makes it effective, and does not merely translate it" (Merleau-Ponty 1962, 183).

and symbolic expression. He adeptly diagnoses our nearly universal tendency to think of human thought only in terms of patterns, structures, and forms, while ignoring or even denying the qualitative, feeling aspect that makes all our thinking possible. In Gendlin's words, his project is "to think—about, and with—that which exceeds patterns (forms, concepts, definitions, categories, distinctions, rules . . .)" (1992, 21). Note the radical character of Gendlin's mission. He is interested not just in developing a theory of the embodied, feeling dimensions of thought. In addition, he wants us to think *in* and *with* these nonformal dimensions, as a means of becoming alive to the emergence of meaning in our lives.

Gendlin sees that modes of thinking that employ only forms, distinctions, patterns, and rules will necessarily miss large parts of the embodied situational experiences that make these forms meaningful in the first place. The fateful error, which Gendlin attributes not just to Western philosophy but also to our general cultural understanding and practices, is to overlook much of what goes into making something meaningful to us. Then we are seduced into mistaking the forms for that which they inform, and we fool ourselves into thinking that it is the forms alone that make something meaningful, real, and knowable. We think that if we have succeeded in abstracting a form—conceptualizing some aspect of our experience—then we have captured the full meaning.

Moreover, this exclusive attention to stable structures can entice us to succumb to the illusion of fixity, that is, the illusion that meanings are fixed, abstract entities that can float free of contexts and the ongoing flow of experience. Such a strategy of exclusion leaves out the body and our situated, embodied practices, along with all their intricate meaning. One of Gendlin's favorite examples of the all-pervasive working of embodied meaning—as a process of symbolic expression and felt sense working together—is his tale of a poet searching for the right words to finish a line:

> The poet reads the written lines over and over, listens, and senses what these lines need (want, demand, imply, ...). Now the poet's hand rotates in the air. The gesture says *that*. Many good lines offer themselves; they try to say, but do not say—*that*. The blank is *more precise*. Although some are good lines, the poet rejects them.
>
> That .... seems to lack words, but no. It knows the language, since it understands—and rejects—these lines that came. So it is not pre-verbal; Rather, it knows what must be said, and knows that these lines don't precisely say that. It knows like a gnawing knows what was forgotten, but it is new in the poet, and perhaps new in the history of the world.

Now, although I don't know most of you, I do know one of your secrets. I know you have written poetry. So I can ask you: Isn't that how it is? This ‥‥ must be directly referred to (felt, experienced, sensed, had, . . .). Therefore, whatever term we use for such a blank, that term also needs our direct reference.

The blank brings something new. That function is not performed by the linguistic forms alone. Rather, it functions *between* two sets of linguistic forms. The blank is not just the already written lines, but rather the *felt sense* from re-reading them, and *that* performs a function needed to lead to the next lines. (Gendlin 1991, 38)

Whether in poetry or in the activities of our day-to-day lives, we all know the kind of experience Gendlin is describing—the experience, first, of coming up with new candidate words for completing the line; second, of testing them by monitoring how *these words* feel in our present situation; and third, of sometimes hitting—and sometimes not hitting—upon the words or other symbolic forms that seem appropriate and that carry us forward in our thinking. Consider, for example, a situation in which a close friend has done something that you consider ill-advised, if not downright immoral. You don't want to alienate him, but you feel the need to speak forthrightly about your discomfort at what he has done. Before you meet him, you rehearse in your mind what you might say. You try out, in imagination, various ways of expressing your distress, sensing whether the particular words you are proposing say what you want to say in a way that keeps your friendship intact. These rehearsals of meaning are "tested" in your felt sense of how well the meaning is carried forward. Then, when all of the rehearsing is over and the time for straight talk arrives, you employ the same ongoing feeling of meaning as you struggle with the precise articulation of your thoughts in the face-to-face encounter.

Several important points need to be emphasized regarding such experiences and the ways they reveal important aspects of meaning and reasoning.

(1) There is a nonlinguistic dimension—the nonformal, nonconceptual side of the relation between our intricate experience and our words, symbols, or other patterns—that gets its fulfillment in and through the words we try out as candidates to complete the line. This felt sense of the situation is not the words or forms alone.

(2) Yet neither is the felt sense of the situation utterly distinct or separable from the words or forms or distinctions. That is why Gendlin says it is not preverbal, since we feel the appropriateness of certain linguistic

or symbolic expressions relative to the developing meaning of a situation. Gendlin cautions us against the mistake of thinking that there are two distinct and autonomous sides of any experience—the felt sense (the implicit) and the formal expression (the explicit)—each of which might exist wholly apart from the other. These are not two independent entities that are only externally related. Instead, they are two dimensions of a single, ongoing activity of meaning-making, each one intrinsically related to the other.

Thus, Gendlin argues, we must never think of the formal, patterned, "objective" side as somehow copying the "subjective" side, for that would entail that the words could stand in for, or represent, the subjective side, and thereby replace it.[4] As he says, "Between the subjective and objective sides there is not a relation of representation or likeness. The words don't copy the blank. . . . The explication releases *that* tension, which was the ......ı. But what the blank was is not just lost or altered; rather, *that* tension is *carried forward* by the words" (1991, 38). So, we do not have two independent entities externally related, but rather one continuously developing meaning of a particular situation that we identify, via reflection, as having these two intimately interwoven or blended dimensions—the formal-structural and the felt-qualitative. It is for this reason that the words or formal distinctions are not adequate in themselves. If they copied the "subjective" side, then that side would be eliminable, replaceable by the forms and patterns. Conversely, the subjective side, the ......ı, is what it is only in relation to the forms that give expression to it.

(3) Notice especially that this nonformal side is not vague, mushy, empty, or chaotic. It is, as Gendlin says, extremely *precise*. Its meaning is carried forward only by quite specific words or forms. The nonformal dimension is so precise that it rejects many candidate expressions as inadequate. When you are considering how to continue a line of poetry, or a line of thought in a philosophical argument, or an episode within a narrative, or an argument with a friend, the felt sense of the qualitative whole is what determines how well various candidates for the next thought, word, or symbol will carry forward the thought. This qualitative, felt sense is vague, but only in a rich, positive sense—namely, it is full of possibilities

4. I hope it will become clear, as my argument develops, that I share the pragmatist suspicion of rigid dichotomies such as objective/subjective and formal/material. Such distinctions can usefully mark out aspects of our experience, but, as James and Dewey showed us, they must not be treated as substantial entities or independent aspects of a situation.

that are not yet realized, and so it only *seems* to lack precision. I would say that it is full of embodied *structure,* if Gendlin had not lumped that term together with *form* and distinguished them from the felt sense.

(4) The blank, the ...., that the poet seeks to realize or fulfill, carries forward the meaning that has been developing in the poem, or in some ongoing experience we are having, and it points toward what is to come next. Gendlin says that the situation "implies" (in a very broad and enriched sense) what is to come next as the situation develops. It implies various possibilities for experience, not in the sense that they are logically deducible from the situation as it is presently formed, but rather insofar as the situation can be carried forward by our pursuing one or more of these possibilities.

So, we are living in and through a growing, changing situation that opens up toward new possibilities and that is transformed as it develops. That is the way human meaning works, and none of this happens without our bodies, or without our embodied interactions within environments that we inhabit and that change along with us. A "situation," as Gendlin uses the term, thus has as two of its abstract aspects an organism and its environment. But it would be a mistake, as Richard Levins and Richard Lewontin observe, to think of the organism and its environment(s) as autonomous, independent entities that are only externally related. Rather, organisms and environments are co-evolving aspects of the experiential processes that make up situations (Levins and Lewontin 1985, 89).

This explains why we should not think that our embodied meaning, understanding, and reasoning could ever be adequately thought or grasped by our concepts, symbols, rules, or patterns. Our situations, with all of their summing up, implying, and carrying forward, are *embodied situations.* Meaning, therefore, is embodied. And neither the nonformal, nonconceptual, implicit aspects nor the explicit forms, patterns, words, and concepts are the meaning in themselves. Meaning resides in their situational relation as that relation develops and changes.

In the passages cited above, Gendlin repeatedly aligns the formal and structural with the "linguistic." However, he is not speaking of language only in the sense of linguistic symbols. What Gendlin calls the "linguistic" pertains to all forms of symbolic interaction, from music to painting to dance to ritual to gesture to sign language. The formal and structural are aligned with the symbolic, but in the broad and very rich sense that encompasses all of the ways we use signs to think and to communicate.

From the point of view of our encounter with the pervasive quality of a situation and our felt sense of how thought can be carried forward, it is perfectly acceptable to say that *the body carries forward the meaning of a situation.* Via our embodied understanding, we learn how to go on with our thinking, how to carry a situation forward in a fulfilling way. Gendlin sums up this embodiment of meaning and thought:

> The body implies what we want to do *and say.*
>
> Therefore sophisticated linguistics and philosophical details can make *our bodies* uncomfortable. From such a discomfort the body can project (imply . . .) [ellipsis in the original] finely shaped new steps to deal with such a situation. . . . Our bodies shape the next thing we say, and perform many other implicit functions essential to language.
>
> That is how our next words "come" from the body, just as hunger, orgasm, and sleep *come* in a bodily way, and just as food-search comes in an animal. It is familiar that after inhaling the body implies exhaling, and when in danger it totals up the situation and its muscles and blood circulation imply fighting, or quite differently, may imply running, or again differently, it may paralyze itself and freeze. . . .
>
> *Our bodies imply the next words and actions to carry our situations forward.* (Gendlin 1997, 28)

What is most compelling about Gendlin's method of philosophizing is the way it calls us back to the meaning of our situation. He always tries to reinvigorate our felt sense of the situations out of which meaning and thought emerge. He does this by helping us be more attentive to what our bodies tell us. He invites us to listen to our embodied experience—to be "present to our experience," as some Buddhists would say. He challenges us to gather the embodied meaning of our situation, just as William Stafford does in the following poem, the first stanza of which I used to open this chapter.

YOU READING THIS, BE READY
Starting here, what do you want to remember?
How sunlight creeps along a shining floor?
What scent of old wood hovers, what softened
sound from outside fills the air?

Will you ever bring a better gift for the world
than the breathing respect that you carry
wherever you go right now? Are you waiting
for time to show you some better thoughts?

When you turn around, starting here, lift this
new glimpse that you found; carry into evening
all that you want from this day. This interval you spent
reading or hearing this, keep it for life—

What can anyone give you greater than now,
starting here, right in this room, when you turn around?

CHAPTER 5

Feeling William James's "But"

The Aesthetics of Reasoning and Logic

If thinking—conceptualizing, imagining, and reasoning—isn't an activity of disembodied mind, a product of the workings of a nonbodily ego, then where does it come from? Following Dewey, I have so far claimed that it arises within and emerges out of the pervasive qualitative situations that make up the moments of our lives. If thought doesn't drop down from the realm of pure spirit, then it must arise from bodily perception, feeling, and action.

But how do we move from the feeling of a situation all the way to thought, including abstract conceptualization and inference? This is a long and complicated story, but I hope to begin it in this chapter and carry it forward in succeeding chapters, all the way up to the highest levels of abstract thinking.

THE EMERGENCE OF CONCEPTS: THE INTERTWINING OF PERCEPT AND CONCEPT

Let us begin with a particular situation, say, eating a meal together with one's family. From the point of view of ourselves as embodied neural organisms, an experience of a meal is one vast, continuous flow of neuronal activations, serially and in parallel, that give rise to neural and chemical activities in our bodies that result in our perceptions, feelings, thoughts, and movements. These bodily processes never cease so long as we are alive, and their result is our rich experience of a complex physical, social, and cultural experience of having a meal, with objects (food, dishes, utensils, furniture), people (family members), and actions (of cooperative food sharing, social communication, planning, arguing, playing, etc.). How, out of this incessant flow of our perceptions, feelings, thoughts, and actions, does our conceptual understanding of the situation arise?

One traditional way of thinking about this process, a way shared by our commonsense theories of mind and many revered philosophical theories alike, is that *percepts* and *concepts* are two radically different kinds of things. This is a foundational part of an objectivist theory of cognition. Percepts, on this view, are the result of our body's capacity to have our sensory receptors affected by things both external and internal to our bodies, thereby giving rise to sense impressions (or sensations). Concepts, on the other hand, are taken to be forms by which we organize our experience by unifying our atomic sense impressions into qualities, objects, people, motions, etc. According to the objectivist view, then, sensations are perceptual givens that arise when the outside world impinges on our sense organs, whereas concepts are supplied by the mind to allow us to recognize what is given in sensation.

What this objectivist view of cognition gets right is that concepts do indeed help us understand, or make sense of, our sensory experience. But what's wrong about this view is the way it treats concepts either as discrete mental entities ("representations") or as abstract entities—in either case, as something *different in kind* from sensations, perceptions, and feelings. To accept this traditional objectivist view of concepts, along with its attendant representationalist theory of mind, is to presuppose an absolute ontological and epistemological gap between percepts and concepts—a gap that parallels the alleged separation between body and mind. As the history of Western philosophy has amply—and tediously—documented, once you assume such a gap, there is no way to bridge it.

In his amazing two-volume work *The Principles of Psychology* (1890) and in his later essay "Percept and Concept" (1911), William James explored a way to conceive of concepts without succumbing to the dualistic ways of thinking that underlie the objectivist view of cognition. The key, he realized, was to not fall into the dualistic trap of thinking of percepts and concepts as different in kind and to see them, rather, as two aspects of a continuous flow of feeling-thinking.

> The great difference between percepts and concepts is that percepts are continuous and concepts are discrete. Not discrete in their *being,* for conception as an *act* is part of the flux of feeling, but discrete from each other in their several *meanings.* Each concept means just what it singly means, and nothing

else; and if the conceiver does not know whether he means this or means that, it shows that his concept is imperfectly formed. The perceptual flux as such, on the contrary, *means* nothing, and is but what it immediately is. No matter how small a tract of it be taken, it is always a much-at-once, and contains innumerable aspects and characters which conception can pick out, isolate, and thereafter always intend. It shows duration, intensity, complexity or simplicity, interestingness, excitingness, pleasantness or their opposites. (James 1911/1979, 32)

As I sit at the dining table, I am engaging a situation that, at any given moment, has a pervasive qualitative unity that marks it off in my experience. Tonight's dinner situation is characterized by our quiet conversation over a light meal, very different from last night's raucous, humor-filled free-for-all of everyone in the family talking at once and reaching for food. It is within, or from, this pervasive quality that discrete things and substances emerge—silverware, tomatoes, bread and butter, balsamic vinegar, olive oil. These things are what stand forth, for a creature like me, out of the background of the whole situation of the meal. They are affordances for a creature with my perceptual makeup, with my capacities for moving my body and manipulating objects, and with my physical and social environments. We say that we have "concepts" for each of these things and substances that populate my dinner table—and so we do. We also have concepts for the physical actions we perform and the social interactions that are occurring as we eat and converse. However, concepts are not themselves things or quasi-things. They are not mysterious abstract entities with a special ontological significance that sets them over against sensations or percepts. Our language of "concepts" is just our way of saying that we are able to mark various meaningful qualities and patterns within our experience, and we are able to mark these distinctions in a way that permits us to recognize something that is *the same* over and over across different experiences and thoughts.

James cautions us in *The Principles of Psychology* not to hypostatize these discriminations within our experience into ethereal entities called "concepts." We should speak of conceptualizing (as an act), rather than of concepts (as quasi-things). Conceptualizing is one of the things we *do* in and with our experience, which is just another way of saying that conceptualizing makes it possible for us to make sense of and to manage our experience. Conceptualizing involves recognizing distinctions within the flow of our experience. From the perceptual continuum, we select an aspect, typically an aspect that recurs across many experiences and many types of experience. We select things that matter for us, things that have value, meaning, and significance, such as various qualities, shapes, and relations. James says that our experience is rich and deep, characterized by "much at once" blending together in a continuous flow. We identify parts of the "much-at-onceness" of our perceptual experience and mark them for use in understanding and transforming our past, present, and future experience: "Out of this aboriginal sensible muchness, attention carves out objects, which conception then names and identifies forever—in the sky 'constellations,' on the earth 'beach,' 'sea,' 'cliff,' 'bushes,' 'grass.' Out of time we cut 'days' and 'nights,' 'summers' and 'winters.' We say *what* each part of the sensible continuum is, and all these abstracted *whats* are concepts" (James 1911/1979, 32–33).

When you "select" some quality or aspect from a much-at-onceness, there is inevitably a great deal that is not selected in that moment. That is precisely what abstraction consists in, namely, attending to some aspect of a continuous situation in such a way that a quality or pattern stands out as distinguished from other patterns or aspects of the situation. James says that these concepts are discrete, but he takes great pains to remind us that percepts and concepts are intermixed and interfuse in our actual thinking. The very notion *concept,* in other words, is itself an abstraction, since it leaves behind the interfusing of feeling and thought that goes on when we conceptualize.

The chief difference between James's naturalistic view and traditional dualistic views is that James denies any ontological separation between feeling, sensation, and perception on the one hand and conceptualization and thought on the other. For James, we must always begin with the full richness of an experience (Dewey's pervasive qualitative unity), out of which arise whatever differentiations are salient for us.

The principal problem with James's account is his use of agency terms, such as "selects," "cuts," and "carves." Though James does not intend this, these terms suggest the need for a mental homunculus (a mini-conceptualizer in the "mind") who does the selecting, cutting, and carving from experience. From the perspective of cognitive neuroscience, we know that there is no single neural ensemble, network, or system that conceptualizes, decides, chooses, or acts, and there is certainly no single locus of any faculty of thinking or willing. Thus, it would be more accurate to say, for example, that at the dinner table *we* don't "select" or "carve up" the situation into *bread* and *butter* and *conversation* (or any of the other concepts we have for what is going on over dinner). Instead, our situation affords us *bread,* just as it affords us various aromas, tastes, sights, textures, and possibilities for interaction and engagement. We are creatures with neural capacities for discriminating various qualities within our situation, and the qualities for which we have so-called concepts are those important enough to us to merit being marked for use.

The hard problem here is how to explain perception and conceptualization without resorting to a homunculus within the mind that does the perceiving and conceptualizing. These processes are neither entirely passive nor entirely active; rather, they are a blending of passivity and activity in an organism-environment transaction. To avoid the error of treating perception as mere passive reception of sensations, we focus on the active engagement of the organism with its surroundings, but this then tempts us to employ the language of human agency in describing how we think. Once we are on this path, we end up replacing thoughtful activity with some "thing" that thinks—that is, with an inner source of spontaneity and activity. Dewey's solution is to grant that activity is a fundamental capacity of certain types of living creatures, but without positing a conscious inner, agent-like source of that activity. This requires us to think of conceptualization as a process of discrimination within an ongoing flow of experience.

Talk about "concepts" has sometimes done far more harm than good to our understanding of mind, thought, and language. No sooner does *concept* (used as a noun) make concepts into things than we must find a *place* for concepts to exist or be. Either they get housed in some mysterious thing we call "the mind," or they are billeted in a Platonic realm of ideas. Even worse, concepts then achieve the exalted status of independently existing entities, and we have in full swing the dualism of concept versus percept, thought versus feeling, and mind versus body. We are seduced into the illusion that concepts are fixed entities—universals—that stand apart from and above the vicissitudes of bodily perceptual experience.[1] James sums up this transcendent view of concepts:

1. I remember quite well my embarrassing experience as a graduate student in a seminar on Frege's philosophy taught by a distinguished philosopher of language. One day I naively expressed my puzzlement at the Fregean notion of "sense," which Frege claimed existed neither in the physical realm nor the mental realm, but in some third realm, along with other entities like numbers, functions, propositions, and thoughts. When I expressed skepticism over the existence of such a realm, the professor accused me of succumbing to "that creeping disease of Midwestern empiricism—if you can't see or touch something, then it doesn't exist!" That, of course, silenced me for the rest of the term. But to this day, I still cannot make any sense of a transcendent realm of concepts, functions, or senses that just *have to be real* if we are to make sense of the universality of shared meanings.

Greek philosophers soon formed the notion that a knowledge of so-called 'universals,' consisting of concepts of abstract forms, qualities, numbers, and relations was the only knowledge worthy of the truly philosophic mind. Particular facts decay and our perceptions of them vary. A concept never varies; and between such unvarying terms the relations must be constant and express eternal verities. Hence there arose a tendency, which has lasted all through philosophy, to contrast the knowledge of universals and intelligibles, as god-like, dignified, and honorable to the knower, with that of particulars and sensibles as something relatively base which more allies us with the beasts. (James 1911/1979, 34)

To counteract this transcendent, disembodied, objectivist view of concepts, we need to bring concepts back into the body-mind. We need to understand *cognition as action* and conceptualizing as a continuous process of attending to various aspects of our experience and putting them to use as part of inquiry. Toward this end, James distinguished what he called the "substantive" aspects of a concept from its "functional" aspects, as follows:

A. *Substantive part*
   1. Sign or symbolic expression (a word or other symbolic form)
   2. Image or sensory presentation (the image called up by the sign)
B. *Functional part:* what the concept leads to by way of thought or action

To illustrate these distinctions, consider our human concept of a dog. The substantive part includes the word or sign (e.g., *dog* in English, *Hund* in German) and a more or less rich image or sense presentation (either a concrete or schematic image) of a dog. The functional part is what dogs afford us by way of possible interactions with them, such as that they can be petted, will greet us cheerfully when we arrive home, can be operated on surgically to repair certain injuries or illnesses they might have, will mate with other members of their species, etc. These interactions are both physical and intellectual.

In what we call "concrete" concepts, the substantive dimension is typically quite vivid and immediately evoked, whereas for "abstract" concepts the functional connections dominate, often almost exclusively. In humans, it is our capacity for abstract thought—for discerning functional relations and implications—that permits us to plan, reason, and theorize. Herein lies a certain evolutionary advantage that we have accrued when it comes to our ability to identify and solve certain highly complex problems (physical, social, moral, spiritual) that we encounter. James explains, "Now however beautiful or otherwise worthy of stationary contemplation the substantive part of a concept may be, the more important part of its significance may naturally be held to be the consequences to which it leads. These may lie either in the way of making us think, or in the way of making us act" (1911/1979, 37).

It is our ability to abstract a quality or structure from the continuous flow of our experience and then to discern its relations to other concepts and its implications for action that makes possible the highest forms of inquiry, of which humans are uniquely capable. My dog, Lucy, has concepts and solves problems, but she lacks the full abstractive capacities that open up the possibility of discovering general explanations of phenomena in the ways we humans do.

At the heart of all pragmatist philosophy is the fundamental understanding that thinking is doing, and that cognition is action. Pragmatism recognizes that thought can be transformative of our experience precisely because thought is embodied and interfused with feeling. Thinking is not something humans "bring" to their experience from the outside; rather, it is *in* and *of* experience—an embodied dimension of those experiences in which abstraction is occurring. Our ability to conceptualize is our chief means for being able to respond to the problems we encounter, to adapt to situations, and to change them when it is possible and desirable, via the use of human intelligence. This conception of mind and thought is the basis for James's famous pragmatic rule of meaning, which states that the meaning of a concept is a matter of its consequences for our present and future thought and action.

JAMES'S PRAGMATIC RULE OF MEANING

The pragmatic rule is that the meaning of a concept may always be found, if not in some sensible particular which it directly designates, then in some particular difference in the course of human experience which its being true will make. Test every concept by the question, "What sensible difference to anybody will its truth make?" and you are in the best possible position for understanding what it means and for discussing its importance. (James 1911/1979, 37)

There are far-reaching implications of this pragmatist view of meaning, one of the most stunning of which is that even our most abstract concepts will have a meaning grounded in perception and bodily experience. This is the only way it can be, if concepts are not disembodied.

Our capacity to abstract farther and farther away from the concrete rich-ness of felt experience is still always and only *abstraction* and selection from the flow of perception. The more we abstract, the more we are left only with perceived relations among qualities or shapes or internal structures of things. We pay the price of losing connection to the specific felt quali-ties of things, in order to gain the reward of generalization over aspects of experience: "The substitution of concepts and their connections, of a whole conceptual order, in short, for the immediate perceptual flow, thus widens enormously our mental panorama. Had we no concepts we should live simply 'getting' each successive moment of experience, as the sessile sea-anemone on its rock receives whatever nourishment the wash of the waves may bring" (James 1911/1979, 39).

Our human glory—abstract thinking and the possibility for enhanced inquiry and creativity that comes with it—involves our ability to select aspects of our experience in so many different ways, from so many differ-ent perspectives, for so many different purposes. When we do this, we de-emphasize our perceptual experience, but we *never* leave it wholly behind. Even our most abstract concepts (such as *cause, necessity, freedom,* and *God*) have no meaning without some connection to felt experience. In a re-markable passage, James follows his pragmatic rule of meaning in tracing some of our most abstract and formal concepts back to possible perceived situations, operations, and consequences.

> That A and B are 'equal,' for example, means either that 'you will find no difference' when you pass from one to the other, or that in substituting one for the other in certain operations 'you will get the same result both times.' 'Substance' means that 'a definite group of sensations will recur.' 'Incom-mensurable' means that 'you are always confronted with a remainder.' 'In-finite' means either that, or that 'you can count as many units in a part as you can in the whole.' 'More' and 'less' mean certain sensations, varying according to the matter. 'Freedom' means 'no feeling of sensible restraint.' 'Necessity' means that 'your way is blocked in all directions save one.' 'God' means that 'you can dismiss certain kinds of fear,' 'cause' that 'you may ex-pect certain sequences,' etc. etc. (James 1911/1979, 38)

These "meanings" that James gives of some of our most abstract con-cepts are not intended by him to be exhaustive (e.g., "God," of course, means far more than "Have no fear"!). He presents these meanings to give examples of how terms (or concepts) have meanings only insofar as they make some perceivable difference (either now or possibly in the future) in how and what we think or do. James is thus claiming that what we tend to regard as purely formal structures are *not* purely formal, but rather are patterns of embodied interactions. On this view, the logical principle known as transitivity (as in "All *A* are *B;* all *B* are *C;* therefore, all *A* are *C*") is not a law of allegedly "pure thought," but rather a principle of embodied experience. If my car keys are in my hand, and my hand is in my pocket, then my keys are in my pocket. James characterizes this as "what contains the container contains the contained of whatever material either be made" (1911/1979, 41). In chapter 7, I will describe such patterns of conceptualization and reasoning based on image schemas, showing their indispensable role in our ability to grasp the meaning of situations and to reason about them. For now, it is enough to see that these patterns are experiential, existing at the level of feeling and thinking interfused.

JAMES AND THE GROUNDING OF LOGIC IN FEELING

In his justly famous chapter from *The Principles of Psychology* titled "The Stream of Thought," James pushes his theory of the embodiment of conceptualization and reasoning to its limits when he stresses that even logical relations are *felt* and not just *thought*. He moves from the bodily nature of conceptualization to the embodiment of consciousness and thought. Human thinking is an embodied, continuous flow, and what we call our "ideas" are phases of that ongoing flow. The idea that thinking is embodied is not the relatively obvious claim that in order to think, one needs a body and a brain. Instead, it entails that the nature of our embodiment shapes both what and how we think, and that every thought implicates a certain bodily awareness.

> Our own bodily position, attitude, condition, is one of the things of which *some* awareness, however inattentive, invariably accompanies the knowledge of whatever else we know. We think; and as we think we feel our bodily selves as the seat of the thinking. If the thinking be *our* thinking, it must be suffused through all its parts with that peculiar warmth and intimacy that make it come as ours. (James 1890/1950, 1:241–42).

Take note of James's radical thesis: "As we think we feel our bodily selves as the seat of the thinking." He is not merely asserting that bodily states must accompany and be the basis for all of our thinking; rather, he is asserting that in all thinking, we are in some degree aware, however vaguely, of our bodily states, as they result from our interactions in the world.

If James is right, then as you read these very words, there should be a way it feels to think the thoughts they express. What could he possibly mean by this? His answer is that since *thought flows,* there must be a quality of this flow that we can experience. James's metaphor is that thought has the structure of the flightings and perchings of birds. Thought moves *from* one temporary "resting place" (one substantive image or idea) *to* another. In between, there is the feeling of the direction, rhythms, and pulses of our transition from one "place" (stable image or idea) to another. *What we feel are the patterns and qualities of this transitional flow of thought,* even though most of the time we have lost the habit of noticing these feelings.

As an example, consider your own process of writing something. Whenever your writing is going well, there is a certain direction, force, and momentum established by your first thoughts. The words pour out, as we say, and your thinking flows too, moving from one thought to the next in smooth transition. But then you get stuck for a moment. You are not sure what to say next, what comes next. Notice the arrested development of your thinking and the accompanying bodily-mental tension. Things were going swimmingly, then you got stopped, and now you need to figure out how to carry on with a new train of thoughts that resolve the felt tension in the situation. Your problem is how to reestablish fluid thought that will run its course to some resolution or fulfillment (when you have "expressed your idea"). As you try out various ways to carry the thought forward, you start and stop, trying first one thought and then another, seeking to realize the felt tendencies of what you are thinking, in just the way described by Eugene Gendlin in his account of the felt sense of thinking (in chapter 4). If you start out with an *if*-thought, then a *then*-thought must soon follow, completing the passage from one place to another on the metaphorical path of your thinking. The *if* aspect of your thought (as in the previous sentence) creates a felt anticipation of something that follows, in a way that moves you to a new thought-location. You move in thinking from the *if* location toward some other place (the *then* location), along a narrow mental path that you must traverse. The feeling of *if* is a feeling of expectancy of something to come, taken in light of the character of a present situation. The expectancy is not just a feeling that you *may* move from the *if*-thought to the *then*-thought, but rather that you *must* make this movement in thinking. It is important to keep in mind that our metaphorical description of this *movement* of thought is not merely a fictional description. It is trying to capture an embodied process of the felt movement (change) of our thinking.

There are, then, feelings of the developing processes of thinking, or rather there are ways it feels to think different thoughts and their relation in a process of inquiry. Thinking is a process, and since it occurs over time, it involves the felt experience of the forward motion from one stage of the process to another. Logical relations are felt as transitions from one thought to another. James thus boldly asserts:

> If there be such things as feelings at all, *then so surely as relations between objects exist in rerum natura, so surely, and more surely, do feelings exist to which these relations are known.* There is not a conjunction or a preposition, and hardly an adverbial phrase, syntactic form, or inflection of voice, in human speech, that does not express some shading or other of relation which we at some moment actually feel to exist between the larger objects of our thought. . . .
>
> We ought to say a feeling of *and,* a feeling of *if,* a feeling of *but,* and a feeling of *by,* quite as readily as we say a feeling of *blue* or a feeling of *cold.* (James 1890/1950, 1:245–46)

Can you feel William James's "but"? If you can't, then there is something wrong with you, something repressed or submerged in your understanding. To feel James's "but" is to feel the quality of a situation as a kind of hesitancy or qualification of something asserted or proposed. When you think "I may go to the party, but I won't have fun," you are expressing some unsatisfactory qualification of your anticipated situation. You are feeling that if your situation should develop in a certain way (i.e., if you go to the party), then there will follow a certain unresolved quality of your situation as it has developed to that point in time (i.e., you feel the dis-ease of not having fun). In addition to this feeling of hesitancy, "but" also marks a feeling of conjunction. In the example above, the not-having-fun is tightly connected to having attended the party. To say "*x* but *y*" asserts that both *x* and *y* are taken together, but *y* is taken (or given) with some hesitancy.[2] Notice how this explains why most contemporary logicians usually translate *but* with *and*—they strip away the peculiar felt quality in order to focus only on the relation of connection between *x* and *y*. Since modern logic does not and cannot recognize a role for feeling, it must ignore anything but "pure" formal relation. Consequently, it interprets logical relations as empty formal relations lacking any felt connection or direction in our thinking.

---

2. I am indebted to Scott Pratt for this analysis and its connection to uses of *but* in modern logic.

Because most of us are not in the habit of attending to these subtle, nuanced feelings of direction and relation in our thinking, we are inclined to deny that they play any serious role in logic. However, once you grant that logic is grounded in human inquiry (as James and Dewey insisted), and once you start to pay attention to how you feel as you think, you will notice an entire submerged continent of feeling that supports, and is part of, your thoughts. You will begin to notice "that ...."—the felt sense—that Gendlin describes as supporting and carrying the meaning of our forms, concepts, and logical relations. Reasoning is not the manipulation of abstract, meaningless symbols according to purely formal syntactic and logical rules. Rather, reasoning is our intelligent-animal way of working through the implications of situations in pursuit of an embodied understanding that allows us to function successfully, more or less, within the problematic situations that we inhabit. Feelings of "furtherance" and "hindrance" of our thinking play a key role in how we know *what follows from what* in our thinking. Thinking moves in a direction, *from* one thought *to* another, and we have corresponding feelings of how this movement is going: we feel the halt to our thinking, we feel the tension as we entertain possible ways to *go on* thinking, and we feel the consummation when a line of thought runs its course to satisfactory conclusion. Such are the aesthetic dimensions of our thinking.

James makes exploratory forays into the vast, uncharted territory of qualitative experience. Logical relations, he explains, are denoted by mere logical skeletons, such as verbal formulas or written symbols, but the relations themselves are *in* experience and *in* the situation. "*A* is *B*, but . . ." has a "difference in felt meaning" from "either *A* or *B*." James summarizes:

> The truth is that large tracts of human speech are nothing but *signs of direction* in thought, of which direction we nevertheless have an acutely discriminative sense, though no definite sensorial image plays any part in it whatsoever. . . . These bare images of logical movement . . . are psychic transitions, always on the wing, so to speak, and not to be glimpsed except in flight. Their function is to lead from one set of images to another. (James 1890/1950, 1:252–53)

Once again, just as Gendlin argued, the feeling of relation is not a mere accompaniment of thought. There are not two things—the abstract, logical thought and an attendant feeling—but only one continuous stream of thought that is at once formal, qualitative, and emotional. "If *X*, then *Y*" doesn't *mean* anything by itself. It only means something as a tendency of an embodied, continuous process of thought. It means that when the antecedent is thought, then something more, and something connected to the antecedent, is anticipated as forthcoming.

LOGIC AND THE FEELING BRAIN

I suspect that most logicians, as well as most philosophers of mind and language, will find these claims about the relation of logic to feeling ludicrous. They will protest that logic has nothing to do with feelings, because it is about pure formal relations and algorithms that can be run on computing machines. True as this might be for the so-called logic of computers, it is utterly false as a statement about human logical inference. Human thinking is a continuous feeling-thinking process that is forever tied to our body's monitoring of its own states. One way to see this is to examine the cognitive neuroscience of the brain. In the very same chapter in which James is describing the feeling of logical relations, he turns to the brain science of his day for confirmation of his claim that we sometimes feel the flow of thought:

> We believe the brain to be an organ whose internal equilibrium is always in a state of change—the change affecting every part. The pulses of change are doubtless more violent in one place than in another, their rhythm more rapid at this time than at that. . . . In the brain the perpetual rearrangement must result in some forms of tension lingering relatively long, whilst others simply come and pass. . . . The lingering consciousnesses, if of simple objects, we call 'sensations' or 'images,' according as they are vivid or faint; if of complex objects, we call them 'percepts' when vivid, 'concepts' or 'thoughts' when faint. For the swift consciousnesses we have only those names of 'transitive states,' or 'feelings of relation,' which we have used. (James 1890/1950, 1:246–47)

James is here trying to connect his view of the flow of thought—which consists of points of relative stasis (images, percepts, concepts) alternating with felt transitional motions (logical relations)—with the brain's monitoring of its processes and internal equilibrium. Today, we have more detailed and well-supported neuroscience accounts of the brain's monitoring of the body's equilibrium. In chapter 3 we considered Damasio's argument that emotions result from the body's monitoring of changes in its states in response to our interactions with our environment. In our systems for monitoring changes in bodily equilibrium, emotions (and subsequent feelings) initiate internal changes in our bodies that sometimes lead us to bodily movements in the world. Damasio's basic hypothesis is that

> the body, as represented in the brain, may constitute the indispensable frame of reference for neural processes that we experience as the mind; that our very organism rather than some absolute external reality is used as the ground reference for the constructions we make of the world around us and for the construction of the ever-present sense of subjectivity that is part and parcel of experiences; that our most refined thoughts and best actions, our greatest joys and deepest sorrows, use the body as a yardstick. (Damasio 1994, xvi)

Don Tucker, a psychologist and cognitive neuroscientist who studies the role of various brain structures in processes of feeling, perception, thought, motivation, and action, has even more forcefully affirmed the grounding of abstract thinking in sensorimotor processes:

> The brain evolved to regulate the motivational control of actions, carried out by the motor system, guided by sensory evaluation of ongoing environmental events. There are no "faculties"—of memory, conscious perception, or music appreciation—that float in the mental ether, separate from the bodily functions. If we accept that the mind comes from the brain, then our behavior and experience must be understood to be elaborations of primordial systems for perceiving, evaluating, and acting. When we study the brain to look for the networks controlling cognition, we find that all of the networks that have been implicated in cognition are linked in one way or the other to sensory systems, to motor systems, or to motivational systems.
> There are no brain parts for disembodied cognition. (Tucker, forthcoming, 58)

In *Mind from Body: Experience from Neural Structure,* Tucker focuses on the basic architecture of the brain as the key to the nature of our cognitive abilities, and he is especially interested in the role of feelings and emotions in all aspects of cognition. He explores the parallel processing that results from three general architectural features of the brain: front-back orientation, hemispheric laterality (right-left organization), and core-shell relationships. I want to focus on just one part of Tucker's account—the core-shell structure—because it reveals possible neural bases for Dewey's notion of a pervasive quality, and it also suggests that both James and Dewey were correct when they argued that concepts arise from a global grasp of a situation that leads to processes of discrimination and differentiation.

Tucker argues that we have not fully appreciated the value of nine-teenth-century studies of the evolutionary and ontogenetic development of the brain. With contemporary neuroimaging technology, we can now get a much more detailed understanding of the complex relations and in-teractions of these various brain architectures. To vastly oversimplify, our brain developed through evolution by adding new structures and layers on top of more primitive parts shared with some other animals. The present-day result is a brain with core limbic structures (mostly responsible for body monitoring, motivation, emotions, and feelings) that are connected to "higher" cortical layers that have ever more differentiated functions, such as perception, body movement, action planning, and reasoning. One striking feature of this core-shell organization is that structures in the core regions are massively interconnected, whereas structures in the shell are more sparsely interconnected. An important consequence of this is that there is more functional differentiation and more modularity of brain ar-eas in the cortical shell than in the limbic core. Tucker summarizes:

> First, *connections stay at their own level.* With the exception of "adjacent" con-nections (paralimbic connects to higher-order association, higher associa-tion connects to primary association, etc.), connections from one level go primarily to other brain areas of that same level. . . .
>
> Second, *the greatest density of connectivity within a level is found at the limbic core.* There is then a progressive decrease in connectivity as you go out toward the primary sensory and motor modules. . . . In fact, the primary sensory and motor cortices can be accurately described as "modules" because each is an isolated island, connected with the diencephalic thalamus but with no other cortical areas except the adjacent unimodal association cortex of that sensory modality or motor area.
>
> The exception is that the primary motor cortex does have point-to-point connections with the primary somatosensory cortex. (Tucker, forth-coming, 78)

The structures and functions Tucker is describing here would make sense of Dewey's claim that our experience always begins with a pervasive unifying quality of a whole situation, within which we then discriminate objects, with their properties and relations to one another. The limbic core, with its dense interconnections and emotional valences, would present us with a holistic, feeling-rich, emotionally nuanced grasp of a situation. The more modular and highly differentiated sensory and motor regions of the shell (cortical) structure would permit the discrimination and differentiation that we call conceptualization. Just as James and Dewey argued, the meaning of a situation grows as we mark more differences, similarities, changes, and relations—that is, as we make finer discriminations within the ongoing flow of experience: "The meaning, or semantic function, of a network may be allowed greater complexity as its architecture becomes more differentiated" (Tucker, forthcoming, 97).

Cognitive processing does not occur merely in a linear direction from core to shell structures. There are reentrant connections, so that what occurs at "higher," or more differentiated, levels can influence what happens in the limbic areas; these areas then affect shell regions, in a never-ending dance of changing experience. But the core-to-shell movement of cognition helps explain why (and how) there can be pervasive qualities that then issue in acts of discrimination and conceptualization. Tucker summarizes the structural basis for this growing arc of experience that Dewey described as the movement from a holistic pervasive qualitative situation to conceptual meaning:

> At the core must be the most integrative concepts, formed through the fusion of many elements through the dense web of interconnection. This fusion of highly processed sensory and motor information[,] . . . together with direct motivational influences from the hypothalamus, would create a *syncretic* form of experience. Meaning is rich, deep, with elements fused in a holistic matrix of information, a matrix charged with visceral significance. Emanating outward—from this core neuropsychological lattice—are the progressive articulations of neocortical networks. Finally, at the shell, we find the most differentiated networks. . . . The most differentiated networks of the hierarchy are the most constrained by the sensory data, forming close matches with the environmental information that is in turn mirrored by the sense receptors. (Tucker, forthcoming, 169)

Conceptual meaning arises from our visceral, purposive engagement with our world. Conceptualization recruits structures of sensorimotor processing (discussed more fully in chapter 8), and it operates within a motivational framework that evolved to help us function successfully within our complex environments. Recall Damasio's claim that the body's most important life-sustaining function is to assess and control bodily states. As we saw, this monitoring is not merely registering our "inner" subjective states. Instead, these states are already the consequence of continual organism-environment interactions, so that managing these states always involves a reaching out beyond our internal milieu to our surrounding situation. Therefore, the monitoring of our bodily states is simultaneously an assessing of the patterns of our interaction with our world. You might say that we are taking the measure of our world-as-we-are-engaging-it. Our mind-brain, in evaluating the flow of its interactions with its environment, will need to identify changes of state and then initiate internal bodily processes to maintain an overall systemic balance within the organism in relation to its environment. Damasio thus describes feelings as "the sensors for the match or lack thereof between nature and circumstance" (1994, xv).

This is where felt logical relations of the sort described by James, Dewey, and Gendlin come into play, for they allow us to manage our inquiries into various possibilities for action within a problematic situation. We actually *feel* how our thinking is "going." We feel when it is blocked, we feel when it moves forward and how it moves, and we feel whether it resolves the problematic situation we were in that gave rise to our thinking about what to do. If we could get over the mistaken idea that logic is only about meaningless formal operations on symbols, and if we could instead see it as being about the structures of embodied inquiry, then it would begin to make sense to describe the "feeling" of logical inference. James saw that logic, being about relations and tendencies, concerns the swift transitions we experience as we move from one thought (as a relatively substantive and stable embodied state) to another. He saw that logic lives and moves in embodied experience, and that it cannot be understood apart from actual purposive human inquiry, which depends on the workings of our brain in our body in our environment. Real logic is embodied—spatial, corporeal, incarnate.

PUTTING LOGIC BACK INTO THE WORLD

If logic doesn't merely fall down from the Platonic heavens above, then it must surely rise up from our embodied experience as functioning organisms within changing environments. Better than anyone before or since, James and Dewey saw that the recognition of this fact requires a serious reconsideration of the very nature of human concepts, thinking, reasoning, logic, and mind.

Just how radical is the thesis of the embodiment of logic and reason? There are at least two possible interpretations of the thesis. The weak interpretation is that feelings *accompany* our cognition of logical relations. While this might be a surprising fact, it would not challenge traditional views of logic as purely formal and meaningless. The skeptic—someone who still wants to hold onto the idea that reason is autonomous, disembodied, purely formal, and wholly transcendent—could easily embrace this weak version. Such a skeptic will protest that even though we might have feelings associated with our grasping of logical relations, those relations themselves remain transcendent structures of pure reason (or the essence of thought as such).

This transcendent, absolutist view of logic is precisely what James and Dewey are rejecting when they espouse the stronger version of the embodied logic hypothesis. Feeling, they are saying, is never merely a concomitant of an autonomous logic; rather, feelings of quality, connection, and direction lie at the heart of logical reasoning, as it is carried out in actual inquiry. To say that reason is embodied means that you can never fully understand its capacities and workings without reference to facts about human bodies, brains, and environments. On this view, formal relations are not meaningless and arbitrary, but instead are highly motivated and meaningful. Meaningful form comes from the nature of our bodies and the patterns of interaction we have with our environment, and it is therefore shaped by our values, interests, and purposes as active agents. As Dewey insisted—and as cognitive science confirms—thought is never wholly divorced from feeling, value, and the aesthetics of our embodied experience. There is always a feeling of our rational thought:

> Hence *an* experience of thinking has its own esthetic quality. It differs from those experiences that are acknowledged to be esthetic, but only in its materials. The material of the fine arts consists of qualities; that of experience having intellectual conclusion are signs or symbols having no intrinsic quality of their own, but standing for things that may in another experience be qualitatively experienced. . . . The experience itself has a satisfying emotional quality because it possesses internal integration and fulfillment reached through ordered and organized movement. . . . What is even more important is that not only is this quality a significant motive in undertaking intellectual inquiry and in keeping it honest, but that no intellectual activity is an integral event (is *an* experience), unless it is rounded out with this quality. Without it, thinking is inconclusive. (Dewey 1934/1987, 38)

Anyone who has ever reflected on their own thought processes, and certainly any writer or teacher, will know immediately what Dewey is talking about when he speaks of the aesthetics of thinking. How many times have you felt the frustration, tension, and dissonance of thinking that is not going well? And how many times have you felt the joy of fulfillment when you do "get it right," when thoughts flow and meaning (or even argument) is carried forward in a satisfactory (satisfying) way? There are aesthetic qualities to our thinking, just as much as there are aesthetic qualities of accomplished creative performances in sports, music, painting, dance, and sculpture. On Dewey's view, all thought is situated, embodied, and value-laden, and so every instance of thinking is guided by its own distinctive aesthetic quality. We *feel* the quality of the situation and thus grasp the tendencies and directions carrying forward the meaning of our present situation. We feel "how to go on" connecting one thought to another.

The embodied character of reasoning and logic is perfectly consistent with the fact that logical relations can seem to transcend particular situations and have a universal or absolute character. We tend to abstract structures from situations and then attempt to apply them to situations that seem to us to be similar in kind to the former ones. Sometimes this will work, especially when the next context we have to think about is mostly stable and continuous with previous contexts in which the logical relations arose. The mistake, one that is deeply etched in our intellectual tradition, is to think that just because certain logical relations "transcend" particular instantiations by applying to many different situations, it would be possible to erase the embeddedness of thought in concrete, actual situations and their concrete qualities. But actual human logic is always situated in value-laden contexts of inquiry. In the arc of inquiry, we start with problematic situations, move reflectively through symbols in acts of reasoning, and return to experience by way of testing our reasoning and by embodied carrying forward of meaning and resolution of difficulties.

Dewey's *Logic: The Theory of Inquiry* (1938/1991) is a monumental attempt to give naturalistic accounts of thinking and logic, bringing these back into the world from which centuries of absolutist thinking had tried to extract them. In a nutshell, Dewey's claim is that our grand illusion has been to think of mind as disembodied, reason as transcendent, and logic as pure form. This extraction of logic from the world is a consequence of our abstracting away from the lived context of actual human inquiry and fooling ourselves into thinking that logic floats free of our action in the world. In Dewey's words, "The idea that any knowledge in particular can be instituted apart from its being the consummation of inquiry, and that knowledge in general can be defined apart from this connection is, moreover, one of the sources of confusion in logical theory" (1938/1991, 16).

Change, chance, and contingency are a fundamental part of life that can sometimes leave us feeling helpless and out of control. In our desperation over this inescapable flux of existence, we reach out for anything we think might lift us above change to some eternal realm of fixed forms and standards of value. We go so far as to fool ourselves into thinking that there must exist absolute, unchanging forms and principles against which all our finite, changing, embodied experience can be measured, once and for all. If these forms actually did exist, then our job as knowers would be simply to discover these eternal patterns and learn how to apply them to guide our lives. The history of Western philosophy, from the early Presocratics to the present day, reveals a succession of attempts to identify and describe these universal, eternal norms. Whether they are believed to come from the mind of God, from Nature, or from Universal Reason, their function is supposed to be that of providing us with an always-fixed mark by which to navigate our way through the ever-changing, ever-flowing waters of our temporal existence.

But Nietzsche, James, Dewey, and a host of subsequent thinkers have shown us that *life is change* and *existence is an ongoing process*. There is no eternal logic, no absolute form that could save us from grappling with change every moment of our lives. The logic we humans have is an embodied logic of inquiry, one that arises in experience and must be readjusted as situations change. Dewey correctly defines human inquiry as an embodied, situated, ongoing process that begins with a problematic or indeterminate situation, employs intelligence and symbolic resources of thought to clarify and seek to resolve the tension in the situation, and, when successful, transforms the character and quality of the situation. *Logical thinking can thereby actually change experience, because it is in and of that experience.* Logic comes from patterns of inquiry that have proved useful in dealing with the kinds of problems we encounter, given our biological and cultural makeup, our history, and our interests and purposes. What we call logical principles (such as the law of noncontradiction, the law of the excluded middle, modus ponens, and modus tollens) are based on habits of inquiry. They are summaries of habits of thinking that have moved inquiry forward and kept it more or less successful under certain perceived conditions. Following in the footsteps of Charles Sanders Peirce, Dewey understands that habits of inquiry are characteristic modes of *action* in dealing with perceived problems: "But when it is found that there are habits involved in *every* inference, in spite of differences of subject-matter, and when these habits are noted and formulated, then the formulations are guiding or leading principles. The principles state habits operative in every inference that tend to yield conclusions that are stable and productive in further inquiries" (Dewey 1938/1991, 20).

The disastrous error that is so characteristic of much of Western epistemology and logic is to equate "conclusions that are stable and productive" with principles that are absolute, a priori, universal, unchanging. Our quest for certainty and our desire for fixed standards tempts us into hypostatizing our principles as absolute forms. In other words, we abstract logical principles from incarnate inquiry and attempt to safely ensconce them in the Museum of Eternal Forms. Once this fateful move has been made, it is a short step to the related mistaken views that (1) logical principles are absolute, (2) logical forms are pure and disembodied, and (3) the normative character of logic comes from its origins in pure reason.

The facts, however, are just the opposite. First, logical principles are not absolute; rather, they are structures of habits of thought that we have found useful in the types of inquiries we engage in. This is a point that W. V. O. Quine (1951) argued strenuously for when he insisted that even logical principles might, in light of changing circumstances, need to be revised. In championing pragmatist views of logic, inquiry, knowledge, and truth, Hilary Putnam (1981, 1995) has challenged traditional claims to a priori knowledge and absolute foundations of logic, arguing instead for fallibilistic, yet antiskeptical, views of human knowing and logic. Second, logical forms are not disembodied. On the contrary, they emerge from the nature of our embodied experience, shaped by our sensorimotor capacities, our feelings, and our modes of inquiry. Third, logical norms come not from pure reason, but from the very value-laden situations in which our inquiries are carried out. Good reasoning is the use of methods and patterns of inference that allow us to deal constructively with the problematic situations we encounter.

Anybody who espouses an objectivist view of cognition will no doubt protest that logic and mathematics *must* be eternal and universal, simply because the principles, laws, and proofs of logic and mathematics hold true across all times, cultures, and practices. Arithmetic and geometry, for example, are believed to work in and apply to the world in itself. The amazingly complex mathematics that made it possible for us to put humans on the moon surely must attest to the fact that there is a correct mathematics that lies at the heart of a correct physics of the natural world.

None of these assertions about the beauty, magnificence, and universal applicability of mathematics is incompatible with the embodiment of human understanding. In their book *Where Mathematics Comes From,* George Lakoff and Rafael Núñez have shown how large parts of mathematics make use of garden-variety structures and processes of everyday human cognition, structures such as images, image schemas, metaphors, metonymies, radial categories, and various kinds of conceptual blending (these will be discussed in later chapters). Mathematics works for us precisely because mathematical ideas can be understood by us using these ordinary conceptual resources. Lakoff and Núñez summarize the human, embodied character of mathematics:

> The effectiveness of mathematics in the world is a tribute to evolution and to culture. Evolution has shaped our bodies and brains so that we have inherited neural capacities for the basics of number and for primitive spatial relations. Culture has made it possible for millions of astute observers of nature, through millennia of trial and error, to develop and pass on more and more sophisticated mathematical tools—tools shaped to describe what they have observed. There is no mystery about the effectiveness of mathematics for characterizing the world as we experience it: That effectiveness results from a combination of mathematical knowledge and connectedness to the world. The connection between mathematical ideas and the world as human beings experience it occurs within human minds. It is human beings who have created logarithmic spirals and fractals and who can "see" logarithmic spirals in snails and in palm leaves. (Lakoff and Núñez 2000, 378)

Mathematics (like logic) is just as universal as our environment and our cognitive equipment are stable and effective for cognizing situations. In other words, if our basic modes of understanding were to change, due primarily to changes in our bodies, our brains, or our world, then our mathematics would change also, and along with it the ways we would apply mathematics to our experience of nature and the universe. From the perspective of embodied cognition, mathematics remains as beautiful and amazing and stable as it always has been, but it also remains dependent on our ability both to sustain it and to extend it creatively as part of processes of inquiry.

A NATURALISTIC GROUNDING OF LOGICAL NORMS AND PRINCIPLES IN THE EXPERIENCE OF INQUIRY

Dewey's theory of logic is naturalistic in the sense that it seeks logical patterns and norms *within our experience of inquiry.* He explains that naturalism "means, on one side, that there is no breach of continuity between operations of inquiry and biological operations and physical operations. 'Continuity,' on the other side, means that rational operations *grow out of* organic activities, without being identical with that from which they emerge" (Dewey 1938/1991, 26). This form of naturalism denies that what we call "mind" and "body" are two ontologically different kinds of entities or processes. A naturalistic logic would therefore have to discover inferential structures within our sensorimotor interactions that are appropriated for reasoning about abstract domains. As we will see in part 2, evidence from cognitive linguistics and cognitive neuroscience suggests that abstract thinking does indeed use the resources of our sensorimotor experience. Such a view would also be consistent with an evolutionary point of view. Does it make sense that we would develop an entirely new set of inferential patterns and capacities for abstract thinking that parallels the structures of the sensorimotor system when we could more economically appropriate the workings of the sensorimotor system to do abstract inferences? The hypothesis of just such a logic-system doppelgänger has certainly held sway historically, under the guise of the existence of pure reason and, more recently, of syntax or form-generating modules. However, I will argue in chapter 8 that this doppelgänger view is at least not a necessary hypothesis, since there is an alternative hypothesis—tying logic to sensorimotor inferences—that has some support from cognitive neuroscience.

The standard, time-honored objection to naturalistic accounts of logic is to call up the hoary specter of the "is/ought" distinction. Logic, it is claimed, has a normative dimension. It tells us not merely how we *do* reason, but also how we *should* reason. On this view, then, no account of *what ought to be* can be derived from *what is*.

This is/ought argument is simply mistaken, and so the right strategy for the naturalist is to call its bluff. Hilary Putnam (1981, 1987), among others, has famously challenged the alleged fact/value (is/ought) dichotomy upon which so much contemporary normative philosophy rests. I shall not embark on an excursion into the various arguments challenging the fact/value dichotomy more than to say that many of them are based on showing that our standards of inquiry in different sciences and areas of practice are always and only assessable relative to the purposes, interests, and values served by those forms of inquiry. As Putnam says, "The procedures by which we decide on the acceptability of a scientific theory have to do with whether or not the scientific theory as a whole exhibits certain 'virtues'" (1981, 133). Values such as prediction, consistency, adequacy, testability, relevance, perspicuousness, and importance are variously built into and realized by different methods and theories. Moreover, there is no value-neutral perspective from which to hierarchically order various values, goods, and purposes in cases where they might conflict.

Putnam's pragmatist orientation squares nicely with Peirce's, James's, and Dewey's views, upon which it is based. Dewey explains how to understand the is/ought distinction from a naturalistic perspective:

> The way in which men *do* "think" denotes, as it is *here* interpreted, simply the ways in which men at a given time carry on their inquiries. So far as it is used to register a difference from the ways in which they *ought* to think, it denotes a difference like that between good and bad farming or good and bad medical practice. Men think in ways they should not when they follow methods of inquiry that experience of past inquiries shows are not competent to reach the intended end of the inquiries in question. . . . We know that some methods of inquiry are better than others in just the same way in which we know that some methods of surgery, farming, road-making, navigating or what-not are better than others. It does not follow in any of these cases that the "better" methods are ideally perfect, or that they are regulative or "normative" because of conformity to some absolute form. They are the methods which experience up to the present time shows to be the best methods available for achieving certain results, while abstraction of these methods does supply a (relative) norm or standard for further undertakings. (Dewey 1938/1991, 108)

It would be difficult to put this point more clearly or cogently. We reason for various purposes and goals, influenced by various interests, commitments, needs, and values. What we call reason serves, at a given point in time, some of these values, and it can only criticize them by assuming some other set of values or standards. What it cannot do is take a value-neutral stance. *The so-called norms of logical inference are just the patterns of thinking that we have discovered as having served us well in our prior inquiries, relative to certain values, purposes, and types of situations.* They are presumptive principles that we hold normatively until and unless they cease to serve our inquiries over the long run (and not merely because of some short-term difficulty or tension). They "transcend" given situations just insofar as they provide useful norms across a broad range of contexts and situations. Their alleged objectivity can only be established relative to some set of values presupposed—values that at some future time may themselves be open to scrutiny and criticism.

Thus, logic is not an unchanging, universal structure of reason as such. Rather, logic is a tool, consisting of rational patterns of inquiry that help us reflect upon, think through, and transform our experience. Logic is embodied, and this embodiment is what keeps logic grounded in, and connected to, experience.

Objectivists about logic might protest, once again, that they are not concerned with the emergence of logic in modes of inquiry; rather, they will insist, their only interest lies in the internal structure of a self-enclosed logical system. To this I answer that the objectivist is entitled to the puzzle-solving and exploratory exercises of formal logic. It is always possible to run the system "off-line," as it were, disengaged from the context of actual human inquiry. But let no one be deceived about what makes it possible for logicians to focus exclusively on logical form and logical operations. The structures, concepts, and rules of their logic first emerged as meaningful only in and through inquiry, even though they now can be somewhat abstracted from those concrete inquiries. The apparent universality and for-all-time-ness that make logic seem so eternal and wonderful are the consequences of embodied sources and processes of human thinking.

PART II

Embodied Meaning and the Sciences of Mind

In part 1, we took a phenomenological and reflective look at how meaning is grounded in our embodied interactions with our environment. I described some of the ways in which the nature of our bodies in interaction with their surroundings provides the basis for how things are meaningful to us and how we begin to make sense of our experience. However, phenomenological description and analysis can tell only part of the story of human understanding, namely, the part that shows itself in our awareness of how things have meaning for us. By telling us what it means to be an embodied person in the "lifeworld," phenomenology reveals many of the structures and processes of human meaning-making. But not every dimension of meaning and understanding can be brought to conscious awareness via self-reflection. A large part of human understanding operates more or less automatically and beneath the level of conscious awareness. It is at this point that the cognitive sciences—the sciences of mind—can begin to work cooperatively with phenomenology, by showing how the body and brain actually perform their marvelous feats of human cognition.

Part 2 is thus a brief expedition—a scouting party, if you will—into the vast frontier of the contemporary sciences of mind. My highly limited purpose in making this voyage of discovery is to suggest that recent empirical research in biology, in cognitive neuroscience, and in cognitive linguistics not only supports the embodied meaning hypothesis but also begins to reveal how our brains play their crucial role in some of our remarkable acts of understanding.

One of the greatest obstacles to a general acknowledgment of the embodiment of mind, meaning, and thought is the persistence—in commonsense, scientific, and philosophical models alike—of the representational theory of mind. As we will see in the next chapter, the representational theory claims that the "mind" operates on "internal representations" (ideas, concepts, images) that can re-present (and thereby "be about") external objects and events. The representational theory had its source in dualistic metaphysical views that mind is separate from and different in kind from body, that what is inner is different in kind from what is outer, and that we have a direct access to the inner that is not available to us for the outer. Even today, some proponents of nondualistic views nevertheless allow a dualistic ontology to creep back into their theory whenever they accept some version of the representational theory.

The naturalistic theory of embodied meaning, mind, and language that I am developing is thus directly at odds with classical representational theories of mind. One major theme of part 2 of this book is that we can provide a philosophically and scientifically realistic alternative to the representational theory of mind. What is required is an outline of how we might begin to explain conceptualization and reasoning without assuming a representational perspective. Chapters 6 and 7 place human cognition in a broader context of animal cognition, drawing on research in the biological sciences about the embodied, situated, goal-directed nature of animal and human cognition. The key point is to see how organism-environment couplings do not require an internal mind that manipulates symbols referring to external things and events. I argue for the continuity of human thinking with these less sophisticated, less complex engagements of animals with their world. Chapter 8 investigates some of the neural bases for our ability to process both concrete and abstract concepts. I draw on recent research in cognitive neuroscience about the role of neural ensembles in conceptualization. Then, in chapter 9, I make a case for the embodied character of abstract concepts, drawing evidence from cognitive linguistics and neuroscience concerning the central role of image schemas and metaphor in abstract thinking.

In short, part 2 fleshes out some of my central claims about the body's role in conceptualization and reasoning by showing that there are neural mechanisms that might plausibly underlie and make possible the cognitive acts I have described in earlier chapters. Part 2 presents a challenge to the representational theory of mind by sketching key parts of an alternative view of cognition and meaning—one that is embodied, nondualistic, and naturalistic.

CHAPTER 6

The Origin of Meaning in Organism-Environment Coupling

A Nonrepresentational View of Mind

A naturalistic theory of mind, thought, and language must, as we have seen, explain conceptual thinking without introducing immaterial mind or a transcendent ego. According to the embodiment view I am developing here, meaning and thought emerge from our capacities for perception, object manipulation, and bodily movement. The chief challenge is to explain the phenomena of thought and symbolic interaction without resorting to a dualistic mind/body ontology that would violate Dewey's principle of continuity, insofar as it would deny continuity between so-called "bodily" processes and "mental" acts. What must be avoided, to paraphrase Hilary Putnam (1987), is the Kantian view that an adequate account of human mind and thought requires the keeping of two sets of books—one for the phenomenal world of things as appearances to us, and the other for the mysterious, noumenal world of things in themselves.

An embodied cognition view must avoid one of the most dangerous dualistic traps of Western philosophy, namely, asking how something inside the "mind" (i.e., ideas, thoughts, mathematical symbols) can represent the outside (i.e., the world). This trap is a consequence of the mistaken view that mind and body are two ontologically different kinds of entities, substances, or events. And this dualism then defines the problem of meaning as that of explaining how disembodied "internal" ideas can possibly represent "external" physical objects and events.

THE REPRESENTATIONAL THEORY OF MIND

Mind/body dualism often generates what are known as representational theories of mind and cognition. Representationalism in its most general sense (as I am using the term here) is the view that cognition (i.e., perceiving, conceptualizing, imagining, reasoning, planning, willing) operates via internal mental "representations" (e.g., ideas, concepts, images, propositions) that are capable of being "about" or "directed to" other representations and to states of affairs in the external world. The technical term for this "aboutness" relation is *intentionality*. In commonsense language, we would simply say that we think with ideas and that our ideas can be about things in the world—things that are past, present, or future. To most people, this view of mind will seem self-evident. For example, if right now I'm thinking about fishing for rainbow trout, I must be entertaining ideas that have as their representational content *fishing* and *rainbow trout*. My idea of *fishing* picks out certain kinds of activities in the world that involve fishing rods, fishing lines, hooks, casting, and various other aspects of angling for fish. My idea of *rainbow trout* picks out certain members of the finny tribe that populate cold, freshwater streams and lakes. What could be more obvious?

Nevertheless, in spite of the widespread and long-standing appeal of the representational view of mind and its apparent obviousness, in its stronger versions it is an extremely problematic view of meaning and thought. Several centuries of struggling with the problem of how "internal" ideas can be related to "external" things should suggest that once you assume a radical mind/body dichotomy, there is no way to bridge the gap between the inner and the outer. When "mind" and "body" are regarded as two fundamentally different kinds of being, no third, mediating thing can exist that possesses both the metaphysical character of inner, mental things and simultaneously the character of the outer, physical things. Otherwise, we wouldn't even need a distinction between two radically different metaphysical kinds, since there would exist something (the mediating third) that could account for both what we attribute to inner mind and what we attribute to the external world (including our bodies).

At the end of this chapter, I will acknowledge some proper uses of the term *representation,* uses that support an extremely modest representational view. However, it is important to get clear about what is false and very misleading in strong representationalist theories that posit an inner world of ideas that get their meaning from their relation to external objects, events, and states of affairs. I am going to urge that whenever possible, we should avoid using "representation" talk, because it tends to foster the illusion of inner mental space populated by mental quasi-entities (such as concepts, propositions, and functions).

As an example of how easily we can be led astray, I am going to argue that the most popular contemporary version of the representational theory of mind—the very strong version articulated by Jerry Fodor and his supporters—is a false and misleading view of human cognition and meaning. Fodor is well known for his spirited defense of a technical version of what he calls folk psychology, which is, roughly, the commonsensical view that we can explain human thought and behavior by attributing mental states (such as beliefs and desires) to people. For example, I might say that the reason Scott is at this moment casting an artificial caddisfly on the surface of Otter Lake is that Scott *desires* to catch a trout and he *believes* (among other things) that there are rainbow trout in Otter Lake, that they often feed on caddisflies, and that an artificial caddisfly pattern is a decent mimic of an actual caddisfly on the surface of the water. Fodor's special version of this belief-desire psychology assumes the operation of what he calls a "language of thought" that provides the meaning of particular tokens of sentences in a person's natural language. Fodor describes his representational theory of mind as follows: "At the heart of the theory is the postulation of a language of thought: an infinite set of 'mental representations' which function both as the immediate objects of propositional attitudes and as the domains of mental processes" (Fodor 1987, 16–17). A propositional attitude is a mental state, such as belief or desire, directed toward a propositional content. For example, to think the thought (described in English) "The rainbows are rising to caddisflies" is to activate in one's language of thought a set of mental symbols or representations that constitute the appropriate proposition, *the rainbows are rising to caddisflies.* Now, it is an essential part of Fodor's view that the alleged mental representations that provide the structure and content of our thinking are not themselves intrinsically meaningful. Rather, they are symbols that can be related and arranged according to their syntactic (or formal) characteristics. Fodor explains:

> Mental states are relations between organisms and internal representations, and causally interrelated mental states succeed one another according to computational principles which apply formally *to the representations.* This is the sense in which internal representations provide the domains for such data processes as inform the mental life. It is, in short, the essence of cognitive theories that they seek to interpret physical (causal) transformations as trans-

formations of information, with the effect of exhibiting the rationality of mental processes. (Fodor 1975, 198)

As Fodor sees them, mental processes operate like a computational program that performs formal operations on symbols. A major problem for this kind of view is to explain how this inner language of thought (or "mentalese," as he sometimes calls it) can get meaning by being related to things in the world. A simplified version of Fodor's answer is that symbols in the language of thought get their meanings by virtue of their lawlike relations to events in the world that cause the appropriate symbols to be "tokened" in the language of thought. As Fodor says, "In such cases the symbol tokenings denote their causes, and the symbol types express the property whose instantiations reliably cause their tokenings. So, in the paradigm case, my utterance of 'horse' says *of* a horse that it *is* one" (Fodor 1987, 99).

William Bechtel, Adele Abrahamsen, and George Graham (1998) have concisely characterized Fodor's position as follows:

> To be a cognizer is to possess a system of syntactically structured symbols-in-the-head (mind/brain) which undergo processing that is sensitive to that structure. Cognition, in all of its forms, from the simplest perception of a physical stimulus to the most complex judgment concerning the grammaticality of an utterance, consists of manipulating innate symbols-in-the-head in accord with that syntax. The system of primitive, innate symbols-in-the-head and their syntactic combination in sentence-like structures is sometimes called "mentalese." (Bechtel, Abrahamsen, and Graham 1998, 63–64)

I am specifically addressing Fodor's theory for four reasons: First, it is the most influential contemporary version of the representational theory of mind. Second, it is a paradigmatic functionalist theory of mind, since it treats mind as a computational program that can be run on any suitable "hardware." Third, it thus regards the "hardware" of mind as relatively incidental to the content of thought. Fourth, it therefore denies any intrinsic meaning to mental states (such as meaning that might arise from the nature of human embodiment). In this and subsequent chapters, I do not intend to criticize Fodor's version of the representational theory directly.[1] Instead, I will attempt to elaborate an alternative, naturalistic ac-

---

1. In a series of essays over several years, but especially in *Representation and Reality* (1988), Hilary Putnam has shown precisely why language of thought views and other

count of mind, concepts, and meaning that is more compatible with the sciences of the mind and that does not presuppose supernatural or non-embodied entities or processes.

EMBODIMENT THEORY'S CHALLENGE TO THE REPRESENTATIONAL THEORY OF MIND

Embodiment theory, in contrast to representationalist theories, requires a radical reevaluation of dualistic metaphysics and epistemology, and it challenges Fodor's representational view that cognition and thought consist of symbolic representations inside an organism's mind-brain that refer to an outside world. According to Dewey's principle of continuity, what we call "body" and "mind" are simply convenient abstractions—shorthand ways of identifying aspects of ongoing organism-environment interactions— and so cognition, thought, and symbolic interaction (such as language use) must be understood as arising from organic processes. I want to trace the rejection of mind/body dualism from the philosopher-psychologists known as the early American pragmatists (especially James and Dewey) forward through contemporary cognitive scientists (e.g., Francisco Varela, Humberto Maturana, Gerald Edelman, Edwin Hutchins, George Lakoff and Vittorio Gallese, and Rodney Brooks). The key to this reconceiving of mind is to stop treating percepts, concepts, propositions, and thoughts as quasi-objects (mental entities or abstract structures) and to see them instead as patterns of experiential interaction. They are aspects or dimensions or structures of the patterns of organism-environment coupling (or integrated interaction) that constitute experience. The only sense in which they are "inner" is that my thoughts are mine (and not yours), but they are not mental objects locked up in the theater of the mind, trying desperately to make contact with the outside world. As we will see, thoughts are just modes of interaction and action. They are *in* and *of* the world (rather than just being *about* the world) because they are processes of experience.

In the remainder of this chapter and in subsequent chapters, I argue for a nondualistic, nonrepresentational view of mind as a process of organism-environment interactions. My *interactionist* (or *transactional* or *enactionist*) view will provide the beginnings of an account of the bodily grounding of meaning and concepts in sensorimotor experience, including the role of

---

forms of functionalism will not work. He has also shown why so-called causal theories of meaning and reference are misguided attempts to connect words to things.

neural maps.[2] In this chapter, I cite evidence from comparative neurobiology of organism-environment coupling for nonhuman animals; then, in chapters 7 and 8, I turn to parallels in human cognition, based on research in recent cognitive science, cognitive neuroscience, and computational neural modeling that supports a theory of embodied cognition and an interactionist view of mind. In chapter 9, I then suggest how this conception of embodied meaning makes it possible to explain even abstract concepts, concepts that have traditionally been thought to be completely disembodied.

WHAT DIFFERENCE DOES EMBODIMENT THEORY MAKE?

When a young child crawls toward the fire in the hearth and a mother snatches up the child before it can get burned, is that cognition? When a team of British mathematicians decodes enemy ciphers during wartime, is that cognition? When ants carrying food back to their nest lay down chemical signals and thereby mark trails to a food source, is that cognition?

Note the commonalities among these situations. First and foremost, in each case the body (individual and social) is in peril. The well-being and continued successful functioning of various organisms are at risk. To survive and flourish, the organism must make adjustments in its way of acting, both within its current environment and in its relations with other creatures. The child must be snatched from the imminent danger of the flames, the mathematicians work desperately to prevent their country from being overrun by the enemy, and the ants must find food and bring it back to the queen in order for the colony to survive. Second, note that in each case the cognition is social, composed of multiple organisms acting cooperatively in response to problems posed by the current environment. And finally, all of these situations have been taken by theorists as emblematic of cognition par excellence (Dewey 1925/1981; Hodges 1983, 160–241; Deneubourg, Pasteels, and Verhaeghe 1983; Brooks and Flynn 1989).

2. I use the term *interactionist* with great trepidation, for it carries the misleading implication that there are two or more independent "things" that are interacting, whereas the view I am presenting treats the "things" within the interaction as just abstracted dimensions of the basic, continuous process of experience. Dewey used the word *transactional* precisely to avoid this dualistic suggestion, and Varela, Thompson, and Rosch (1991) use the nice term *enactionist* to stress the active, dynamic, directed process of experience.

Embodiment theory is now well supported by research in the cognitive sciences, yet there remains considerable debate as to what exactly the term *embodiment* might mean (Rohrer 2001a, forthcoming). Is the "body" merely a physical, causally determined entity? Is it a set of organic processes? Is it a felt experience of sensations and movement? Or is it a socially constructed artifact? I will suggest, in the final chapter of this book, that the body is *all* of these things. In previous chapters, we have seen how parts of the pragmatist view of thought help explain how meaning is grounded in our embodiment. We can now begin to sketch the broader nonrepresentational view of mind that emerges from this naturalistic perspective.

Embodiment theory shares several key tenets of the pragmatist view of cognition. Embodied cognition

- is the result of the evolutionary processes of variation and selection;
- is situated within a dynamic, ongoing organism-environment relationship;
- is problem-centered and operates relative to the needs, interests, and values of organisms;
- is not concerned with finding some allegedly perfect solution to a problem but, rather, one that works well enough relative to the current situation; and
- is often social and carried out cooperatively by more than one individual organism.

Pragmatists advance a view of cognition radically different from the one we are most familiar with from classical (or first-generation) cognitive science. For classical cognitive science, it is assumed that cognition consists of the application of universal logical and formal rules that govern the manipulation of "internal" mental symbols, symbols that are supposedly capable of representing states of affairs in the "external" world. Fodor's representational theory, which treats mind as a computational program, is an exemplary instance of such a first-generation view of cognitive science.

The internal/external split that underlies this view presupposes that "mentalese," construed as part of a functional program, could be detached from the nature and functioning of specific bodily organisms, from the environments they inhabit, and from the problems that provoke cognition. Given this view, it would follow that cognition could take place in any number of suitable media, such as a human brain or a computing machine. This theoretical viewpoint was instrumental in the development of the first electronic calculating machines and general-purpose computers.

In fact, these machines were originally developed by the British military to reduce the tedious workload of military mathematicians (or human "computers"—in the sense of humans who compute). But this thought experiment did not end merely with offloading the tedium of calculation onto electronic machines. From its original conception in the work of Alan Turing (1937), the idea of a universal computing machine became the metaphor of choice for future models of the mind and brain. For example, Allen Newell and Herbert Simon (1976), in their conception of the brain as a physical symbol system, consider the human brain to be just a specific instance of a Turing-style universal machine. In short, *for classical, first-generation cognitive science, cognition is defined narrowly as mathematical and logical computation with intrinsically meaningless internal symbols that can supposedly be placed in relation to aspects of the external world.*

The pragmatist alternative to this classical cognitive science view of mind is to argue that *cognition is action,* rather than mental mirroring of an external reality. Cognition is a particular kind of action: a response strategy that involves both nonconscious processes and occasional conscious processes that apply some measure of forethought in order to solve some practical, real-world problem. In the 1940s, during World War II, the problem of breaking the German codes was of utmost importance to the British war effort, and this led to the development of a series of machines (the Bombes) that could try a vast number of possible cipher keys against intercepted German communications. These decoding machines were among the predecessors of the modern computer. Early computers were designed to model human action—*computing* possible cipher keys—so that machines would replace human labor (Hodges 1983, 160–241).

However, this success in the modeling of a very specific intellectual operation was soon mistakenly regarded as the key to understanding cognition in general. If one thinks that mathematical and logical reasoning are what distinguish human beings from other animals, one might erroneously assume that any computational machine that could model aspects of this peculiarly human trait could also be used to model cognition in general. Hence the MIND AS COMPUTER metaphor swept early (first-generation) cognitive science.[3]

By contrast, on the pragmatist view, we human beings *are* animals. Our rationality is not something apart from our animal bodies, but instead

---

3. For a conceptual analysis of the MIND AS COMPUTER metaphor and some of its fateful implications for contemporary analytic philosophy, see Lakoff and Johnson 1999, chapters 12 and 21.

emerges from, and is shaped by, our embodied engagement with our environment. Thus, Dewey famously asserted that "to see the organism *in* nature, the nervous system in the organism, the brain in the nervous system, the cortex in the brain is the answer to the problems which haunt philosophy" (Dewey 1925/1981, 198).

THE CONTINUITY OF EMBODIED EXPERIENCE AND THOUGHT: JAMES AND DEWEY

We have already seen some of the ways that James and Dewey provide us with exemplary nonreductionist and nonrepresentational models of embodied mind. Their models combined the best biological and cognitive science of their day with nuanced phenomenological description and a commitment that philosophy should address the pressing human problems of our lives. I contend that James and Dewey thus provide us today with ideals of a philosophy that maintains a constructive dialogue with the sciences that can guide us in how to live. The fundamental assumption of the pragmatists' naturalistic approach is that everything we attribute to "mind"—perceiving, conceptualizing, imagining, reasoning, desiring, willing, dreaming—has emerged (and continues to develop) as part of a process in which an organism seeks to survive, grow, and flourish within different kinds of environments. As James puts it:

> Mental facts cannot be properly studied apart from the physical environment of which they take cognizance. The great fault of the older rational psychology was to set up the soul as an absolute spiritual being with certain faculties of its own by which the several activities of remembering, imagining, reasoning, and willing, etc. were explained, almost without reference to the peculiarities of the world with which these activities deal. But the richer insight of modern days perceives that our inner faculties are *adapted* in advance to the features of the world in which we dwell, adapted, I mean, so as to secure our safety and prosperity in its midst. (James 1900, 3)

This evolutionary embeddedness of the organism within its changing environments, and the development of thought in response to such changes, ties mind inextricably to body and environment. The changes entailed by such a view are revolutionary, relative to classical dualistic views of mind and thought. From the very beginning of life, the problem of knowledge is *not* how so-called internal ideas can re-present external realities, because the mind was never separate from its environment in the first place. In Dewey's words, "Since both the inanimate and the human environment are involved in the functions of life, it is inevitable, if these functions evolve to the point of thinking and if thinking is naturally serial with biological functions, that it will have as the material of thought, even of its erratic imaginings, the events and connections of this environment" (Dewey 1925/1981, 212–13).

Another way of expressing this rootedness of thinking in bodily experience is to say that there is no ontological rupture in experience between perceiving, feeling, and thinking. More complex levels of organic functioning are just that—levels, and nothing more, although there are emergent properties of "higher" levels of functioning. Dewey describes the connectedness of all levels of cognition via his principle of continuity, according to which "rational operations *grow out of* organic activities, without being identical with that from which they emerge" (Dewey 1938/1991, 26).

The notion of continuity is fundamental for Dewey, because it is the key to avoiding ontological and epistemological dualisms. Dewey employs at least two different senses of the term. *Higher-lower continuity* is the twofold claim that "higher" organisms are not the result of some additional ontological *kind* emerging in the history of the world, and also that our "higher" self (reason, will) is not utterly different in kind from our "lower" self (perception, emotion, imagination). *Inner-outer continuity* is the denial that what is inner (e.g., mental) needs ontological principles for its explanation that are different from those used to explain the outer (e.g., the physical). The continuity thesis is the basis of Dewey's claim that we can provide a naturalistic explanation of events in our world without reference to the alleged activities and powers of supernatural agents or causes. Dewey's views on continuity thus collide head-on with religious and moral traditions that posit disembodied souls and spirits or that regard "mind" as nonnatural.

The principle of continuity entails that any explanation of the nature and workings of mind, even the most abstract conceptualization and reasoning, must have its roots in the embodied capacities of the organism for perception, feeling, object manipulation, and bodily movement. The continuity hypothesis, however, does *not* entail that there are no demarcations, differentiations, or distinctions within experience. Of course there are demarcations, and they are real and important! The continuity hypothesis insists only that wherever and whenever we find actual working distinctions, they are explicable against the background of continuous processes. Furthermore, social and cultural forces are required to develop our cognitive capacities to their full potential, including language and symbolic reasoning. Infants do not speak or discover mathematical proofs at birth. Dewey's continuity thesis thus requires both evolutionary and developmental explanations. For James and Dewey, this meant that a full-fledged theory of human cognition must have at least three major components:

(1) There must be an account of the connections between humans and other animals as regards the emergence and development of meaningful patterns of organism-environment interactions—patterns of sensorimotor experience shared by all organisms of a certain kind and meaningful for those organisms. Such patterns must be tied to the organism's attempts to function within its environment. The continuity here is between what we call "lower" and "higher" organisms. (This is the subject of the present chapter.)

(2) There must be an account of how we can perform abstract thinking using our capacities for perception and motor response. There would need to be bodily processes for extending sensorimotor concepts and logic for use in abstract reasoning, as well as an account of how the processes embodying such abstract-reasoning capacities are learned during an organism's development. This story has at least two parts: (a) an evolutionary and physiological account explaining how an adult human's abstract reasoning utilizes the brain's perceptual and motor systems; and (b) a developmental and anthropological account of how social and cultural behaviors educate the sensorimotor systems of successive generations of children so that they may communicate and perform abstract reasoning. The continuity here pertains to both higher/lower and inner/outer.[4]

(3) Because judgments of value are essential to an organism's continued functioning, there must be an account of the central role of emotions and feelings in the constitution of an organism's world and its knowledge of it. Again, this will involve a continuity between the "higher" (rational) and the "lower" (emotional) aspects of the self, and also a continuity between the inner (associated with disembodied reason) and the outer (associated with the emotional body).

ORGANISM-ENVIRONMENT COUPLING

Dewey's principle of continuity states that there are no ontological gaps between the different levels of functioning within an organism. One way to see what this entails is to survey a few representative types of organism-

---

4. In the present chapter and in chapters 7 and 8, I can only address part (a) of this complex issue.

environment couplings, starting with single-celled organisms and moving up to more complex animals and eventually to humans. In every case, we can observe the same adaptive process of interactive coordination between a specific organism and recurring characteristics of its environment.

But does that mean that we can trace human cognition all the way back to the sensorimotor behavior of single-celled organisms? On the face of it, this seems preposterous; and indeed, from an evolutionary biologist's perspective, there are clear differences in the size, complexity, and structural differentiation of human beings as compared with single-celled organisms such as bacteria. The behavior of single-celled organisms is not ordinarily relevant to the behavior of multicellular organisms, except insofar as there might be structural, morphological analogies between the sensorimotor activity of single-celled organisms and particular sensorimotoric cells within multicellular bodies.

From Chemotaxis to Cognition

In fact, just this sort of morphological analogy plays a key role in the argument by Humberto Maturana and Francisco Varela that central nervous systems evolved in multicellular organisms to coordinate sensorimotor activity (Maturana and Varela 1998, 142–63). In a single-celled organism, locomotion is achieved by dynamically coupling the sensory and motor surfaces of the cell membrane. When an amoeba engulfs a protozoan, its cell membranes are responding to the presence of the chemical substances that make up the protozoan, causing changes in the consistency of the amoeba's protoplasm. These changes manifest as pseudopods—digitations that the amoeba appears to extend around the protozoan as it prepares to feed upon it. Similarly, certain bacteria have a tail-like membrane structure called a flagellum that is rotated like a propeller to move the bacterium. When the flagellum is rotated in one direction, the bacterium simply tumbles; reversing the direction of rotation causes the bacterium to move. If a grain of sugar is placed into the solution containing this bacterium, chemical receptors on the cell membrane sense the sugar molecules. This causes a membrane change in which the bacterium changes the direction of rotation of its flagellar propeller and gradually moves toward the greatest concentration of the sugar molecules, a process known as chemotaxis. For both the amoeba and the bacterium, changes in the chemical environment cause sensory perturbations in the cellular membrane, which invariably produces movement. The key point here is that *without any awareness of anything like an internal representation,* single-celled organisms engage in sensorimotor coordination in response to environmental changes. Even at this apparently primitive level, there is a finely tuned, ongoing coupling of organism and environment.

Multicellular organisms also accomplish their sensorimotor coordination by means of changes in cellular membranes. However, the cellular specialization afforded by multicellularity means that not every cell needs to perform the same functions. Maturana and Varela (1998) discuss the example of an evolutionarily ancient metazoic organism called the hydra (a coelenterate). The hydra, which lives in ponds, is shaped like a two-layered tube with four or six tentacles emanating from its mouth. On the inside layer of the tube, most cells secrete digestive fluids, while the outside layer is partly composed of radial and longitudinal muscle cells. Locomotion is accomplished by contracting muscle cells along the body of the organism, some of which cause changes in the hydrostatic pressure within the organism, changing its shape and its direction of locomotion.

Between the two layers of cells, however, are specialized cells—neurons—with elongated membranes that can extend over the length of the entire organism before terminating in the muscle cells. These tail-like cellular projections are the axons, and evolutionarily speaking they are the flagella of the multicellular organism.[5] Changes in the electrochemical state of other, smaller cellular projections (known as dendrites) of the neurons cause larger changes in the electrochemical state of the axonal membrane, which in turn induces the muscle cells to contract. These neural signals typically originate in either the tentacles or the "stomach" of the hydra, such that these structures' electrochemical state responds to molecules indicating the presence or absence of food and/or excessive digestive secretions. The neurons consistently terminate in the longitudinal and radial muscles that contract the hydra body for locomotion or for swallowing. The topology of how the nerve cells interconnect is crucial: when a tentacle is touched, a chain of neurons fires sequentially down the tentacle toward the hydra's mouth and causes the muscle cells to curl the tentacle about the prey. The structural coupling between the hydra (with its changes in electrochemical states) and its environment (e.g., prey that touches its tentacle) is what allows the hydra to function adaptively in its environment—this allows the hydra to contract the correct muscles to swallow or to move up or down, right or left.

5. Recent research shows that this may be more than a surface morphological analogy: all microtubular cellular projections stem from a common ancestor (Erickson et al. 1996; Goldberg 2003).

It is clear that the hydra does not experience internal representations of an external world that it could use as a basis for operating within its environment. A protozoan swims into the grasp of its tentacles and the neurons fire as they have been wired to do, stimulating adjacent muscle cells so that the tentacles curl about the food and bring it to a mouth that is simultaneously preparing to swallow. Now, it is obviously quite a jump from the hydra to humans, but Dewey's principle of continuity requires an account of human cognition that is not different in kind—though it would certainly differ massively in complexity—from the story of organism-environment coupling that applies to the simpler multicellular animals. In general, "higher" human cognition is evolutionarily continuous with sensorimotor coordination, because all nervous systems "couple the sensory and motor surfaces through a network of neurons whose pattern can be quite varied" (Maturana and Varela 1998, 159). At the human level, cognition is action—we think in order to act, and we act as *part of* our thinking.

Here the skeptic will interrupt my account of organism-environment coupling with an obvious objection: while these reflexive behaviors are examples of patterns of meaningful sensorimotor activation for coelenterate organisms, what would constitute similar patterns for humans? The whole point, they will say, is that it is precisely the human capacity for abstract representational thinking that distinguishes us from the lower animals. There is no continuum here, but rather a radical ontological gap that separates humans from all other creatures. Surely human cognition is something more complex, and of a different order, than what occurs in the simple reflex of a hydra.

From Neural Maps to Neural Plasticity

Obviously, human cognition involves orders of complexity that far exceed those of primitive organisms. But even though human cognition is a little more like what happens in frogs, owls, and monkeys, it is nevertheless surprisingly continuous in important ways with that of the hydra functioning within its environment. Frogs, for example, must couple with their environment via primitive reflexes. They have a certain regularly occurring life-maintenance problem: they need to extend their tongues to eat flies. This was the subject of a classic experiment in the history of neurobiology (Sperry 1943). When a frog is still a tadpole, it is possible to rotate its eye 180 degrees (making sure to keep the optic nerve intact). The tadpole is then allowed to develop normally into a frog. When a frog whose eye was rotated goes for a fly, its tongue extends to the point in its visual field that is exactly opposite the point where the fly is located. No amount of failure will teach the frog to move its tongue differently; the nervous system acts entirely on the basis of the connections between the retinal image and the tongue muscles. Maturana and Varela conclude that for frogs, "there is no such thing as up or down, front and back, in reference to an outside world, as it exists for the observer doing the study" (1998, 125–26). The frog has no access to our notion of the external world and our 180-degree rotation of its eye; it has only an environmentally induced change of state in the neurons constituting its retinal map.

One of the most profound findings in neuroscience is that nervous systems exploit topological and topographic organization. In other words, organisms build neural "maps." In neural maps, adjacent neural cells (or small groups of neural cells) fire sequentially when a stimulus moves across adjacent positions within a sensory field. For example, scientists have manipulated the visual field of the frog and measured the electrical activity of a region of its brain to show that as one stimulates a frog's visual field, the neurons of its optic tectum will fire in coordination with the visual stimulus. Scott Fraser (1985) covered the frog's optic tectum with a grid of twenty-four electrodes, each one recording electrical activity that was the sum of the signals from a receptive field containing many optic nerve fiber terminals. When a point of light was moved in a straight line in the frog's right visual field, from right to left and then from bottom to top, the electrode grid recorded neuronal activity in straight lines with sequential firing, first from the rostral (front) to the caudal (back) areas and then from the lateral to the medial areas. We call this pattern of activation the frog's retinal map, or retinotectal map, because it encodes environmental visual stimuli in a topographically consistent manner. The spatial orientation of this topography is rotated in various ways; thus, visual right-to-left movement becomes front-to-back in the retinotectal map, and so on. But the topographic mapping between movement in the vertical visual plane and the plane of the retinotectal neural map remains consistent. Even though there is considerable spatial distortion in the neural map, the key relational structures are preserved. In some other cases, such as some auditory maps and color maps, the correspondences are less about shape and position, and the organization is more properly called topologic than topographic; but the organizing principle of the neural mapping of sensation still holds. In the auditory regions of human brains, for example, successive rising pitches activate contiguous areas in the auditory cortex, so that "adjacent" pitches (such as B going to A) activate regions of the auditory cortex immediately next to one another.

The degree to which such neural maps might be plastic and subject to reorganization has been the subject of much recent study. It is important to remember that in the case of the frog, Sperry performed a radical and destructive intervention that is outside the realm of "normal" Darwinian deviation. In other words, if this were to occur by natural selection, such a frog would be unable to catch flies and would die quickly, without passing on its genes. Interventions that are more subtle and perhaps more likely to occur in nature, such as cutting the optic nerve of a goldfish and destroying part of the optic tectum, result in a recovery of function; the goldfish's optic-nerve axons will regenerate and make a complete retinal map in the remaining part of the tectum (Gaze and Sharma 1970).

Or consider another, even more subtle intervention: suppose we were to make a barn owl wear glasses that changed its perception of its visual field? Like frogs, owls have developed an extremely accurate method of attacking prey. The owl hears a mouse rustling on the ground and locates the mouse primarily by using the tiny difference in time that it takes for a sound to reach one ear as opposed to the other. This establishes the mouse's approximate position in the owl's retinotectal map, and the diving owl then looks to find the exact location of its prey as it strikes. Eric Knudsen (2002) put prismatic glasses on adult and juvenile owls that distorted the owls' vision by twenty-three degrees. After wearing the glasses for eight weeks, the adult owls never learned to compensate, although juveniles were able to learn to hunt accurately. However, when the glasses were re-introduced to adult owls who had worn them as juveniles, they were able to readjust to the glasses in short order.

This behavioral plasticity has anatomical underpinnings in the organization of neural maps. When the experimental owls were injected with an anatomical tracing dye, comparison of the neural arbors—the patterns of neural connections—from normally reared and prism-reared owls revealed greatly differing patterns of axonal projections between auditory and spatial neural maps, "showing that alternative learned and normal circuits can coexist in this network" (Knudsen 2002, 325). In other words, in order to deal with wearing glasses, the owl brain had grown permanent alternative axonal connections in a cross-modal neural map of space located in the external nucleus of the inferior colliculus (ICX). The ICX neural arbor of prism-reared owls is significantly more dense than in owls that developed normally, with neurons typically having at least two distinct branches of axons (DeBello, Feldman, and Knudsen 2001). By contrast, the retinotectal maps of the visual modality alone do not seem to exhibit quite the same plasticity, neither in owls (whose retinotectum did not change)

nor in frogs. Anatomical research on frogs reared and kept alive with surgically rotated eyes has shown that after five weeks, the retinotectal neural
arbors exhibited a similar pattern of "two-headed" axons—that is, they
had two major axonal branches. However, after ten weeks, the older axonal connections started to decay and disappear, and after sixteen weeks
no two-headed axons could be traced (Guo and Udin 2000). Apparently,
the frog's single-modal retinotectal maps do not receive enough reentrant
neural connections from other sensory modalities to sustain the multiple
branching neural arbors found in the cross-modal map of an owl who develops normally at first and subsequently with glasses.

Working on adult squirrel and owl monkeys, Michael Merzenich and
colleagues (1987; reviewed in Buonomano and Merzenich 1998) have
shown that it is possible to dynamically reorganize the somatosensory
cortical maps subject to certain bodily constraints. Similar to the owls and
frogs that grew dual arborizations, these monkeys exhibited a plasticity
based on their brains' ability to select which parts of their neural arbors
to use for what kinds of input. In a series of studies, Merzenich and colleagues altered the monkey's hand sensory activity by such interventions
as (1) cutting a peripheral nerve, such as the medial or radial nerve, and
(1a) allowing it to regenerate naturally or (1b) tying it off to prevent regen-
eration; (2) amputating a single digit; and (3) taping together two digits so
that they could not be moved independently. The results show that cortical areas now lacking their previous sensory connections (or independent sensory input, in the third condition) were "colonized" in a couple of
weeks by adjacent neural maps with active sensory connections. In other
words, the degree of existing but somewhat dormant neural-arbor overlap was large enough that the cortex was able to reorganize. And in the
case of (1a), where the nerve was allowed to regenerate, the somatosensory map gradually returned to occupy a similar-sized stretch of cortex,
albeit with slightly different and filtering boundaries. These experiments
illustrate that learning in adults is accomplished in part by neural gating—
sequencing of neural firings—between redundant and overlapping neural
arbors.

All of these examples of ontogenetic neural change suggest that there
is a process of neural-arbor selection akin to natural selection taking place
in concert with specific patterns of organism-environment interactions.
On precisely these grounds, the neurobiologist Gerald Edelman (1987) has
proposed a theory of "neural Darwinism," or "neuronal group selection,"
to explain how such neural maps are formed in the organism's embryonic
development. Different groups of neurons compete to become topobio-

logical neural maps as they migrate and grow during neural development. Successful cortical groups, driven primarily by regularities in the environment passed on from those neurons that are closer to the sensory apparatus, will fire together and wire together in a process of axonal sprouting and synaptogenesis. Some neuronal groups will fail to find useful topological connections, and they eventually die and are crowded out by the successful neuronal groups, while others will hang on in something of an intermediate state of success (Edelman 1987, 127–40). In the adult organism, these latent axonal arbors remaining from only partly successful attempts to wire together lie dormant, ready to reorganize the map as needed by means of further synaptogenesis. Edelman (1987, 43–47) calls these latent reorganizations of the neuronal groups *secondary repertoires,* as distinguished from their normal *primary repertoires.*

Like frogs, owls, and monkeys, humans have sets of visual, auditory, and somatosensory maps. The more obvious of these map perceptual space in fairly direct analogs—preserving topologies of pitch, the retinal field, color, the parts of the body, and so on. But subsequent maps preserve increasingly abstract topological structure (or even combinations of structure), such as object shape, edges, orientation, direction of motion, and even the particular degree of the vertical or horizontal. *Like the frog, we live in the world significantly (but not totally) defined by our maps. Topologically speaking, our bodies are in our minds.* Our "minds" are processes that arise through our ongoing coupling with our environment. Mind is in and of this embodied experiential process, not above it all.

ARE NEURAL MAPS INTERNAL REPRESENTATIONS? NO, AND YES!

Some people might suppose that talk of neural maps would necessarily engender representational theories of cognition. On this view, the map would be construed as an internal representation of some external reality. But the account given above *does not* entail any of the traditional metaphysical dualisms that underlie representational views—strict dichotomies such as subject/object and mind/body. Such dichotomies might describe aspects of organism-environment interactions, but they do not indicate ontologically different entities or structures. According to our interactionist view, maps and other structures of organism-environment coordination are prime examples of nonrepresentational structures of meaning, understanding, and thought. Maturana and Varela (1998, 125–26) remind us that we must not read our scientific or philosophical perspectives (i.e., our theoretical stance) on cognition back into the experience itself that we are theorizing about. William James called this error the "Psychologist's Fallacy," namely, "the *confusion of his own standpoint with that of the mental fact* about which he is making his report" (1890/1950, 1:196). In observing something scientifically, one must always consider the standpoint of the scientist in relation to the object of study. When scientists use terms such as *retinal maps, pitch maps, sensorimotor maps,* and *color maps* to describe the operations of various neural arrays in a frog's or a human's nervous system, they do so from their standpoint as observers and theorists who can see mappings and isomorphisms between the neural patterns and their own experience of the "external world." But for the engaged frog, and for the human in the act of perceiving, that map *is* the external world, or at least the topological structure of the world as currently experienced! It is not some internal representation of that world. The reason is that if you took the neural map out of the situation, that situation would not exist as it now does—it would be a different situation. The frog's neural map has its origin not in the immediate mappings that we observers see in the moment, but in a longitudinal evolutionary and developmental process during which those neural connections were "selected for" by Darwinian or neo-Darwinian mechanisms.

In short, what we (as scientists) theoretically recognize and describe as an organism's maps are not—*for that organism*—internal representations that can correspond to external realities. Rather, what we call sensorimotor and somatosensory maps (whether in multicellular organisms, monkeys, or humans) are *for that organism* precisely its structures of experience and reality. Consequently, we must be careful not to be misled by philosophers of mind and language who, in speaking of the intentionality (the "aboutness") of these maps and other neural structures, surreptitiously introduce an inner/outer split that does not exist in reality for the organism. What must be avoided is the illusory setting up of an inner theater of the mind, in which immaterial ideas parade on the stage of consciousness, to be seen by the mind's eye.

I must acknowledge at least one sense in which neural maps—a certain neuronal cluster that is activated as an organism perceives and moves within its environment—may properly be called a representation, which is why that term is widely (though uncritically) used by neuroscientists. Just insofar as a specific neural map is loosely isomorphic with some structure of an organism's environment-as-experienced, neuroscientists are prone to call these maps representations. Something "in the brain" appears to correlate structurally with patterns of the "external environment," even though the environment is not, strictly speaking, independent of the organism. So, from the point of view of the scientist (but *not* from the perspective of the experiencing organism), the neural map represents some structure in the world. It is in this sense that a neuroscientist might say that adjacent neural assemblies in parts of the auditory cortex "represent" adjacent tonal relations. However, we must always be clear that an organism never actually experiences its neural maps as internal mental structures. We do not experience the *maps,* but rather *through them* we experience a structured world full of patterns and qualities.

In challenging the representational theory of mind, I am in no way denying that human beings have images, feelings, and thoughts that they experience as *theirs* and that they understand to be "about" something in their world. But it is quite a leap from such a claim to the very much stronger claim that thought is the mental entertaining and manipulation of internal representations. What I am denying is that we have mental *entities* called "concepts" or "representations" in our "minds" and that thinking is a matter of manipulating these entities by surveying their properties, discerning their relations to each other and to mind-external objects, and arranging them in internal acts of judgment. To say that we have concepts is to say, with James, that within the continuous flow of our perceptual experience, we can attend to aspects of the flow for purposes of understanding our situation, planning what to do, and then acting. Concepts, on this view, are stable patterns of neuronal activation, but they are *not* quasi-entities. Of course, we have the ability to abstract aspects of our experience and then to consider how these so-called abstract concepts relate to one another. There is nothing wrong with this way of talking, unless it leads us to suppose that there must be some center of thought, conceptualization, reasoning, or consciousness that "sees" or "grasps" (i.e., understands) the concepts and compares them to one another, as if we were holding up one juicy red tomato and comparing it to another tomato.

IN WHAT SENSES ARE THERE MENTAL REPRESENTATIONS?

The classical representationalist picture of thought and how the mind works is so powerful and so deeply rooted in our self-understanding that it is hardly likely to ever be dislodged, either in how we think about thought or in how we talk about our thinking. Nevertheless, it is a mistaken picture that is not supported by what we are learning about how brains work and what cognition and conceptualization are. The empirical evidence from neuroscience suggests that there is no single center of mind and thinking and that scientifically, conceptualization has to depend on activated neural connections. I want to be clear that I am, of course, not denying that we conceptualize; I am only denying that we do so by manipulating mental entities that have the remarkable capacity to be "about" external things. It is also perfectly acceptable to say that we have "mental states," just as long as we don't define these by means of the representational model.

I am not recommending that we launch a massive campaign to expunge the term "mental representation" from our vocabularies. Such a campaign would be an impossible undertaking, doomed to failure. There are some perfectly acceptable uses of the word *representation,* and here is a short list of those uses.

1. *Patterns of sensorimotor neural activation.* As we saw in the previous section, scientists often identify recurring patterns of neural activation that correlate with what the scientist perceives as structural features of the organism's environment. The scientist is likely to call these neural patterns representations. The neural maps just discussed, and also images and image schemas (to be discussed in the next chapter), are examples of representations in this limited sense.

2. *Conceptual structures.* We have described concepts not as abstract, internal mental entities, but as selective discriminations from the ongoing, continuous flow of our experience. In chapter 8, we will see how there is no discontinuity between concrete and abstract concepts. As long as we understand concepts in this nondualistic manner, we can think of them as representations of various aspects of our experience. However, I am inclined always to avoid calling concepts "representations," simply because that term too easily activates a cognitive frame with all of the classical representationalist architecture.

3. *External systems of symbolic interaction.* It is perfectly acceptable to say that linguistic signs and other symbols (which can be regarded as either objects or events in the world) can represent various things and events. The word *dog* can be said to pick out or represent dogs. A photograph of Grace Kelly can be said to represent Princess Grace. A topological map of Oregon can be said to represent the topography of Oregon. An elaborate coronation ritual can be said to represent the grandeur, authority, and royalty of the newly crowned king. Picasso's painting *Guernica* can be said to represent the horror and terror of some incident in 1937 during the Spanish civil war. Even though these are all distinct senses of the term *represent,* and they need to be carefully distinguished and analyzed to identify the key differences, they are appropriate uses.

4. *Theoretical models.* In the sciences, mathematics, and philosophy, we develop theoretical models to help us explain natural and human phenomena. By virtue of structural isomorphism, analogies, and propositional models, we attempt to represent entities, events, states, relations, and processes. Such models are representations of what they purport to be about.

In sum, people are never going to stop using the term *representation*. Nor should they. The term should be used when it is appropriate, which means whenever it does not activate any strong form of the representational theory of mind. The representational theory is incompatible with cognitive neuroscience and out of touch with evolutionary accounts of mind, thought, and language. It is philosophically problematic, because it reinforces a set of ontological and epistemological dualisms that make it impossible to explain meaning, understanding, knowledge, and values without relying on supernatural, or at least transcendent, realities. In our theories of meaning and mind, we must exercise due caution to avoid falling back into any form of the representational view of mind.

CHAPTER 7

The Corporeal Roots of Symbolic Meaning

In the previous chapter, I described patterns of organism-environment coupling mostly for nonhuman animals and argued that a strong representational theory of mind is of no use in explaining how such interactions work. For nonhuman animals, meaning is fully embodied. However, for human animals as well, meanings arise from organism-environment interactions, and we too have neural maps. The structural features and relations that shape our encounters with aspects of our environment are preserved in our neural maps.

In general, every aspect of our spatial experience will be defined by recurring patterns and structures (such as up-down, front-back, near-far, in-out, on-under) that constitute the basic contours of our lived world. It should not be surprising, therefore, that we have evolved to take special notice of these recurring shapes, relations, and patterns, and that these patterns exist as topological features of our neural maps. Such patterns are the structural elements of our ongoing engagement with our environment. They are one of the primary ways we are in touch with our world, understand it, and can act within it.

Since the earliest episodes of ancient Greek philosophy, humans have been inclined to distinguish themselves from "brute" animals and all lower organisms by their supposedly unique capacities for abstract conceptualization and reasoning that are typically associated with the possession of language. According to this view, human reason is a unique capacity having a different source than our capacities for perception, motor activities, feeling, and emotion. Therefore, the problem for an embodied view of cognition is to explain our marvelous human feats of meaning-making, abstraction, reasoning, and symbolic interaction, but without positing an ontological rupture between "lower" animals and humans, or between human "bodily" and "mental" processes. The question is, How can meaning emerge in our bodily experience (i.e., in sensorimotor activity) and still be the basis for abstract thought?

The key to ontological continuity is the coupling (the interactive coordination) of an organism (here, a human one) and its environment. Recurring, adaptive patterns of organism-environment interaction are the basis for our ability to survive and flourish. They are also the ground of meaning. Let us consider some of the most basic kinds of structural couplings that make up our human experience of our world.

IMAGE SCHEMAS AND CROSS-MODAL PERCEPTION

The character of our experience is delineated in large part by the nature of our bodies and brains, the kinds of environments we inhabit, our social interactions, and the values and purposes we have. The patterns of our ongoing interactions, or enactions (to use the term from Varela, Thompson, and Rosch 1991), define the contours of our world and make it possible for us to make sense of, reason about, and act reliably within this world. What George Lakoff (1987) and I (Johnson 1987) called image schemas are precisely these basic structures of sensorimotor experience by which we encounter a world that we can understand and act within.

An image schema is a dynamic, recurring pattern of organism-environment interactions. As such, it will reveal itself in the contours of our basic sensorimotor experience. Consequently, one way to begin to survey the range of image schemas is via a phenomenological description of the most basic structural features of all human bodily experience. When I speak of a "phenomenological" survey of image schemas, I do not mean the use of anything like a formal Husserlian method of "transcendental reduction,"[1] but merely a reflective interrogation of the contours of our lived experience. Ask yourself what are the most fundamental structures of perception, object manipulation, and bodily movement, given that human bodies share several quite specific sensorimotor capacities that are keyed

---

1. Husserl proposed a method of "suspending" one's practical engagement with everyday experience in order to allow the fundamental structures of experience to reveal themselves. I do not think we should try to suspend our practical embeddedness; rather, we should survey the patterns of this practical interaction.

to the size and constitution of our bodies and to the common characteristics of the various environments we inhabit. Certain obvious patterns
immediately stand out.[2] For example, because of our particular bodily
makeup, we project right and left, front and back, near and far, throughout the horizon of our perceptual interactions. As Mark Turner (1991) observes, if we were nonsymmetric creatures floating in a liquid medium
with no up or down, no right or left, and no front or back, the meaning
of our bodily experience would be quite different from the ways we actually *do* make sense of things. For instance, there would be no "right" or
"left" for us, neither in our experience nor in our conceptual system (if we
had one).

Another fundamental organizing structure is tied to the fact that our
perceptual fields have focal areas that fade off into a vague horizon of possible experiences that are neither currently in focus nor at the center of
our conscious awareness. Hence, it comes as no surprise that we have a
CENTER-PERIPHERY image schema, based on this horizonal character
of our perception. Other image schemas are equally obvious. Because of
our ongoing bodily encounter with physical forces that push and pull us,
we experience the image-schematic structures of COMPULSION, AT-
TRACTION, and BLOCKAGE OF MOVEMENT, to name but a few aspects of what Leonard Talmy (1985) calls "force dynamics." The bodily
logic of such force schemas will give rise to specific inferences that we
draw, based on the internal structure of the schemas. For instance, objects
move at varying speeds, they move along trajectories, there is a rhythmic
flow to their movement, they start and stop, etc. Based on these and other
characteristics of moving objects, the internal structures of the image
schemas for forced movement support and constrain the precise inferences
we make about our experience.

There are thus quite distinctive patterns and logics to these dimensions
of our perception of moving objects, our kinesthetic sense of our own motion, and our proprioceptive sense of the position and movement of our
body parts. Because we exist within a gravitational field at the earth's surface, and because of our ability to stand erect, we give great significance to
standing up, rising, and falling down. Our understanding of these bodily
experiences involves a VERTICALITY (UP-DOWN) schema and a BAL-
ANCE schema. Our experience of rectilinear motion gives rise to the inferences we draw about straight-line movement (Cienki 1998), and we draw

2. A survey of some of the structure and semantics of some of the more important
image schemas is presented in Johnson 1987, chapters 2–5.

different inferences about curved motions, deviating motions, or motions that have no obvious goal (relative to a SOURCE-PATH-GOAL schema).

Because we must continually monitor our own changing bodily states, we are exquisitely attuned to changes in degree, intensity, and quality of feelings. Such experiences are the basis for our sense of the scalar intensity of a quality (the SCALARITY schema). In other words, because the qualities (e.g., redness, softness, coolness, agitation, sharpness) of our experience vary continuously in intensity, there is a scalar vector that applies to every aspect of our qualitative experience. For example, lights can grow brighter or dimmer, sounds can increase or diminish in loudness, stoves can get hotter or cooler, iced tea can get sweeter as we add sugar or more tart as we add lemon.

Because we must constantly interact with containers of all shapes and sizes, we naturally learn the "logic" of containment (for the CONTAINER schema). Containers have at least the minimal structure of a boundary, an interior, and an exterior. Through many experiences each day, we learn what the word *into* means, as we encounter the movement of objects as they pass from the exterior of a container across or through its boundary, finally coming to rest in its interior. We know, in a bodily way, that something that is inside a container is not outside it. We learn that if something starts moving within a container toward its boundary and eventually crosses over the boundary, then it is at least temporarily outside of the container.

Through this type of informal phenomenological analysis of the structural dimensions of our sensorimotor experience, most of the basic image schemas will show themselves. However, we must keep in mind that phenomenological analysis alone is never enough, because image schemas typically operate beneath the level of conscious awareness. That is why we must go beyond phenomenology to employ standard explanatory methods of linguistics, psychology, and neuroscience that allow us to probe structures within our unconscious thought processes. A great deal of our current knowledge of image schemas comes from linguistic analyses of their role in the semantics of spatial terms and bodily operations and of their role in conceptualizing and reasoning about abstract domains. Originally, Lakoff (1987) and I (Johnson 1987) hypothesized the existence of various image schemas in order to frame explanatory generalizations concerning syntactic, semantic, and pragmatic aspects of language and other forms of symbolic interaction. Over the past two decades, a burgeoning body of empirical linguistic research has explored the role of image-schematic structures in a vast array of syntactic and semantic phenomena in languages around the world.[3] Raymond Gibbs (1994) has described the main types of empirical evidence currently available for image schemas (see also Gibbs and Steen 1999). And there is considerable evidence concerning the role of image schemas in inference (Lakoff 1987; Lakoff and Johnson 1999; Lakoff and Núñez 2000).

Three important aspects of image schemas relating to the grounding of meaning can now be emphasized. First, image schemas are an important part of what makes it possible for our bodily experiences to have meaning for us. The meaning is that of the recurring structures and patterns of our sensorimotor experience. As such, it typically operates beneath the level of our conscious awareness, although it also plays a role in our discrimination of the contours of our bodily orientation and experience. Meaning structures of this sort are part of what Lakoff and I (1999) call the *cognitive unconscious*. For example, humans will share certain general understandings of what it means for something to be located within a container, and they will understand at least part of this without having to reflect upon it or think about it. Seeing a container, manipulating one, or hearing or reading the word *in* will activate a CONTAINER image schema in our understanding of a particular scene. Certain types and sizes of containers will offer different specific affordances—possibilities for interaction—for creatures with our types of bodies, brains, and environments.

Second, there is a *logic* of image-schematic structure. Consider a case in which you are moving along a linear path toward a destination, and at time T1 you are halfway to the destination. If you then travel farther along the path and reach time T2, you will be closer to your destination at T2 than you were at T1. This is part of the spatial logic of the SOURCE-PATH-GOAL schema. Or consider what follows if your car keys are *in* your hand and you then place your hand *in* your pocket. Via the transitive logic of containment, the car keys end up *in* your pocket. Such apparently trivial spatial logic is *not* trivial. On the contrary, it is just such spatial and bodily logic that makes it possible for us to make sense of, and to act intelligently within, our ordinary experience.

The third moral is that image schemas are not to be understood as either merely "mental" or merely "bodily," but rather as contours of what Dewey called the body-mind. Dewey recognized the underlying continuity that connects our physical interactions in the world with our activities

---

3. The journal *Cognitive Linguistics* is the principal source for cross-cultural analyses of image schemas in languages across the world, but see also Hampe and Grady 2005.

of imagining and thinking. He summarized the body-mind continuity as follows:

> But body-mind simply designates what actually takes place when a living body is implicated in situations of discourse, communication, and participation. In the hyphenated phrase body-mind, "body" designates the continued and conserved, the registered and cumulative operation of factors continuous with the rest of nature, inanimate as well as animate; while "mind" designates the characters and consequences which are differential, indicative of features which emerge when "body" is engaged in a wider, more complex and interdependent situation. (Dewey 1925/1981, 285)

If we could only disabuse ourselves of the mistaken idea that thought must somehow be a type of activity *ontologically* different from our other bodily engagements (such as seeing, hearing, holding things, and walking), then our entire understanding of the so-called mind/body problem would be transformed. We would cease to interpret the problem as how two completely different kinds of things (body and mind) can be united in interaction. Instead, we would rephrase the problem as that of explaining how increasing levels of complexity within organisms can eventually result in the emergence of progressively more reflective and abstractive cognitive activities, activities we associate with "mind."

I am suggesting that the very possibility of abstract conceptualization and reasoning depends directly on the fact that "body" and "mind" are not two separate things, but rather are abstractions from our ongoing, continuous, interactive experience. Although Dewey did not have the benefit of the elaborate analyses from today's cognitive science showing how meaning and thought are based on patterns of sensorimotor experience, he understood that what we think of as "higher" cognitive activities are grounded in, and shaped by, activities of bodily perception and movement:

> Just as when men start to talk they must use sounds and gestures antecedent to speech, and as when they begin to hunt animals, catch fish or make baskets, they must employ materials and processes that exist antecedently to these operations, so when men begin to observe and think they must use the nervous system and other organic structures which existed independently and antecedently. That the use reshapes the prior materials so as to adapt them more efficiently and freely to the uses to which they are put, is not a problem to be solved: it is an expression of the common fact that

anything changes according to the interacting field it enters. (Dewey 1925/ 1981, 285)

If you treat an image schema as merely an abstract, formal cognitive structure, then you leave out its embodied origin and its arena of operation. On the other hand, if you treat the image schema as nothing but a structure of a bodily (sensorimotor) process, you cannot explain abstract conceptualization and thought. Only when image schemas are seen as structures of sensorimotor experience that can be recruited for abstract conceptualization and reasoning (see chapter 9) does it become possible to answer the key question: how can abstract concepts emerge from embodied experience without calling upon disembodied mind, autonomous language modules, or pure reason? Failure to recognize the nondualistic, mental-bodily reality of image schemas would cause the collapse of the whole project of utilizing image-schematic logic to explain abstract thought.

Image schemas are thus a crucial part of our nonrepresentational coupling with our world, just as barn owls and squirrel monkeys have image schemas that define their types of sensorimotor experience. One of the chief ways that humans are different is that we have neural mechanisms for metaphorically extending image schemas as we perform abstract conceptualization and reasoning. Moreover, we are capable of becoming aware of the way the dynamic flow of our experience and thought is structured by the CONTAINER, VERTICALITY, COMPULSIVE FORCE, SCALARITY, SOURCE-PATH-GOAL, and many other image schemas.

Image-schematic structure is the basis for our understanding of spatial terms and all aspects of our perception and motor activities. An example from Lakoff and Núñez (2000) illustrates how to conceive this image-schematic basis of spatial concepts and spatial language in humans. What we (speakers of English) call our concept *in* is defined for us by a CONTAINER image schema that consists generically of three parts:

1. a boundary, which demarcates
2. an interior
3. from an exterior.

When we say "The car is in the garage," we understand the garage as a bounded space; we profile (Langacker 1986) the interior of that space, and we regard the car as a Trajector within that space, with the garage (as container) serving as a Landmark in relation to which the Trajector is located.

Similarly, when we hear the sentence "Grandpa walked *from* the outhouse *to* the garage," we understand that situation via a SOURCE-PATH-GOAL schema that consists of

1. a starting point,
2. a destination (endpoint), and
3. a path from the starting location to the destination.

In other words, the *from-to* construction in English is image-schematic.

Many of our basic prepositional compounds are based on a compositional blending of two or more image schemas. The English word *into* (as in "Grandpa went *into* the barn") is understood via a superimposition of the CONTAINER schema and the SOURCE-PATH-GOAL schema, as follows:

• *In* activates a CONTAINER schema with the interior profiled.
• *To* activates a SOURCE-PATH-GOAL schema with the destination (endpoint) profiled.
• The destination (endpoint) is mapped onto the interior of the CONTAINER schema.
• We thus understand Grandpa (as Trajector) as moving from outside (source point of the SOURCE-PATH-GOAL schema) into, and terminating his motion within, the barn (which is a container and also the Landmark for the motion). The result is our simple understanding of motion along a path from the exterior to the interior of a container.

Into in English is thus an elementary composition of two image schemas.

Image schemas appear to be realized as activation patterns (or "contours") in human topological neural maps. As with much interdisciplinary research in the neurosciences, this finding was first discovered by intracranial neuronal recordings in monkeys and was later extended by analogous neuroimaging studies on humans. When Giacomo Rizzolatti and colleagues (Fogassi et al. 2001; see review in Rizzolatti and Craighero 2004) showed macaques visual images of another monkey grasping a banana with its hand, the researchers were able to record activity from "mirror" neurons in the same secondary somatomotor maps that would be implicated if the monkey itself were performing the particular grasping action. Analogous human neuroimaging experiments (Buccino et al. 2001), in which participants watched a video clip of another person performing a grasping action, showed increased activation in the secondary somatomotor cortices that are known to map hand and arm grasping motions. Rizzolatti and colleagues thus showed that these neural maps contain image-schematic sensorimotor activation patterns for grasping.

An explicit attempt to model image schemas using known facts about our neural maps can be found in the neurocomputational literature. Terry Regier (1996) has developed what he calls "structured" or "constrained" connectionist neural models for a number of image schemas. "Constrained" connectionism builds into its neural models a small number of structures that have been identified in research on human visual and spatial processing. These include center-surround cell arrays, spreading activation, orientation-sensitive cells, and neural gating. Regier shows how these constrained connectionist models of image schemas can learn spatial-relation terms in different languages.

In addition to the evidence from the neurosciences, there is a growing body of research from developmental psychology suggesting that infants come into the world with capacities for experiencing image-schematic structures. Recall my earlier discussion (in chapter 2) of Daniel Stern's description (1985) of certain types of sensorimotor structures that infants are able to detect from birth. He argues, first, that these capacities form the basis for meaning and the infant's sense of self; and, second, that these capacities continue to play a central role in meaning, understanding, and thinking even in adults, who are capable of propositional thinking. The patterns of cross-modal perception, such as the infant's ability to correlate the pacifier he was sucking on with the pacifier he later sees, require intermodal connections between brain areas responsible for tactile and visual processing. Although Stern speaks of these structures of cross-modal perception as "abstract representations," his account does not necessarily entail a strong representational view. Rather, these are "representations" in the first of the four acceptable senses I discussed in chapter 6, since these perceptual structures are not inner mirrorings of external things, but rather the very contours of our experience itself.

Like infants, we adults have a ROUGH-SMOOTH image schema, which we use as we anticipate a change in surface texture as we walk. For example, we can see where we will step from the rough carpet of the hallway onto the slippery tile of the bathroom, and we transfer this information from the visual to the somatomotor system so that our feet will not slip. Such patterns of cross-modal perception are especially clear examples of how image schemas differ from being just a topographically mapped image in a neural map; they are sensorimotoric patterns of experience that are instantiated in and coordinated between the neural maps.

A second type of pattern that makes up the infant's (and adult's) image-schematic experience is Stern's vitality-affect contours, illustrated earlier with the notion of a "rush," or the swelling qualitative contour of a felt experience. We can experience an adrenaline rush, a rush of joy or anger, a drug-induced rush, or the rush of a hot flash. Even though these rushes are felt in different sensory modalities, they can all be characterized as a rapid, forceful building up or swelling contour of the experience across time. Stern notes that understanding how such affect contours are meaningful to creatures like us gives us profound insight into meaning generally, whether that meaning comes via language, vision, music, dance, touch, or smell. We crave the emotional satisfaction that comes from pattern completion, and witnessing even a portion of the pattern is enough to set our affect contours in motion. The infant needs only to see the parent *begin* to reach for the bottle, and she already begins to quiet down—the grasping schema does not even need to be completely realized in time before she recognizes the action. When as adults we hear a musical composition building up to a crescendo, this causes increasing emotional tension that is released at the musical climax. The emotional salience of the vitality-affect contours in image schemas shows that image schemas are not mere static "representations" (or "snapshots") of one moment in a topographic neural map. Instead, image schemas operate dynamically in and through time.

At this point, I can summarize my conception of image schemas as

1. recurrent, stable patterns of sensorimotor experience;
2. "image"-like, in that they preserve the topological structure of the perceptual whole;
3. operating dynamically in and across time;
4. at once "bodily" *and* "mental";
5. predicated on interaction with a wider environment;
6. realized as activation patterns (or "contours") in topologic neural maps;
7. structures that link sensorimotor experiences to conceptualization and language; and
8. having internal structures that give rise to constrained inferences.

Image schemas constitute a preverbal and mostly nonconscious, emergent level of meaning. They are patterns instantiated in the topologic neural maps we share with other animals, though we as humans have particular image schemas that are more or less peculiar to our types of bodies and the characteristics of the environments we inhabit. Although they are preverbal, they play a major role in the syntax, semantics, and pragmatics of natural language. They lie at the heart of meaning, and they underlie language, abstract reasoning, and all forms of symbolic interaction.

IMAGE SCHEMAS BIND BODY AND MIND

Let us take stock of the argument so far. This chapter and the previous one are crucial steps in setting out the ontological framework that is required for a theory of cognition as embodied. It is a nondualistic ontology built around the principle of continuity, according to which there are no ontological ruptures or gaps between different levels of complexity within an organism. "Higher" cognitive processes have to emerge from complex interactions among "lower"-level capacities. If you start by assuming a radical difference in kind between the higher and lower forms of cognition, you will never bridge the gap between the two types (i.e., between the mental and the physical). As the history of Western philosophy has repeatedly demonstrated, once you break Humpty-Dumpty apart, you'll never put him back together again. Once you separate mind from body, inner from outer, conception from perception, reason from emotion, you will never find an ontological hermaphrodite in which these allegedly separate and distinct metaphysical kinds can be united.

The grounding assumption of the embodied cognition view is that Humpty-Dumpty was never broken, so there is no need to try to put him back together. As the pragmatists argued, experience was never ontologically bifurcated in the first place, even though we can always identify aspects of our unified experience and abstract them as if they were separate and distinct entities, structures, or processes. Experience comes whole and continuous. We make distinctions and abstract out patterns from this qualitative whole. On this view, cognition is an organic, embodied process of enaction in which the organism is dynamically engaged with its surroundings and is not separated or alienated from them. So, there is no need for inner ideas that could somehow capture what is outer and other (the world). We are, instead, *in* and *of* the world. The patterns of our engagement are sensorimotor patterns, image schemas, conceptual metaphors, and other imaginative structures.

Recalling my discussion of representations at the end of the previous chapter, we can now acknowledge the sense in which it would be appropriate to call image schemas "representations." For example, as mentioned earlier, a neural map in the brain does map topological aspects of experience. An image schema would be instantiated as a particular pattern within this map, and so one could speak of the image schema as representing some pattern "in the world." However, great caution is required in speaking of representations, for it is too easy to slide back into the classical representationalist doctrine of mind/body dualism. As soon as you turn from speaking of a "representation in the brain" (such as a neural map) to speaking of a "representation in the mind," you are off and running again with full-blown dualism. The concept of representation comes loaded with dualistic metaphysical and epistemological baggage that it ultimately cannot carry. It is true that naturalistic philosophers and most neuroscientists use the term *representation* in talking about cognition. But if you look carefully at second-generation (embodied) cognitive science, you will discover that they do not use this term to indicate the existence of purely *mental* entities (called "ideas" or "concepts"). As we will see in chapter 8, the neural activations that we call concepts are not re-presentations of experience. Rather, they are just structures of experience! Only if we stand back, as theorists, looking first at the neural patterns and then at what the organism under study is encountering in its environment (as perceptual input), can we regard the pattern, model, or activation as representing something else. For example, we think we know scientifically what is present to a person's retina, and we correlate that with neural connections activated in the various areas of the visual cortex. However, this sense of "representing" is innocuous—patterns in the visual cortex map patterns in the retina—and it does not support a classic representational theory of mind, because there is no "inner idea" re-presenting an "outer reality," since the outer reality is the world *as experienced*.

This having been said, there still remains a justifiable reason to use the term *representation* whenever we want to speak of words, signs, symbols, or actions as representations. For a scientific account of cognition, we don't need representations. But the term may be useful whenever we have formalisms that claim to capture the structure of something. In a colloquial sense, we can speak of a sign like *dog* as representing, or standing for, a certain furry canine. We can construct formal models and then place elements of those models in one-to-one relations with other symbols or things, and we can say that the first set of elements and structures "represents" the second set. Notice, however, that this sense of the term does not require or lend credence to the representational theory of mind, because it need not presuppose internal mental symbols.

THE SOCIAL, INTERSUBJECTIVE CHARACTER
OF EMBODIED COGNITION

I have been presenting evidence for the embodied character of cognition, suggesting an appropriate pragmatist philosophical framework for interpreting that evidence. Contra representationalism, I have argued that cognition is not some inner process performed by "mind," but rather is a form of embodied action. I argued this by giving examples of how cognition is located in organism-environment interactions, instead of being locked up in some alleged private mental sphere of thought. However, an exclusive focus on the organism's engagement and coupling with its environment can lead to the mistaken impression that thought is individual, not social. Therefore, we must at least briefly address the crucial fact that language and abstract reasoning are socially and culturally situated activities. I cannot do justice to this important dimension here, but I want at least to identify the social dimension as essential to our capacity for meaning and thoughtful inquiry.

Thus far, I have discussed only one sociocultural dimension, that of cognitive development. My brief discussion of development was framed more within the context of nervous systems than within sociocultural interactions. I stressed the point that epigenetic bodily interactions with the world are what shape our neural maps and the image schemas in them. For humans, a very large and distinctive part of such engagement involves interacting with other humans. In other words, human understanding and thinking are social. This raises the question: how do socially and culturally determined factors come to play a role in human cognition?

In framing an answer to this question, two important mistakes must be avoided. The first mistake is to assume that humans are fundamentally different from other animals with respect to socially and culturally transmitted behaviors. In fact, human sociocultural influences are continuous with those of other animal species, even if there are distinct characteristics that arise with the acquisition of a human language. Second, having challenged the split between "inner mind" and "outer body," we must be careful not to replace it with another, equally problematic dichotomy—that between the individual and the social. We must recognize that cognition does not take place only within the brain and body of a single individual but is instead partly constituted by social interactions, social relations, and cultural artifacts and practices. The evidence to which I now turn comes from cognitive ethology and distributed cognition. Of course, there are ways in which our sociocultural behaviors are peculiarly human, but the story is, once again, much more complex and multidimensional than classical representationalists suppose.

Following Humberto Maturana and Francisco Varela (1998, 180–84), I would define social phenomena as those phenomena arising out of recurrent structural couplings that require the coordinated participation of multiple organisms. Maturana and Varela argue that just as the cell-to-cell interactions in the transition from single to multicellular organisms afford a new level of *intercellular* structural coupling, so also recurrent interactions between organisms afford a new level of *interorganismic* structural coupling.

The social insects are a good basic example of this kind of recurrent interorganismic behavior. For example, ants must feed their queen for their colony to remain alive. Individual workers navigate their way to and from the nest and food sources by leaving trails of chemical markers. When seeking food, an individual ant moves away from markers dropped by other ants. Naturally, the density of such markers decreases in proportion to the distance from the nest. But when one ant finds food, it begins to actively seek denser clusters of markers, thus leading the ant back to the nest. Furthermore, whenever a worker ant eats, its chemical markers change slightly. These markers attract, rather than repel, other ants. Thus, the ants gradually begin to form a column leading from a food source to the nest. Note that the ants' cognition is both social, in that it takes place between organisms, and distributed, in the sense that it offloads much of the cognitive work onto the environment. No single ant carries around an "internal representation" or neural map of where the ant colony is. Ant cognition is thus nonrepresentational in that it is both intrinsically social and situated in organism-environment interactions.

I am not claiming that ants have language or symbolic interaction of any sort. Quite the contrary; their "communication" is wholly unconscious and automated. Moreover, the social cognition of insects does not include the capacity for spontaneous imitation, which is so central to human abstract cognition. For a social behavior to become a learned behavior and then continue across generations, a capacity for spontaneous imitation is crucial. However, zoological ethologists have long known that this imitative capacity is not unique to humans. Researchers studying macaques left sweet potatoes on the beach for a colony of wild monkeys who normally inhabited the jungle near the beach. After gradually becoming habituated to the beach and becoming more familiar with the sea, one monkey discovered that dipping the potatoes in a tide pool would cleanse them of the sand that made them unpalatable. This behavior was imitated throughout the colony in a matter of days, although the researchers observed that older macaques were slower to acquire the behavior than the younger ones (Kawamura 1959; McGrew 1998). Maturana and Varela (1998, 203) define cultural behavior precisely as this kind of relatively stable pattern of transgenerational social behavior.

The culturally acquired behavior most often held up by classical representationalists as the hallmark of the distinctively human is language. However, even here there is not a clear break from the animal kingdom in terms of basic cognitive capabilities, as we see when considering the results of researchers who have been trying to teach symbolic communication to other primates. Instead, their observations are consonant with our theory of how language and image schemas emerge from bodily processes involving cross-modal perception. In experiments done by Sue Savage-Rumbaugh, Rose Sevcik, and William Hopkins (1988), three bonobo chimpanzees who had been trained in symbolic communication were able to make not only cross-modal associations (i.e., visual to tactile), but also symbolic to sensory-modal associations. For example, Kanzi was able to hear a spoken English word and accurately choose either the corresponding visual lexigram or a visual picture for the word. Sherman and Austin were able to choose the appropriate object by touch when presented with a visual lexigram, with 100 percent accuracy. Conversely, they were also able to choose the appropriate visual lexigram when presented with a tactile-only stimulus (Sherman, 96 percent correct; Austin, 100 percent correct) or olfactory-only stimulus (Sherman, 95 percent correct; Austin, 70 percent correct). Their ability to perform such symbol to sensory-modality coordination enhanced their performance on tasks measuring solely cross-modal coordination; as the researchers observe, "These symbol-sophisticated apes were able to perform a variety of cross-modal tasks and to switch easily from one type of task to another. Other apes have been limited to a single cross-modal task" (Savage-Rumbaugh, Sevcik, and Hopkins 1988, 623). Although these bonobos will never approach the linguistic capabilities of humans, the results show that our human capacity for abstract, cross-modal thought is shared by at least some members of the animal kingdom.

In fact, related recent research on primates has shown that it is the distinctively human sociocultural environment (and not some great discontinuity in comparative cognitive capacity) that facilitates the capabilities underlying language and abstract reason. We have already noted that the neural development of the cross-modal maps of juvenile owls can be modified by epigenetic stimulation, but it is equally important to realize that the cross-modal basis for many of our image schemas requires epigenetic stimulation of the kind presented by human parents. Michael Tomasello, Sue Savage-Rumbaugh, and A. C. Kruger (1993) compared the abilities of bonobo chimpanzees and human children to imitatively learn novel actions with novel objects. They tested three conspecific (mother-reared) chimpanzees and three enculturated (human-reared) chimpanzees, along with eighteen- and thirty-month-old human children. They introduced a new object into the participant's environment, and after observing the participant's natural interactions with the object, the experimenter demonstrated a novel action with the object with the instruction "Do what I do." Their results showed that the mother-reared chimpanzees were much poorer imitators than the enculturated chimpanzees and the human children, who did not differ in their results. From these two studies taken together, we can conclude that a human-like sociocultural environment is an essential component not only for the development of our capacity for imitation, but also for the development of our capacities for cross-modal image schemas, language, and abstract reasoning.[4]

Finally, there is also considerable evidence from cognitive anthropology that adult humans do not think in a manner consistent with the dichotomies posed by classical representationalism. Like the social insects, we tend to offload much of our cognition onto the environments we create. We tend to accomplish this in two ways: first, we make cognitive artifacts to help us engage in complex cognitive actions (Clark 1998); and, second, we distribute cognition among members of a social organization. As an example of the first way, Edwin Hutchins (1995, 99–102) discusses how medieval mariners used the thirty-two-point compass rose to predict tides. By superimposing onto the compass rose the twenty-four-hour day (in forty-five-minute intervals), the mariners could map the lunar "time" of the high tide (the bearing of the full moon when its pull causes a high tide) to a solar time of day. As long as they knew two facts—the number of days since the last full moon and the lunar high tide for a particular port—they could simply count off a number of points on the compass rose equal to the days past the full moon in order to compute the time of the next high tide. Without the schema provided by the cognitive artifact, computing the next high tide would have been a much more laborious cognitive task.

4. This conclusion is further supported by results showing that human children with specific language impairments show deficiencies in their ability to perform cross-modal tasks (Montgomery 1993).

As an example of the second way of offloading the work of cognition onto our environments, Hutchins (1995, 263–85) discusses how the partially overlapping knowledge of a group of three navy navigation personnel is distributed among the team. Because the participants know the spatial relations and procedures immanent to another team member's job, the overlaps function as a brake on navigational errors that could imperil the ship. In short, both socially distributed cognition and cognitive artifacts are environmental factors that we use in our daily cognitive feats.

A fully adequate treatment of the social and cultural dimensions of thought would require substantially more evidence and analysis. I have only attempted to suggest that cognition cannot be locked up within the private workings of an individual mind. Since thought is a form of coordinated action, it is spread out in the world, coordinated with both the physical environment and the social, cultural, moral, political, and religious environments, institutions, and shared practices. Language—and all forms of symbolic expression—are quintessentially social behaviors. Dewey nicely summarizes the intrinsically social character of all thought in his argument that the very idea of thinking as a kind of inner mental dialogue is only possible because of socially established and preserved meanings, values, and practices:

> When the introspectionist thinks he has withdrawn into a wholly private realm of events disparate in kind from other events, made out of mental stuff, he is only turning his attention to his own soliloquy. And soliloquy is the product and reflex of converse with others; social communication not an effect of soliloquy. If we had not talked with others and they with us, we should never talk to and with ourselves. Because of converse, social give and take, various organic attitudes become an assemblage of persons engaged in converse, conferring with one another, exchanging distinctive experiences. . . . Through speech a person dramatically identifies himself with potential acts and deeds; he plays many roles, not in successive stages of life but in a contemporaneously enacted drama. Thus mind emerges. (Dewey 1925/1981, 135)

Thus mind emerges. It emerges as, and is enacted through, social cognition. I think it is therefore accurate to say that we are not born with minds fully formed and ready for thinking. Instead, we acquire "minds" through our coordinated sharing of meaning and our concomitant ability to engage in symbolic interaction. Infants have primitive cognitive capacities that, through interaction with the world and other people, become functioning minds. On this view, mind is a matter of degree, stretching from the primitive mindedness of new babies to the more developed mindfulness of adults. If a person loses her capacities for consciousness and her abilities to experience meaning, she could be said to "lose her mind." Mind is an achievement, not a pre-given faculty. There is no radical rupture between our higher cognition and our bodily experience of meaning; instead, that meaning is carried forward and given voice through language and other forms of social symbolic interaction and expression.

Finally, meaning does not reside in our brain, nor does it reside in a disembodied mind. Meaning requires a functioning brain, in a living body that engages its environments—environments that are social and cultural, as well as physical and biological. Cultural artifacts and practices— for example, language, architecture, music, art, ritual acts, and public institutions—preserve aspects of meaning as objective features of the world. Without these cultural artifacts, our accumulated meaning, understanding, and knowledge would not be preserved over time, and each new generation would have to literally start over from scratch. Fortunately, because of social and cultural cognition, we do not have to relearn the meaning of our world. Each child, and each social group, can appropriate those objects and activities in which a culture's meanings and values are sedimented. However, we must keep in mind that those sociocultural objects, practices, and events are not meaningful in themselves. Rather, they become meaningful only insofar as they are enacted in the lives of human beings who *use* the language, *live by* the symbols, *sing* and *appreciate* the music, *participate* in the rituals, and *reenact* the practices and values of institutions.

A PRAGMATIST PERSPECTIVE ON EMBODIED MEANING

I have been arguing against disembodied views of mind, concepts, and reasoning, especially as they underlie representational theories of mind and language. My alternative view—that cognition is embodied—has its roots partly in American pragmatist philosophy, and it is being supported and extended by recent work in second-generation cognitive science. Pragmatists like James and Dewey understood that philosophy and empirical science must develop in mutual cooperation and criticism, if we are ever to have an empirically responsible and philosophically sound understanding of the human mind and all of its marvelous capacities and acts. Pragmatism and cognitive science of the embodied mind are characterized by (1) a profound, nonreductionist respect for the richness, depth, and complexity of human experience and cognition; (2) an evolutionary perspective that appreciates the role of dynamic change in all development (as opposed to fixity and finality); (3) a commitment to the embodiment of meaning, tied to the continuity of body and mind; and (4) recognition that human cognition and creativity arise in response to problematic situations that involve values, interests, and social interaction. The principle of continuity marks the fact that apparently novel aspects of thought and social interaction arise naturally via increased complexity of the organism-environment interactions that constitute experience. Pragmatists thus have an embodied cognition perspective, and they argue that all of our traditional metaphysical and epistemological dualisms (e.g., mind/body, inner/outer, subject/object, concept/percept, reason/emotion, knowledge/ imagination, and theory/practice) do not mark irreducible ontological distinctions but are merely abstractions from the continuous interactive (enactive) process that is experience. Such distinctions are not absolute ontological dichotomies. Sometimes they serve us well, but often they serve us quite poorly, depending on what problems we are investigating, what values we have, and what the sociocultural context is.

The themes I have been tracing throughout this and the previous chapter—our engagement and cognition as human animals, our ongoing coupling with and our falling in and out of harmony with our surroundings, and the grounding of meaning in our bodily perception and action—are beautifully encapsulated by Dewey in a passage in which he identifies the whole life process of meaning-making as it is intimately tied to aesthetic dimensions of experience:

> At every moment, the living creature is exposed to dangers from its surroundings, and at every moment, it must draw upon something in its surroundings to satisfy its needs. The career and destiny of a living thing are bound up with its interchanges with environment, not externally but in the most intimate needs.
>
> The growl of a dog crouching over his food, his howl in time of loss and loneliness, the wagging of his tail at the return of his human friend are expressions of the implication of living in a natural medium which includes man along with the animal he has domesticated. Every need, say for hunger for fresh air or food, is a lack that denoted at least a temporary absence of adequate adjustment with surroundings. But it is also a demand, a reaching out into the environment by building at least a temporary equilibrium. Life itself consists of phases in which the organism falls out of step with the march of surrounding things and then recovers unison with it—either through effort or some happy chance. . . .

These biological commonplaces are something more than that [mere biological consequences]; they reach to the roots of the esthetic in experience. (Dewey 1934, 535)

We humans are live creatures. We are acting when we think, perhaps falling in and out of step with the environment, but never are our thoughts outside of it. Via the aesthetics of our bodily senses, the environment enters into the very shape of our thought, sculpting our most abstract reasoning out of our embodied interactions with the world.

CHAPTER 8

The Brain's Role in Meaning

WHY COGNITIVE NEUROSCIENCE MATTERS

Throughout this book, my oft-repeated mantra has been this: in order to have human meaning, you need a human brain, operating in a living human body, continually interacting with a human environment that is at once physical, social, and cultural. Take away any one of these three dimensions, and you lose the possibility of meaning: no brain, no meaning; no body, no meaning; no environment, no meaning. Although the brain alone cannot give us meaning, it is surely the supreme bodily organ in the construction of meaning. That is why I find it disturbing that most traditional accounts of meaning have so little to say about the sciences of the body and the brain. Until quite recently, the vast majority of philosophers of mind and language went cheerfully about their business of constructing theories of syntax, semantics, pragmatics, mental states, representation, and values without so much as a nod toward the neural and bodily bases for these aspects of cognition.[1]

---

1. I am referring here primarily to traditional analytic philosophers of mind and language and to what Lakoff and I (1999) have called "first-generation" or "disembodied" cognitive science. What I find so encouraging is the excellent work appearing over the past two decades by two groups: philosophers attentive to developing cognitive science and cognitive neuroscientists who are philosophically sophisticated. It is now clear that anyone coming into the study of mind and language today must have at least a basic knowledge of recent developments in the cognitive sciences.

One reason for this neglect of neuroscience is the fact that this field is only in its early stages of development, which leads many people to argue that it is therefore premature to draw any conclusions for the philosophy of mind and language based on empirical research on brain processes. Over the past two decades, scientists have made stunning progress in understanding the neural components of cognition, perhaps more progress than in all the prior centuries of the scientific study of mind. However, what we are learning is still surely only the beginning—some highly limited, tentative studies of various cognitive activities—and there is nothing approaching either a widely accepted general theory of thinking or a global account of mind.

In light of this relative immaturity of cognitive neuroscience, one might perhaps be justified in taking a wait-and-see approach. Yet some conclusions *do* seem to be justified, even though the science is nascent. There are certain popular theories of mind and language that are incompatible with empirical evidence about the brain and cognition. If your favorite theory is at odds with this research, then you ought to be worried, and you ought to be asking whether you need to rethink some of your cherished hypotheses. For example, any theory of language that is built completely on neural modularity (or that presupposes an encapsulated syntax module) *has* to be wrong, because there is just too much compelling evidence that the mind-brain does not and cannot work only with modularity (Edelman 1992; Edelman and Tononi 2000; Tucker 2007). Another problematic case would be any theory claiming that concepts are processed in brain regions completely independent of the areas devoted to sensorimotor processing. As we will see below, such a hypothesis is wildly improbable. Although it is of course possible that particular claims in our current neuroscience will be overthrown by subsequent theories and empirical research, there are clearly some results so robust and well supported that they have to be taken seriously by anyone developing a theory of mind and meaning.

The value of neuroscience, however, is not merely negative and critical, for it can also suggest plausible constructive hypotheses about the nature of mind, thought, and language. For example, cognitive neuroscience might actually tell us something about what concepts are and how they work. It might tell us whether there are sensorimotor aspects of even our most abstract conceptualization. It might tell us how emotion plays an essential role in reasoning. These would be positive, theory-constituting insights of cognitive science, not just limiting constraints on the range of possible philosophical views. So, it is now time to make forays into parts of cognitive neuroscience that can shed light on the topics we have been discussing. In this chapter, I want to survey some intriguing, highly suggestive evidence from cognitive neuroscience that lends support to the embodiment of meaning hypothesis.

EMBODIED CONCEPTS

In previous chapters, I have argued for the embodiment of meaning, concepts, and understanding, using mostly evidence from phenomenological description and empirical research from second-generation cognitive science. This includes evidence from linguistics, developmental and cognitive psychology, biology, and emotion research. I now want to examine additional evidence from neuroscience that supports some of my claims about embodied meaning and that also suggests some of the neural bases of conceptualization. The naturalistic, nonrepresentational, embodied view of meaning I am proposing has to include at least a rudimentary account of the neural (and neurocomputational) components. From a neural perspective, we need to know what concepts are and how they work.

The obvious challenge for a theory of embodied meaning is twofold. First, if concepts are not disembodied symbolic representations, then what are they, from a neural perspective? Second, can *all* concepts be embodied, that is, grounded in sensorimotor aspects of experience? This second question requires an account of both concrete concepts (i.e., concepts of concrete objects, persons, events, and bodily actions) and abstract concepts (e.g., mind, knowledge, ideas, justice, rights, freedom) that are not about concrete, physical entities. My argument progresses in two steps. First, we must examine evidence that the meaning of concrete concepts is grounded in activations of sensorimotor areas of the brain. Second, we must suggest how abstract concepts (concepts not tied to specific sensory experiences) also rely on sensorimotor areas of the brain and are thus embodied.

I have been arguing that the key to an embodied, nonrepresentational view is this: concepts are not inner mental entities that re-present external realities. Rather, concepts are neural activation patterns that can either be "turned on" by some actual perceptual or motoric event in our bodies, or else activated when we merely think about something, without actually perceiving it or performing a specific action. So in order to understand what concepts are from a neural perspective and how they work, we must examine how they emerge in the process of an embodied organism's ongoing engagement with its environment. I want to begin with an elegant summary of this interactional process by Vittorio Gallese, who describes how energy exchanges between an organism and its environment ultimately result in patterns of activation within functional neuronal clusters:

> If we analyse at the *physical level of description* the relationship between bio-
> logical agents and 'the world outside', we will find living organisms process-
> ing the different epiphanies of energy they are exposed to: electromagnetic,
> mechanical, chemical energy. Energy interacts with living organisms. It is
> only by virtue of this interaction that energy can be specified in terms of
> the 'stimuli' (visual, auditory, somatosensory, etc.) to which every organism
> is exposed. The result of the interaction between energy, now 'stimulus', is
> translated, or better, transduced into a *common informational code*. The recep-
> tors of the different sensory modalities are the agents of the transduction
> process: they convert the different types of energies resulting from organ-
> isms-world interactions into the common code of action potentials. Action
> potentials express the electro-chemical excitability of cells, and constitute
> the code used by the billions of neurons that comprise the central nervous
> system to 'communicate' with each other. (Gallese 2003, 1232)

In short, in the context of organism-environment interactions, patterns of energy become stimuli for the organism; these patterns are converted within the organism to action potentials in neurons, thus initiating vast neuronal "communication." Gallese does not hesitate to call these patterns of organism-environment interactions and couplings "representations," insofar as they are informationally coded as neural action potentials and activation patterns, but he does not mean by this that they are representa-tions in the classical sense—that is, inner mental entities directed at exter-nal realities. Instead, Gallese suggests that these activation patterns should be thought of as both the vehicle of representation *and* the content, be-cause, as patterns of organism-environment interaction, they are both the structures of the interactions themselves (the vehicle) and simultaneously what we might call "models" of the world for the organism (the content).

We must resist the strong temptation to think of these structures in the traditional representational way, as though they were internal mental rep-resentations. As explained in chapter 6, this temptation arises from the fact that scientists can stand back and reflect on a certain pattern of neural ac-tivation in the organism and then compare this with what they think the organism is encountering "in the world." This reproduces the inner/outer dichotomy and misleads us into thinking of a neural activation pattern as being some internalized quasi-entity that stands in an intentional rela-tion to some independent pattern in the world. Instead, the correct way of describing an activation pattern is to say, first, that it *constitutes* some part of our experience of an "affordance" (Gibson 1979) of the world for us; and, second, that the pattern is both a model of and a model for possible experience and action. It is a *model of* structures of recurring organism-environment coupling, and it is a *model for* possible perceptions and actions that one might experience. Once again, however, it is *not* a model in the sense of a conceptual or propositional construct that we reflectively entertain in some inner mental theater. Rather, neural activation patterns are merely recurring structures of experiences actual and possible, retained in the organism as synaptic weights (i.e., as the tendency of certain neurons to fire when stimulated by inputs from other neurons).

Furthermore, this entire process is loosely goal-directed and always has a built-in teleological aspect, since organisms have implicit values they are trying to realize (either consciously or unconsciously and automatically)—values such as maintaining homeostasis in their internal milieu, protecting themselves from harm, reproducing, and, in more advanced cases, actualizing their potentialities for growth and fulfillment. This teleological directedness ultimately depends on the organism's ability to control aspects of its environment and its own bodily states:

> Any interaction requires a control strategy. Control strategies are typically *relational:* they can be seen as a way of modeling the interaction between organism and environment. . . . Properties that are constantly coupled with objects or events, and that reliably occur on different occasions, are most useful, because they enable biological agents to acquire and store knowledge that can also be applied to the future. Furthermore, this kind of 'stored knowledge' allows one to anticipate and predict some properties without the need of always verifying them (see Millikan 2000). Abstraction is exactly that: it enables the representation of objects and events in a way that is independent of their full-blown and constant presence. (Gallese 2003, 1234)

What Gallese is describing here is the basis for conceptualization. Just as we saw with James and Dewey, concepts are patterns of interaction that are important enough for the ongoing experience of a person (or an animal) to merit being selected from the flow of experience. Certain neurons and neuronal clusters fire in response to certain patterns (energy exchanges that become "stimuli" for the organism). Larger functional clusters fire together (and wire together), often because they are patterns important to the organism's functioning. Humans, for example, like other animals, have heat receptors, because various degrees of heat can be either helpful or quite harmful to us. We have also developed finely tuned systems for automatically monitoring and controlling temperature within our internal milieu. Our neural makeup, in interaction with the energies available in our surroundings, will result in specific neural connections and tendencies for specific neuronal clusters to fire in the presence of certain specific stimuli. Concepts have to be understood as the various possible patterns of activation by which we can mark significant characteristics of our experience.

Although we do not currently have a fully adequate account of concepts from a neural perspective, there are some promising theories emerging in recent cognitive neuroscience. Vittorio Gallese and George Lakoff (2005), for example, have proposed that conceptualization uses some of the very same sensorimotor processes that are activated in actual perceptual and motor experiences. They thus reject any view that regards thinking as a kind of cognition radically different from perceiving and doing. What I find most exciting about their theory is that it suggests some ways in which even abstract concepts are tied to sensorimotor processes.

Gallese and Lakoff discuss experiments with both monkeys and humans showing that sensorimotor areas involved in perception and action are also activated in conceptualizing those perceptions or actions, and they then try to extend this account to abstract concepts. Their argument proceeds in three steps:

1. To show that the sensorimotor system of the brain is multimodal—that is, that our systems for seeing, touching, hearing, and motor actions, for example, are integrated by cross-modal neural links.
2. To argue that concrete concepts involve the activation of some of the same sensorimotor functional clusters of neurons that are used in the actual perception or bodily motion that is being conceptualized.
3. To suggest how abstract concepts might be tied to the sensorimotor system.

Let us consider each of these three steps in turn.

The Multimodal Character of the Sensorimotor System

When you see a cup sitting on the table in front of you, you are not just having a *visual* experience. In addition to the activation of neuronal clusters in parts of your visual cortices, you are experiencing that cup as something you could reach for, grasp, pick up, and raise to your lips to quench your thirst. The cup affords not just a visual form; it also affords pick-up-ability. This was the point Dewey was making when he observed that there is a depth and richness to our visual experience that calls into play other sensory and motor experiences (1934/1987, 129). We know this is true not just on the basis of subtle phenomenological descriptions, but also because we have strong neuroscientific evidence. Seeing the cup activates what are known as canonical neurons. Studies with monkeys by Giacomo Rizzolatti, Leonardo Fogassi, and Vittorio Gallese (2000; see also Rizzolatti and Craighero 2004) show that these canonical neurons fire both when the monkey reaches for and grasps a particular object and when the monkey simply sees the object that it *could* grasp, even though it does not. In other words, objects are not just visual or tactile or auditory shapes, nor are they merely things that support various motor programs for interacting with them. They are, instead, all of these dimensions together. *Perception at this level is multimodal.* Gallese and Lakoff summarize their notion of multimodality as follows: "To claim, as we do, that an action like *grasping* is 'multimodal' is to say that (1) it is neurally enacted using neural substrates used for both action and perception, and (2) that modalities of action and perception are integrated at the level of the sensory-motor system itself and not via higher association areas" (2005, 459). To cite another example of this cross-modal connectivity, the same neurons that fire when a monkey turns its head to a location in peri-personal space (say, where a graspable object is) will also fire when either an object is presented or a sound occurs in that same location, even though the monkey doesn't actually turn its head to that location (see, e.g., Duhamel, Colby, and Goldberg 1998).

The so-called mirror neurons also support the multimodality hypothesis. In general, mirror neurons fire both when a subject performs a specific motor action (like grasping an object with a certain type of grip) and also when the subject merely sees another subject perform the same precise motor action. There is a rapidly growing body of evidence, including studies on both monkeys and humans, for various manifestations of this phenomenon (for a review, see Rizzolatti, Fogassi, and Gallese 2001; and Rizzolatti and Craighero 2004). One interesting case tested F5 mirror neurons in monkeys that discharged consistently under the following four conditions: (1) when the monkey *performed* a noisy action, such as breaking a peanut apart or tearing a sheet of paper; (2) when the monkey *saw* these same actions performed by someone else; (3) when the monkey *heard* these noisy actions being performed; and (4) when the monkey both *saw and heard* the same actions.

Mirror-neuron phenomena suggest that *understanding is a form of simulation.* To see another person perform an action activates some of the same sensorimotor areas, *as if* the observer herself were performing the action.

This deep and pre-reflective level of engagement with others reveals our most profound bodily understanding of other people, and it shows our intercorporeal social connectedness. Moreover, mirror-neuron research supports the hypothesis that *imagination is a form of simulation*. Research by Marc Jeannerod (1994) shows that *imagining* certain motor actions activates some of the same parts of the brain that are involved in actually performing that action. Imagining a visual scene also activates areas of the brain that would be activated if we actually perceived that scene (Kosslyn 1994).

Concrete Concepts Use Sensorimotor Areas of the Brain

A central tenet of an embodied cognition theory of concepts is that concrete concepts (that is, concepts for concrete objects, events, and actions) are processed using sensorimotor areas of the brain. The embodiment view thus hinges on denying that conceptualization is carried on only in highly specialized brain regions that are physically and functionally separate from areas responsible for perception and motor movements. The Gallese-Lakoff embodiment hypothesis is that concrete concepts are realized neurally as sensorimotor schemas that organize functional neural clusters into meaningful, integrated gestalts. In their words, *"the job done by what have been called 'concepts' can be accomplished by schemas characterized by parameters and their values*. Such a schema, from a neural perspective, consists of a network of functional clusters" (Gallese and Lakoff 2005, 466). The guiding idea here is that thinking using a concrete concept involves activating many of the same sensorimotor neural clusters that would be activated in actually perceiving something, manipulating an object, or moving one's body.

Gallese and Lakoff elucidate the key notions of schemas, functional clusters, and parameters by presenting a model of the schema for the concrete concept *grasp*. *Parameters* are higher-level features of neural organization of the sensorimotor system, characterizing such things as the force with which an action is done, the direction of the action, the objects acted upon, the phase of the action (e.g., initial state, central phase, ending phase, final state), and the agent performing the action. Different *functional clusters* of neurons work together to realize different neural parameters, so one functional cluster might be responsible for the force of the action, another for its direction, and a third for its goal. When you combine all of the relevant parameters for a type of action and specify the particular values for each parameter relative to a particular action, you have the *schema* for that action. The *grasp* schema, as characterized by Gallese and Lakoff, would include at least the following structure:

The *Grasp* Schema

1. Role parameters: agent, object, object location, and the action itself
2. Phase parameters: initial condition, starting phase, central phase, purpose condition, ending phase, final state
3. The manner parameter (i.e., is the object grasped with the whole hand, two fingers only, etc.)
4. The parameter values (and constraints on them):
   - Agent: an individual
   - Object: a physical entity with parameters such as size, shape, mass, degree of fragility, etc.
   - Initial condition: object location:: within peri-personal space
   - Starting phase: reaching, with direction:: toward object location, opening effector
   - Central phase: closing effector:: with force (a function of fragility and mass)
   - Purpose condition:: effector encloses object, with manner (a grip determined by parameter values and situational conditions)
   - Final state:: agent in-control-of object
   (Note: The "::" indicates the content of a phase.)[2]

It is important to see that Gallese and Lakoff are only giving a formal model of the *grasp* schema, a model that would have to be realized in real-time processes by functional neural clusters activated in accordance with certain "values" for the parameters. There is bound to be a certain artificiality, oversimplification, and overly mechanistic (almost robotic) appearance to this model, which is meant to be enacted in a flesh-and-blood organism purposively engaging its environment. The value of the model, however, is that it makes use of known neural architectures, such as the functional clusters responsible for various sensorimotor operations, and it suggests how they can be integrated into a fluid human action, such as grasping a cup. It gives us a good idea of some of what goes into typical motor actions as simple (or, rather, as complex) as grasping.

2. This summary characterization of the *grasp* schema is taken, with minor changes, from Gallese and Lakoff 2005, 467.

Gallese and Lakoff's big hypothesis is that concrete concepts are schemas of this sort. To have the concept *grasp* is just to have this schema with its specific parameters, with their specific values. The *grasp* schema is activated when we actually grasp a cup, and it is activated (with some inhibitory circuits) when we hear or read the word *grasp* or even when we just think about grasping something. Moreover, the inferential structure of a concrete concept is precisely specified by the internal structure of the appropriate schema (with the particular contextually determined values for its parameters). Gallese and Lakoff summarize their bold claim thus:

> Understanding requires simulation. The understanding of concrete concepts—physical action, physical objects, and so on—requires sensory-motor simulation. But sensory-motor simulation, as contemporary neuroscience has shown, is carried out by the sensory-motor system of the brain. It follows that the sensory-motor *is required for understanding at least concrete concepts.* We see this as an insurmountable difficulty for any traditional theory that claims that concrete concepts are modality-neutral, disembodied, and symbolic. (Gallese and Lakoff 2005, 468)

In trying to show how the sensorimotor system might operate to make conceptualization possible, Gallese and Lakoff are able to raise a strong objection to any disembodied view of concepts. Remember that the traditional (disembodied) view requires that conceptualization occur in brain regions different from those dedicated to sensorimotor processing. But we have examined one example of how the structure of specific actions (e.g., grasping) requires neural clusters and parameterizations for all of the parts and dimensions of the action in question (there must be structures for object location, object size, degree of force, manner of action, and so forth). *All of this structure must be present not just in the sensorimotor actions, but also in our concept of the action.* Consequently, on the traditional disembodied concepts view, there must be a massive reduplication, in the alleged concept-processing areas, of all of this structure that is in the actual action. This would mean that we had developed evolutionarily (or perhaps by divine fiat) two exactly parallel systems in the brain, one for sensorimotor actions and the other for concepts of those sensorimotor actions. Although such a conceptual doppelgänger system is not impossible, it is hard to imagine why such a neurally costly duplication would ever have occurred, when the sensorimotor system alone could be the basis for concrete conceptualization. Of course, this argument doesn't prove anything, but it ought to give us compelling reasons for asking whether all our concepts might, indeed, be embodied.

The Embodiment of Abstract Concepts

It may not seem surprising that concrete concepts operate via the sensorimotor areas of the brain. But it is much harder to see how our abstract concepts—concepts for nonphysical entities, institutions, actions, relations, values—could ever be truly embodied. In the next chapter, I am going to sketch a theory of conceptual metaphor as one of our principal imaginative mechanisms for abstraction, whereby we understand abstract domains using sensorimotor structures. Here, obviously, the neuroscientific story gets quite sketchy, very partial, and highly speculative. At present, we have a likely hypothesis (conceptual metaphor and conceptual blending) with some suggestive computational neuroscience models for how it might be realized in the brain.

As we will see in chapter 9, the idea behind conceptual metaphor theory is that our abstract concepts are typically defined by multiple, often inconsistent conceptual metaphors. Each conceptual metaphor consists of a systematic mapping of entities and relations from a sensorimotor source domain to a target domain that is abstract. For example, in English we have multiple metaphors for conceptualizing the act of intellectual understanding. The dominant metaphor is UNDERSTANDING IS SEEING, in which elements of the source domain (vision) are mapped onto the target domain (intellectual understanding), as follows.

UNDERSTANDING IS SEEING

Source domain (vision)	*Target domain (understanding)*
Object Seen	→ Idea/Concept
Seeing An Object Clearly	→ Understanding An Idea
Person Who Sees	→ Person Who Understands
Light	→ "Light" Of Reason
Visual Focusing	→ Mental Attention
Visual Acuity	→ Mental Acuity
Physical Viewpoint	→ Mental Perspective

In the conceptual metaphor UNDERSTANDING IS SEEING, the source domain (vision) activates parts of the visual system in the brain, including the inferential structure of this source domain. For example, if something is obstructing my line of sight, then I will not be able to see the obstructed object. If there is insufficient light, I will not be able to see the object clearly. If I cannot discern the object clearly, I won't perceive the details of its shape and structure. When we then conceptualize understanding as seeing, all of this inferential structure is potentially activated for use in conceptualizing the target domain (understanding). The inferences are carried out via the source-domain activations, and then they carry over into the target domain via the source-to-target mappings. Thus, to utilize the source-domain logic of seeing, if an idea is *obscure* or an explanation is *not clear,* it follows that one cannot understand the idea. *Murky* arguments are hard to understand. Shedding more *light* on a subject makes it easier to understand, and so we value any account that is *illuminating.*

Understanding Is Seeing is but one of several metaphorical concepts for understanding. Another conceptual metaphor is Understanding Is Grasping, which consists of the following mapping.

Understanding Is Grasping

Source domain (grasping)		Target domain (understanding)
Object Grasped	→	Idea/Concept Understood
Grasping An Object	→	Understanding An Idea
Strength Of Grip	→	Depth Of Understanding
Losing One's Grip	→	Failing To Understand
Object Out Of Reach	→	Idea That Cannot Be Understood

Again, notice that there is a source-domain logic, or inferential structure, for this particular metaphor, just as for Understanding Is Seeing. In the source domain (physical grasping), if an object is out of reach, you cannot grasp it. Via the conceptual mapping, if an idea is *beyond you,* you cannot understand it. If your physical grip on an object fails, you will drop or lose the object. So, if your intellectual grip fails, you will not understand the idea (you won't be able to *get a handle on,* or *grasp,* the idea).

The embodied meaning hypothesis proposes that when we conceptualize acts of understanding via the Understanding Is Grasping metaphor, we are activating the *grasp* schema described by Gallese and Lakoff. It is this activated schema that permits us to reason and draw inferences about what it means to understand an idea, sentence, or theory. All of the internal structure of the *grasp* schema is made available for making sense of acts of understanding.

In this account of conceptual metaphor, the term *mapping* is being used in two different senses, depending on whether the context is a conceptual mapping or a neural mapping. A *conceptual mapping* refers to the correlation of items and relations in the conceptual source domain with structure in the target domain. *Neural mapping* refers to patterns and neural connections between and among various functional parts of the brain. A specific neural map is a topographical or topological structure in a neuronal assembly that preserves certain relations in a different neural cluster. From a neural perspective, the conceptual metaphor hypothesis states that neural mapping is the basis for the conceptual mapping that constitutes a conceptual metaphor. Metaphorical mappings are physically realized in stable neural circuitry linking the sensorimotor system to other brain areas. In other words, if there are conceptual metaphors, then there must exist neural connections between sensorimotor areas of the brain and other areas that are involved in thinking.

The big question is whether our brains actually work this way. Do we use our sensorimotor neural circuitry for abstract reasoning, via metaphorical mapping structures? We do not yet know the answer to this question. However, there is at least some evidence from cognitive neuroscience for the plausibility of the embodied meaning hypothesis. The new evidence comes from both the patient-based neurological literature and neuroimaging studies of normal adults. What this evidence suggests is that sensorimotor areas are implicated in our processing of abstract (metaphorically defined) concepts.

While we have long known that patients can develop anomias reflecting selective category deficits in naming, for example, animals, tools, or plants (Warrington and Shallice 1984), several recent studies have reported a selective category deficit for body-part terms (Suzuki, Yamadori, and Fujii 1997; Shelton, Fouch, and Caramazza 1998; Coslett, Saffran, and Schwoebel 2002). The deficit work suggests that lesions in the secondary motor cortices, in regions that likely contain both somatotopic and egocentric spatial maps, can cause difficulties in tasks such as body-part naming and naming contiguous sections of the body. These findings suggest that the comprehension of body-part terms requires the active participation of these neural maps.

Two other neuroimaging studies also show that we can drive the human somatomotor maps with both literal and metaphoric linguistic stimuli relating to the body. In an fMRI study, Olaf Hauk, Ingrid Johnsrude, and Friedemann Pulvermüller (2004) showed that single-word terms such as *smile, punch,* and *kick* differentially activate face, arm-hand, and leg regions within the somatomotor maps, which suggests that literal language can differentially activate *body part–related* somatomotor neural maps. Similarly, an fMRI neuroimaging study by Tim Rohrer (2001b, 2005) shows that both literal and metaphoric sentences using hand terms—for example, "She handed me the apple" (literal) and "He handed me the theory" (metaphorical)—activate primary and secondary hand regions within the primary and secondary sensorimotor maps. After the presentation of the linguistic stimuli, Rohrer also mapped the hand somatic cortex of each study participant, using a tactile hand-stroking task. A comparison between the tactile and the sentential conditions shows a high degree of overlap in the primary and secondary somatomotor cortex for both language tasks (figure 1). These experiments are the strongest evidence to date from neuroimaging for the conceptual metaphor hypothesis.

There is also evidence from neurocomputationally inspired models of conceptual metaphor and abstract reasoning. Building on Terry Regier's work (1996) on modeling the image-schematic character of spatial-relations terms, Srini Narayanan (1997b) and Jerome Feldman and Narayanan (2004) developed a constrained connectionist network to model how the bodily logic of our sensorimotor systems enables us to perform abstract reasoning about international economics using conceptual metaphors. For example, the system was able to successfully interpret sentences such as "In 1991, the Indian government deregulated the business sector" (literal) and "In 1991, the Indian government loosened its stranglehold on business" (metaphorical). Narayanan's model can perform inferences either entirely within the literal sensorimotor domain or in the linguistic domain using common conceptual metaphor mappings.

Taken together with the neuroimaging evidence for image schemas and conceptual metaphors (Rohrer 2005, 2001b), these neurocomputational models support the metaphoric and image-schematic basis of our language and abstract reasoning. At present, however, we simply do not have enough strong evidence to decide the issue of conceptual metaphor on neuroscientific grounds alone. That is why, in chapter 9, I will present nine other types of evidence from cognitive science for the existence of conceptual metaphor as a key to abstract thought. This growing body of evidence convinces me that the conceptual metaphor hypothesis is the best current explanation for large parts of our abstract conceptualization and reasoning.

In order for this account of abstract reasoning as based on image schemas and conceptual metaphor to be tenable, there must be neural connections between sensorimotor areas of the brain and parts of the brain responsible for higher cognitive functioning. Gerald Edelman's account of reentrant mapping for neuronal groups gives a plausible neural story of how image schemas exist and operate and even of how it is possible for there to be metaphoric mappings across different domains. Edelman and Giulio Tononi characterize reentry as

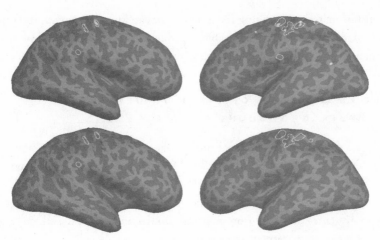

FIGURE I. fMRI activation courses in response to literal and metaphoric activation sentences. Areas active and overlapping from a hand somatosensory task are outlined in white. (Rohrer 2001b)

> the ongoing, recursive interchange of parallel signals between reciprocally connected areas of the brain, an interchange that continually coordinates the activities of these areas' maps to each other in space and time. This interchange, unlike feedback, involves many parallel paths and has no specific instructive error function associated with it. Instead, it alters selective events and correlations of signals among areas and is essential for the synchronization and coordination of the areas' mutual functions. (Edelman and Tononi 2000, 48)

The types of maps Edelman and Tononi are referring to in this passage are primarily sensory and motor maps, such as those that would permit the intermodal connection and correlation of structures in neural maps for both vision and touch. In this way, for instance, there could be a correlation of a visually realized CONTAINER schema with one that is realized in touch, and such connections would make it possible for us to reach out and grasp the cup we see in front of us. Edelman calls such a cross-modal system of connections a higher-order "global mapping," which consists of "a dynamic structure containing multiple reentrant local maps (both motor and sensory) that are able to interact with nonmapped parts of the brain" (Edelman 1992, 89). While this would begin to account for cross-modal image schemas, a further set of mappings to "higher" cortical areas would be needed to account for conceptual metaphor. Although Edelman does not give any detailed explanation of how such metaphoric mappings might be possible, his account of the epigenesis of language postulates reentrant mappings ranging from perceptual and motor maps all the way up to areas of the brain responsible for conceptual categorization, syntax, semantics, and phonology (ibid., 246–52).

THE BODILY BASIS OF OTHER STRUCTURES OF ABSTRACT THOUGHT

Image schemas and conceptual metaphors and metonymies are not the only embodied structures of abstract thinking. All aspects of grammar— the binding of form and meaning—and all aspects of logical relations need to be accounted for through ties to body-based meaning. I want to suggest some strategies that might prove helpful in dealing with the full scope of our capacities for abstract conceptualization and reasoning.

As a key component of what he calls the neural theory of language (NTL), Lakoff has given the name *cogs* to a large number of types of neural circuits that can be used to characterize grammatical constructions. According to Gallese and Lakoff (2005), cogs are structures of sensorimotor processes that can be appropriated for other cognitive functions. I quote at length from their summary account:

1. It (the Cog) provides general structuring for sensory-motor observation, action, and simulation: the specific details for this general structure are filled in via neural connections to other regions of the brain; it is in those regions that the "details" that fill in the Cog structure are characterized. When functioning in this way, the Cog circuit is a natural, normal, seamless part of the sensory-motor system.
2. It presumably evolved for the purposes of sensory-motor integration (cf. phase neurons in monkeys).
3. It performs its neural computations even when the connections to the "specific details" are inhibited.
4. It can be exploited, either as part of a metaphorical mapping or on its own, to characterize the structure of abstract concepts.
5. Its computations, which evolved to serve sensory-motor purposes, also characterize a "logic" and can be used for reasoning.
6. It can function in language as the meaning (or part of the meaning) of a grammatical construction or grammatical morpheme.[3]

Image schemas are prime examples of cogs, since they are recurring patterns of sensorimotor interactions that can be recruited for abstract

---

3. This summary characterization of cogs, quoted from an earlier draft of Gallese and Lakoff 2005, was deleted from the final version.

conceptualization and reasoning. Another excellent example is what David Bailey (1997) and Srini Narayanan (1997a, 1997b, 1997c) call an *executing
schema* (or *X-schema*), which specifies a basic recurring phase structure for
actions. Bailey developed a computational neural model that learns how
to categorize and name verbs of hand motions from various languages
around the world. His model can also give orders to produce the appropriate hand motions for these verbs in a computer model of the body that
can be used in robotics. Bailey's model involves high-level motor-control
schemas (controller X-schemas) that operate dynamically to control and
organize various motor synergies. For example, there would be a specific
X-schema for a simple action like picking up a glass and drinking. The
X-schema for this particular action would be a controller schema with
particular kinds of bindings to certain motor synergies that are part of
picking up and moving a glass (e.g., opening the fingers, forming them
into an appropriate grasping configuration, closing the hand around the
glass, lifting the glass to the lips, etc.).

Narayanan worked with Bailey to model motor schemas of this sort.
They soon recognized that all the motor schemas they were modeling
shared a common high-level control structure with the following dimensions:

1. *Readiness:* Prior to initiating a particular action, your body must satisfy
   certain readiness, or preparatory, conditions. For example, in order to
   lift a chair, you might have to reorient your body posture and stop
   doing some other bodily task.
2. *Starting phase transition:* You have to begin the specific action process in
   an appropriate way. For example, to lift a chair, you must grasp it with
   your hands in a way that will allow you to exert force in an upward
   direction.
3. *Main process (central phase transition):* You then undertake the typical motor movements that constitute the particular kind of action you are
   performing.
4. *Postcentral state:* While engaged in the main process, you might be inter-
   rupted and have to stop, and you can then consider whether to resume
   the same action. Having completed one iteration of the main activity,
   you might choose to repeat that structure over again. In cases where
   there is a goal or purpose for your action, you monitor your progress
   toward the fulfillment of that purpose.
5. *Ending phase transition:* This is the phase when your action is proceeding
   toward completion.

6. *Final state:* You then enter the final state, with whatever results and consequences it brings.

If you look again at the *grasp* schema described earlier, you will see, not surprisingly, that it has all of this phase structure, with various parameters that specify the particular action involved. That is, besides having the general structure of any X-schema, the *grasp* schema is characterized by the parameter values that make it grasping (and this particular act of grasping) rather than, say, walking or waving good-bye.

These dimensions of motor schemas together constitute what in linguistics is called *aspect*. They define the semantic structure of events in general, so they are not specific only to particular motor schemas. Any action a person undertakes—from picking up a cup to preparing a salad to planning a trip to solving a quadratic equation—will manifest this general aspectual structure with its various phases in sequence. Because even our most abstract acts of thought are *acts,* they, too, have these dimensions. Languages around the world have syntactic and semantic devices for coding these aspectual dimensions for all kinds of actions and events. In English, for example, the central phase transition is indicated by *be + ing,* as in "Sarah is cooking dinner." *Have + past* identifies a point in time and indicates that an action was completed (final state) prior to that time, as in "I've hiked up to Otter Lake several times."

Once we have one or more actions that manifest both this generic controller X-schema structure and some more specific X-schema structures (such as *lifting a chair, grasping a cup,* or *pitching a baseball*), we can then build up an indefinite number of larger event and action structures by means of compositional processes of the following sort:

- *Iteration:* You can repeat an action, or some subroutine within an action. You can swing a golf club, swing it again, and then swing it seven more times.
- *Sequences:* Large-scale event structures can be built up by stringing together a series of events or actions. You can go to the store before preparing dinner, which is followed by a walk in the park before coming back home to read a book; all of these combined can form the complex event of spending the evening.
- *Embedding:* One part of an X-schema can embed some other action or part of an action. For example, the *goal* of the action of packing your camping gear might become the *starting point* for your extended action of going backpacking in the mountains.

- *Conditional relations:* One action can provide the condition for the performance or occurrence of another, as in "If you pick up your dirty clothes, your girlfriend or boyfriend won't leave you."

In short, via structures like these for combining, embedding, and sequencing actions, we are able to construct the large-scale actions and narrative structures that make it possible for us to make sense of our actions. Moreover, insofar as the structure of motor programs can also perform abstract inferences, our abstract conceptualization and reasoning manifest sequencing, embedding, iteration, and other structures for building up actions.

Narayanan hypothesizes that controller X-schemas might exist in the premotor cortex, which coordinates various motor synergies into organized actions and action sequences. What Narayanan then proceeds to show is that his neural models for X-schemas are capable of performing inferences about events and actions. For example, let's say you read in the *Wall Street Journal* that Germany had fallen into a deep economic depression but was slowly climbing out, thanks to improved international trade. Narayanan developed a model of conceptual metaphor in which structure from various sensorimotor domains could be recruited to perform inferences for some abstract domain, such as economics. He then showed that certain models of metaphoric thinking based on motor schemas could perform the appropriate abstract inferences for a domain such as international economics.

Building on Narayanan's work, George Lakoff has recently proposed a highly detailed neural model for conceptual metaphor (Lakoff, forthcoming). We do not yet know whether the human brain actually works in precisely the way that these neural models specify. That is, we do not yet have sufficient evidence that motor schemas are recruited for abstract reasoning. What we do have so far are some examples of neural models that can perform appropriate motor actions within a model of the body and can also perform appropriate inferences about abstract conceptual domains. And we have evidence, as noted above, of the existence of cross-modal neural connections. There is a certain evolutionary economy to such a picture of human cognitive functioning. Instead of developing a second set of inferential operations for abstract concepts—a doppelgänger of sensorimotor inference structure—it would be more efficient to recruit sensorimotor programs for so-called higher-level cognitive functions. However, the details of how this might work remain to be developed, and we await additional neuroimaging evidence that would be relevant to the assessment of this hypothesis.

Image schemas, X-schemas, and conceptual metaphors are but three types of cogs that could play a central role in making abstract thinking possible. But it is remarkable how much of our abstract thought can be explained using these resources. Narayanan (1997a, 1997b), for instance, brought all three of these structures together to show how neural circuitry in the premotor cortex that can perform motor control can also compute the general logic of aspect, for concrete and abstract actions alike. Although Narayanan's models do not constitute a proof that the brain actually works this way, they are based on known neural architectures, and they show at least how it might be possible to recruit sensorimotor structures for some types of abstract thinking.

The two major alternatives to this kind of explanation of meaning, conceptualization, and understanding are both distasteful and out of touch with contemporary cognitive neuroscience. One alternative assumes disembodied mind and disembodied thought. The other assumes that conceptualization involves a massive, total duplication of all the inferential structure of the sensorimotor areas. The cog hypothesis, in contrast with these two extreme positions, gives an evolutionarily and cognitively elegant solution to how abstract thought is possible for embodied minds.

In sum, the embodied cognition hypothesis seeks the roots of concrete and abstract conceptualization alike in patterns and qualities of sensorimotor experience. Don Tucker formulates this claim as follows:

> Complex psychological functions must be understood to arise from bodily control networks. There is no other source for them. This is an exquisite parsimony of facts.
>
> There are no brain parts for abstract faculties of the mind—faculties like volition or insight or even conceptualization—that are separate from the brain parts that evolved to mediate between visceral and somatic processes. . . .
>
> If we assume that there is a nested structure of concepts that must take form across the—exactly isomorphic—nested structure of the neural networks of the corticolimbic hierarchy, we can then specify the structure of abstract conceptualization. This is a structure of mind based on bodily forms. Abstraction has one level of representation emergent from syncretic, evaluative, and regulatory representations at the limbic core. It has two intermediate levels, in "association" areas of the cortex. These are levels that very likely provide not only greater structural differentiation but a buffer from the concretizing effect of visceral demands. (Tucker, forthcoming, 202–3)

Conceptualization is thus a complex process of multilevel interactions of brain areas, with reentrant connections among these levels, in an ongoing symphony of meaning-making and thought. Tucker concludes:

> In this dialectical arbitration of opposing constraints, abstract concepts may emerge through recursive, bidirectional exchange across linked, hierarchic, and embedded networks. We can surmise that, at the core, concepts take the form of feelings and intuitive, preconscious constructs. We can further surmise that, through coupled representations across the linked corticolimbic hierarchy, our concepts differentiate toward specific and concrete forms—images and movements—as they are actualized at the sensory and motor interfaces with the world. (Tucker, forthcoming, 196)

As William James claimed more than a century ago, the music of meaning-making is both thought *and* feeling at once, and its notes are the rhythms and tone qualities of our bodily processes.

It is fitting to end this chapter on neuroscientific evidence with a major warning: we must never equate brain with mind. The brain is *not* the mind. The brain is one key part of the entire pattern of embodied organism-environment interaction that is the proper locus of mind and meaning. To repeat what I have said many times, the proper locus of mind is a complex, multilevel, continually interactive process that involves all of the following: a brain, operating in and for a living, purposive body, in continual engagement with complex environments that are not just physical but social and cultural as well. Consequently, my purpose in this chapter has been only to indicate the role of some of the sensorimotor structures in the brain that contribute to the possibility of meaning. And the possibility of meaning—to repeat what I said at the beginning of this chapter, because it cannot be stressed enough—depends on three dimensions. Without a brain, there is no meaning. Without a living, acting body—no meaning. And without organism-environment interaction—no meaning.

CHAPTER 9

From Embodied Meaning to Abstract Thought

Dewey's pragmatist continuity thesis claims that we must be able to move, without any ontological or epistemological rupture, from the body-based meaning of spatial and perceptual experience that is characterizable by image schemas and affect contours all the way up to abstract conceptualization and reasoning. This same notion of ontological continuity underlies most second-generation (embodied) cognitive science. The existence of *abstract* concepts thus poses a fundamental problem for any naturalistic view of meaning as grounded in the qualities and structures of sensorimotor experience. How can thinking about abstract, nonphysical entities possibly be grounded in the body?

CONCEPTUAL METAPHOR

Although there is not yet any fully-worked-out theory of how all abstract thought works, some of the central mechanisms are becoming better understood. One particularly important structure is *conceptual metaphor* (Lakoff and Johnson 1980, 1999). In the previous chapter, I summarized one promising neural model of how conceptual metaphor might work in the brain. In the present chapter, I want to examine how abstract concepts are defined by conceptual metaphors that recruit the semantics and inference patterns of sensorimotor experience. Giving examples of key metaphors that operate in mathematics, science, and philosophy, I will then suggest that metaphor makes it possible to extend body-based meaning and inference into abstract thought. Any philosophy that cannot acknowledge this central role of metaphor in reflective thought is bound to be incapable of explaining human meaning, understanding, thinking, and communication.

The most sweeping claim of conceptual metaphor theory is that what we call abstract concepts are defined by systematic mappings from body-based, sensorimotor source domains onto abstract target domains. Consider, for example, how we understand the expression "We have a long way to go before our theory is finished." Why can we use the phrase *a long way to go,* which is literally about distance and motion through space, to talk about the completion of a mental project (developing a theory), in which there is no literal motion whatsoever? The answer is that there is a conceptual metaphor PURPOSEFUL ACTIVITIES ARE JOURNEYS, via which we understand progress toward some nonphysical goal metaphorically as progress in moving toward some destination. The metaphor consists of the following conceptual mapping of entities and relations in the source domain (physical spatial motion) onto the target domain (purposeful activities, both physical and abstract).

The PURPOSEFUL ACTIVITIES ARE JOURNEYS Metaphor

Source domain (motion in space)	*Target domain (mental activity)*
Starting Point A	→ Initial State
Ending Point B	→ Final State
Destination	→ Purpose To Be Achieved
Motion From A To B	→ Process Of Achieving Purpose
Obstacles To Motion	→ Difficulties In Achieving Purpose

This conceptual mapping also makes use of one of our most basic metaphors for understanding the passage of time (discussed in chapter 1), in which temporal change is understood metaphorically as motion along a path to some location. Recall that, in one version of this metaphor, the observer moves along a time line, with the future arrayed as the space in front of her, the past as the space behind her, and the present as her location (where she is). Consequently, when we hear "We have a long way to go until our campaign fund drive is finished," we understand ourselves metaphorically as moving along a path toward the destination (completion of the fund drive), and we understand that there can be obstacles along the way that could slow our progress.

Primary Metaphor

The PURPOSEFUL ACTIVITIES ARE JOURNEYS metaphor is a fairly high-level, broad-scope metaphor that is typical of our abstract concepts. Conceptual metaphor theory proposes that nearly all abstract conceptualization works via conceptual metaphor, conceptual metonymy, and a few other principles of imaginative extension. These high-level, systematic metaphors are usually complex combinations of more basic metaphors—called "primary metaphors" by Joseph Grady (1997)—that arise naturally from our embodied experience. A primary metaphor is based on an experiential correlation between a particular sensorimotor domain and some domain pertaining to a subjective experience or judgment. For example, each of us has repeated experiences in which being intimate (emotionally and psychologically) with a person is correlated with being physically close to them. The repeated co-activation of neural patterns associated with the subjective experience of intimacy and the sensorimotor experience of being physically close establishes the cross-domain neural connections that define the primary metaphor PSYCHOLOGICAL INTIMACY IS PHYSICAL CLOSENESS. This neural co-activation becomes the basis for a conceptual mapping of entities, structures, and relations from the source domain (physical closeness) onto the target domain (psychological intimacy). We then metaphorically conceive of being emotionally intimate with someone as being physically close to them. This primary metaphorical conception gives rise to the ordinary ways we talk about relationships, as in "We used to *be so close,* but over the past few months we've been *drifting apart,*" "She won't allow anyone to *get close to her,* for fear of being hurt," and "You keep *pushing me away,* no matter how I try to *approach you.*"

Grady hypothesizes that people will acquire hundreds, or even thousands, of primary conceptual metaphors just by going about the daily affairs of their lives. These metaphors are formed primarily because of the nature of our bodies (with their brains, sense organs, motor systems, and emotions) as they interact with our environments. We cannot avoid acquiring these metaphors, because the experiential correlations (and hence the neural co-activations) on which they are based constitute large parts of our mundane experience.

Primary metaphors thus arise naturally via our bodily perceptions and actions, as they come to shape our burgeoning experience as we grow from infancy to adulthood. Most of the time, they are activated automatically and unconsciously to structure our understanding of situations and events. Other, more complex metaphors appropriate, build on, blend, and extend our primary metaphors. We also develop large numbers of these more complex, systematic metaphors, by which we understand the abstract concepts that are held by many to distinguish us from other animals. Grady lists scores of these primary metaphors, along with the neural co-activations that underlie them; some examples are AFFECTION IS WARMTH, IMPORTANT IS BIG, MORE IS UP/LESS IS DOWN, ORGANIZATION IS PHYSICAL STRUCTURE, HAPPY IS UP/SAD IS DOWN, STATES ARE LOCATIONS, CAUSES ARE FORCES, CAUSATION IS FORCED MOTION, PURPOSES ARE DESTINATIONS, TIME IS MOTION, CONTROL IS UP, KNOWING IS SEEING, HELP IS SUPPORT, DIFFICULTIES ARE BURDENS, CATEGORIES ARE CONTAINERS, and UNDERSTANDING IS SEEING.

Metaphorical Logic

The reason that conceptual metaphor is so important, then, is that it is our primary (although not our only) means for abstract conceptualization and reasoning. It lets us appropriate the semantics and knowledge structure of a sensorimotor source domain to understand an abstract target domain. Pragmatism's principle of continuity claims that abstract thought is not disembodied; rather, it must arise from our sensorimotor capacities and is constrained by the nature of our bodies, brains, and environments. From an evolutionary perspective, this means that we have not developed two separate logical and inferential systems, one for our bodily experiences and one for our abstract concepts and reasoning (as a pure logic). Instead, the logic of our bodily experience provides all the logic we need in order to perform every rational inference, even with the most abstract concepts. In our metaphor-based reasoning, the inferences are carried out according to the corporeal logic of our sensorimotor capacities, and then, via the source-to-target mapping, the corresponding logical inferences are drawn in the target domain.

For example, there is a definite spatial or bodily logic of containment that arises in our experience with containers:

(a) An entity is either inside the container or outside it, but not both at once.
(b) If I place object O within physical container C and then put container C inside of container D, then object O is in container D.

In other words, our bodily encounters with containers and objects that we observe and manipulate teach us the spatial logic of containers.

Next, consider the common conceptual metaphor CATEGORIES ARE CONTAINERS, in which a conceptual category is understood metaphorically as an abstract container for physical and abstract entities. For example, we say that "the category 'human' is *contained in* the category 'animals,' which is *contained in* the category 'living things.'" Similarly, we may ask "Which category is this tree *in*?" On the basis of the inferential image-schematic structure of the source domain (spatial containment), and via the source-to-target mapping, we then have corresponding inferences about the logic of abstract concepts:

(a') An entity either falls within a given category or falls outside it, but not both at once. For example: Charles cannot be a man and not a man at the same time, in the same place, and in the same manner. (The law of the excluded middle)

(b') If entity E is in category C', and category C' is in category D', then entity E is in category D'. For example: All men are mortal (C' is in D') and Socrates is a man (E is in C'); therefore, Socrates is mortal (E is in D').

Thus, according to our neural model (from chapter 8), we would predict that the abstract inferences are "computed" using sensorimotor neural structure and activated as target-domain inferences because there are neural connections from sensorimotor areas of the brain to other areas that are responsible for so-called higher cognitive functions. We don't run an inferential process at the sensorimotor level and then perform an entirely different inferential process for abstract concepts like *category* or *set;* rather, we use the inference patterns found in the sensorimotor brain regions to do our abstract reasoning. In accordance with the pragmatist principle of continuity, there is no need to introduce a new kind of reasoning (with a different ontological basis) to explain logical reasoning with abstract concepts.

Conceptual Metaphor as a Basis for Abstract Conceptualization and Reasoning

We are now in a position to address the problem of the bodily grounding of meaning and the nature of abstract thought. The principal philosophical reason why image schemas and conceptual metaphors are important is that they make it possible for us to use the structure of sensory and motor operations to understand abstract concepts and to draw inferences about them. The central idea is that image schemas, which arise recurrently in our perception and bodily movement, have their own logic, which can be applied to abstract conceptual domains via primary and higher-level conceptual metaphors. Image-schematic logic then serves as the basis for inferences about abstract entities and operations.[1] From a neural perspective, this means that certain connections to sensorimotor areas are inhibited, even though the image-schematic structure remains activated and is appropriated for abstract thinking. According to this view, we do not have two kinds of logic, one for spatial-bodily concepts and a wholly different one for abstract concepts. There is no disembodied logic at all. Instead, we recruit body-based, image-schematic logic to perform abstract reasoning.[2]

Excellent examples of this use of image-schematic structure and conceptual metaphor in abstract reasoning come from mathematics, which, ironically, is traditionally conceived as the epitome of disembodied, a priori, universal thinking. In *Where Mathematics Comes From: How the Embodied Mind Brings Mathematics into Being* (2000), George Lakoff and Rafael Núñez provide detailed analyses of scores of image schemas operating within conceptual metaphors that define the basic concepts and operations across a broad range of mathematical fields. They show that mathematics is far from disembodied; indeed, it is grounded in sensorimotor schemas that are the basis for elaborate conceptual metaphors by which we understand mathematical ideas.

To cite just a couple of elementary examples, consider two of the basic metaphors by which we understand the operations of arithmetic, such as addition, subtraction, multiplication, and division. Let's begin with the COLLECTION image schema, which involves the pattern of adding objects to a group or pile or taking them away. We experience correlations between addition and the action of adding objects to a collection and between subtraction and taking objects away from a collection. Such correlations are the basis for a conceptual metaphor, in this case, one whose source domain is object collection and whose target domain is arithmetic

---

1. I am not claiming that an image-schema analysis plus conceptual metaphor is sufficient to tell the whole story of human reasoning. A complete account would include, as we have seen in earlier chapters, the role of pervasive qualities and of emotions and feelings. It would require a general theory of cogs. And, as I suggested briefly in chapters 7 and 8, it would require an explanation of social interactions, as well as of speech-act conditions and the purposes and goals of inquiry and thought.

2. See Dodge and Lakoff 2005 for one possible theory of the neural basis of image schemas.

operations. The metaphor ARITHMETIC IS OBJECT COLLECTION is a mapping of entities and operations from the source domain (object collection) onto the target domain (arithmetic).

The ARITHMETIC IS OBJECT COLLECTION Metaphor

Source domain (object collection)		Target domain (arithmetic)
Collections Of Objects Of The Same Size	→	Numbers
The Size Of The Collection	→	The Size Of The Number
Bigger	→	Greater
Smaller	→	Less
The Smallest Collection	→	The Unit (One)
Putting Collections Together	→	Addition
Taking A Smaller Collection From A Larger Collection	→	Subtraction

Lakoff and Núñez show how several key entailments of this metaphor, which involves the CONTAINER schema, generate various laws of arithmetic:

> Take the basic truths about collections of physical objects. Map them onto statements about numbers, using the metaphorical mapping. The result is a set of "truths" about natural numbers under the operations of addition and subtraction.
>
> For example, suppose we have two collections, *A* and *B,* of physical objects with *A* bigger than *B*. Now suppose we add the same collection *C* to each. Then *A* plus *C* will be a bigger collection of physical objects than *B* plus *C*. This is a fact about collections of physical objects of the same size. Using the mapping Numbers Are Collections of Objects, this physical truth that we experience in grouping objects becomes a mathematical truth about numbers: If *A* is greater than *B,* then *A+C* is greater than *B+C*. (Lakoff and Núñez 2000, 56)

This simple analysis may seem pedestrian, but Lakoff and Núñez go on to show how the analysis explains many important properties of natural numbers, such as magnitude, stability results for addition and subtraction, inverse operations, uniform ontology, closure for addition, unlimited iteration for addition, limited iteration for subtraction, sequential operations, equality of result, preservation of equality, commutativity, associativity, and on and on.

A second fundamental conceptual metaphor for arithmetic is based on a SOURCE-PATH-GOAL schema. This schema underlies our understanding of bodily motion along a path, where there is a starting point (Source) and a continuous set of steps (Path) taken toward the destination (Goal). The SOURCE-PATH-GOAL schema is the foundation for our common understanding of arithmetical operations as motions along a linear path, according to the following mapping.

The ARITHMETIC IS MOTION ALONG
A PATH Metaphor

Source domain (motion along a path)	*Target domain (arithmetic operations)*
Motions Along The Path	→ Arithmetic Operations
Point-Location On The Path	→ Result Of An Arithmetic Operation
Origin Point	→ Zero
A Point-Location	→ One
Further From The Origin Than	→ Greater Than
Closer To The Origin Than	→ Less Than
Moving From Point-Location A Away From The Origin, A Distance That Is The Same As The Distance From The Origin To Point-Location B	→ Addition Of B To A
Moving Toward The Origin From A, A Distance That Is The Same As The Distance From The Origin To B	→ Subtraction Of B From A

Notice an extremely important difference between the ARITHMETIC IS OBJECT COLLECTION metaphor and the MOTION ALONG A PATH metaphor. The logic of the former will *not* support the notion of negative numbers, because we have no experience of anything like a "negative" collection. That simply makes no sense in this metaphor. By contrast, the MOTION ALONG A PATH metaphor *does* support a conception of negative numbers, since we can think of a reverse motion from a starting point (zero) along a path in the "negative" direction. Consequently, these two metaphors are not merely alternative ways of conceptualizing the same arithmetical process. Their ontologies, the entities they posit, and the operations they support are not identical.

Thus, according to the MOTION ALONG A PATH metaphor, we utilize the structure of the SOURCE-PATH-GOAL schema plus our knowledge of the "logic" of motion along a path in order to understand and reason about arithmetical operations in abstract domains and fields. Lakoff and Núñez explore the pervasive use of this foundational metaphor to conceptualize iterative processes like multiplication and the calculation of fractions. They also provide an extensive analysis of the mathematics and geometry of the number line and of the Cartesian coordinate system as it employs the SOURCE-PATH-GOAL schema.

An analysis of the metaphors underlying basic arithmetical operations is just one small part of the Lakoff-Núñez argument for the metaphorical foundations of mathematics. They analyze the image-schematic, metaphoric, and metonymic bases of mathematical ideas such as sets, classes, hypersets, infinity, infinitesimals, real numbers, transfinite numbers, e, points, continuity, Dedekind cuts, and the Cartesian plane. They reveal the metaphorical logic of Euler's equation. Their point is to show that it is precisely image schemas and metaphors that constitute our mathematical ideas and make it possible for us to understand these ideas, perform operations on them, and apply them to aspects of our physical, social, and cultural worlds.

In short, image schemas (operating within conceptual metaphors) make it possible for us to employ the logic of our sensorimotor experience to perform high-level cognitive operations for abstract entities and domains. The resources of our bodily experience are appropriated for abstract thinking. This process of image-schematic and metaphor-based understanding has been demonstrated for many other fields besides mathematics and logic, such as law (Winter 2001; Bjerre 2005), morality (Johnson 1993; Fesmire 2003), politics (Lakoff 1996), analogical problem-solving (Gentner 1983; Craig, Nersessian, and Catrambone 2002), scientific causality (Lakoff and Johnson 1999), psychology (Gibbs 1994; Fernandez-Duque and Johnson 1999, 2002), medicine (Wright 2002), music (Cox 1999; Brower 2000; Zbikowski 2002; Johnson and Larson 2003; Echard 2005), architecture (Johnson 2002; Muller, forthcoming), advertising (Forceville 1994a, 1994b), and many other areas of abstract reasoning and theorizing.

Evidence for Conceptual Metaphor and Its Role in Abstract Reasoning

The principal sources of evidence for the existence of image schemas and conceptual metaphors are studies of language, although the sources are not limited strictly to linguistic research. The following nine types of evidence are now well represented in various fields of study.

1. *Polysemy generalizations.* This evidence consists primarily of linguistic studies of how conceptual metaphors underlie the multiple related senses of a single term, such as the use of *in* for expressions like *in the house, in the Democratic party, in love, in time, in the event of,* and *in the set of all progressive Oregonians* (Lakoff and Johnson 1980; Sweetser 1990; Lakoff and Johnson 1999). There are now scores of articles showing the metaphorical mappings that underlie polysemy in many language groups throughout the world. The journals *Metaphor and Symbol* and *Cognitive Linguistics* are rich sources for such analyses.

2. *Inferential generalizations.* As we have seen above, conceptual metaphors and image schemas generate the inferences we make using metaphorical concepts. For example, falling is an action in which one is out of control. We thus infer that "falling in love" will entail being out of control, being excited, and being scared (Kovecses 2000; Lakoff and Johnson 1980).

3. *Novel extensions.* Novel metaphors, such as those in scientific discovery, poetry, and creative problem-solving, are typically novel extensions of, or else blendings of, existing conventional conceptual metaphors. Lakoff and Mark Turner (1989), for example, analyze the mappings for a number of conventional conceptual metaphors for life and death, and then they show how extensions of these metaphors are at work in poetry and literature around the world. This work and several other studies (e.g., Steen 1997) have spawned the field of cognitive poetics.

4. *Spontaneous gesture.* David McNeill (1992) published the first major study of metaphors in spontaneous gestures, such as when a speaker who is discussing her struggle to make an important life decision holds her hands, palms up, in front of her and slightly out to her sides and alternately raises first one hand and then the other, as if weighing (by balancing) one thing (option) against another (see also Cienki 1998 and Sweetser 1998).

5. *Sign language.* Sarah Taub (1997) has analyzed some of the central metaphors in American Sign Language.

6. *Historical semantic change.* Eve Sweetser (1990) presents evidence of underlying conceptual metaphors that explain aspects of change in word meaning over time.

7. *Language-acquisition studies.* Christopher Johnson (1997) is one of several linguists and psychologists who study children's developing ability to understand and use conceptual metaphor. There is a large and growing field, dating from the early 1980s (including, e.g., Winner, Engel, and Gardner 1980; and Bowdle and Gentner 2005), studying how children ac-

quire metaphorical understanding. Bayta Maring (2003), for example, has analyzed the metaphorical bases of children's developing theories of mind.

8. *Psychological experiments.* Raymond Gibbs (1994, 2003) provides good evidence for conceptual metaphor based on various kinds of psychological experiments.

9. *Discourse-coherence analysis.* Srini Narayanan (1997b) has shown how news stories about international economics use common conceptual metaphors. But it should be noted that even beyond explicit studies of coherence, nearly any analysis of the workings of conceptual metaphor in any field of study provides vast evidence for its role in discourse coherence, so the sources of evidence here are legion.

Recently, additional new sources of evidence have become available to explain the possible neural bases for the image-schematic mappings that operate in conceptual metaphors. Although these studies are not definitive (indeed, they are often highly speculative), they at least have begun to suggest possible neural architecture that could be the basis for conceptual metaphor.

METAPHOR AS THE BASIS FOR PHILOSOPHY

If our abstract concepts are defined primarily by conceptual metaphors, then theoretical and practical reasoning in every conceivable field and discipline should be based on metaphor. They are. As I noted earlier, there are a growing number of studies examining the defining metaphors of fields such as physics, chemistry, psychology, anthropology, philosophy, religion, politics, and law.

I want to exemplify this type of analysis by investigating some of the ways in which philosophy would not exist without the systems of conceptual metaphors that define its key ideas. I suggest that the bodily grounding of philosophical ideas via metaphors is not a liability of the discipline, but rather is what makes philosophy potentially important for our lives. The metaphors define our key philosophical ideas and give us a way of understanding whatever relevance these ideas might have for our lives. Without metaphor, there would be no philosophy, nor any other mode of reflective understanding of our world.

What Is at Issue in the Question of Metaphor?

Philosophy's debt to metaphor is profound and immeasurable. However, philosophy's debt is neither greater nor less than that of any other significant human intellectual field or discipline. Philosophers must use the same conceptual resources possessed by any human being, and the potential for any philosophy to make sense of a person's life depends directly on the fact that all of us are metaphoric animals.

What I have just said is not now, nor has it ever been, widely accepted by philosophers. In fact, for the major part of our philosophical history, the idea that metaphor lies at the heart of human conceptualization and reasoning has been rejected.[3] One could even make a crude distinction between two types of philosophy: (1) objectivist and literalist philosophies, which see metaphor as a dispensable linguistic appurtenance; and (2) philosophies that regard any particular philosophical viewpoint as a creative elaboration of some specific set of basic conceptual metaphors.

The history of Western philosophy is, for the most part, one long development of the objectivist dismissal of metaphor, punctuated rarely by bold declarations (such as Nietzsche's) of the pervasiveness of metaphor in all thought. Where a philosopher stands on this key issue can be determined by their answer to one question: are our abstract concepts defined by metaphor, or not? Once the question is formulated in this manner, it is easy to see the profound philosophical stakes. If our most fundamental abstract concepts—such as those for causation, events, will, thought, reason, knowledge, mind, justice, and rights—are irreducibly metaphoric, then philosophy must consist in the analysis, criticism, elaboration, and creative blending of the metaphorical concepts out of which philosophies are made. If, on the other hand, you believe that our most important philosophical concepts are, in the final analysis, literal, then you will regard metaphor as cognitively insignificant, and you will relegate it to what you disparagingly regard as some distant corner of philosophy, typically the unfairly maligned field of aesthetics.

Anyone who thinks that there is really nothing very important at stake here should consider the following. There are a number of perennial philosophical questions that arise over and over again throughout history, any time you reflect on the nature of human experience. These are questions such as: What is mind, and how does it work? What is meaning? What does it mean to be a person? Is there such a thing as human will, and is it free? What is the nature of reality? What can I know, and how can I go about gaining that knowledge? What things or states are "good" and should therefore be pursued? Are certain actions morally required of us?

---

3. In "Metaphor in the Philosophical Tradition" (1981), I have surveyed some of the more influential expressions in Western philosophy of the denial of a serious cognitive role for metaphor.

Does God exist (and what difference would it make)? Is there any meaning to human existence, or is life absurd? *Both the framing of these questions and the kinds of answers we give to them depend on metaphor. You cannot address any of these questions without engaging metaphor.* Consequently, an adequate philosophy must include an extensive inquiry into the workings of metaphor and how it shapes our most important philosophical ideas.

Philosophical Concepts Are Metaphoric

From a practical standpoint, it is obviously not possible to make an exhaustive survey showing that *all* our philosophical concepts are defined by conceptual metaphors. Instead, I will examine one key concept—causation—to indicate its metaphorical constitution, and I will then suggest that causation is a highly representative example of the role of conceptual metaphor in defining all our abstract concepts.

I have selected causation as the exemplary metaphorically defined concept because it is hard to imagine a metaphysical concept that is more fundamental than causation. It lies at the heart of all of the sciences, it is pervasive in our folk theories of the world, and it is a philosophical linchpin of virtually every ontology. When the first substantial metaphor analysis of our causal concepts emerged within cognitive linguistics over a decade ago, it became clear that the implications of this research were stunning. In my own analytic philosophical training, most of the books and articles I read assumed science to be a superior form of knowledge, partly because of its ability to give causal explanations of events. In one philosophical treatise after another, I was struck by how philosophers referred to "causes" as if they were objective forces or entities and as if there existed basically one kind of natural causation (as revealed in expressions such as "X caused Y" and "The cause of Y is X"). In an attempt to explain human actions, many philosophers also spoke of "agent causality," in order to carve out a space for human "willing"; but in physical nature, natural causes ruled the day. So, there seemed to be at least one type of cause (i.e., physical), but not more than two types (adding agent causation to physical causation), and both conceptions were thought to be literal, not metaphorical. Causes were alleged to be literal entities or forces in the world.

This picture, as we will see, turns out to be mistaken, and badly so. It is a mistake that has disastrous consequences. To see why this is so, let us begin with an analysis of one of our most often used concepts of causation, that of causation as a physical force. Once detailed analyses had been performed on the semantics of our causal terms, the metaphorical nature of this concept became quite evident. In cognitive linguistics, the study of causal concepts emerged from the study of how people conceptualize events generally. The first prominent causal metaphor that was studied involved an understanding of change of state as (metaphorical) motion from one location to another, according to the following general mapping.

The LOCATION EVENT-STRUCTURE Metaphor

Source domain (motion in space)		*Target domain (events)*
Locations In Space	→	States
Movement From One Location To Another	→	Change Of State
Physical Forces	→	Causes
Forced Movement	→	Causation
Self-Propelled Movements	→	Actions
Destinations	→	Purposes
Paths To Destinations	→	Means To Ends
Impediments To Motion	→	Difficulties

The LOCATION EVENT-STRUCTURE metaphor comprises a complex system of several submappings, each of which is what Grady (1997) calls a primary metaphor. In English, the semantics of our terms for events is given by the detailed structure of the mapping. Each submapping supports a large number of expressions whose dependence on metaphor goes largely unnoticed in our ordinary discourse. For example, the submapping Change Of State Is Movement underlies expressions such as "The water *went from* hot *to* cold," "The system is *moving toward* homeostasis," and "The pizza *is somewhere between* warm and cold." The submapping Causation Is Forced Movement is evident in "The fire *brought* the water to a boil," "His treachery *pushed* the king over the edge," and "The candidate's speech *threw* the crowd into a frenzy."

Notice how these submappings code various dimensions of what linguists call *aspect*, which concerns the means and manner of an action. For instance, we say "The fire *brought* the water to a boil" but not *"the fire *threw* the water to a boil," for a very good reason. In the source domain of physical forces and motions, to *bring* something is to apply continuous force to an object to move it from one location to another, causing it to end up in that new place, or in some person's possession. When metaphorically extended to causation in general, the semantics of *bring* thus entails continuous application of force to bring about a change of state. *Bringing* water to a boil entails the constant heating of the water until it boils (i.e., until it arrives at the metaphorical boiling-state location). *Throwing* a physical object, by contrast, involves an initial application of strong force with the object continuing to move to a new location, even after the force is no longer applied. Thus *threw,* according to the submapping, is not appropriate for the case of boiling water, though it is just the right term for "Babe Ruth's home run *threw* the crowd into a frenzy."

Now, how could a literalist philosopher have any adequate account of the semantics of *throw,* as revealed in this case of Babe Ruth's home run? Will she say that there is a purely literal way to express the type of causation involved here? But there isn't. If we say "Babe Ruth's home run *caused* the crowd to get emotionally excited," we lose the key semantic details expressed by *threw.* "Caused to get excited" does *not* capture the *manner* of the causation, which is rapid initial "force" followed by an extended trajectory after the initial event.

The crucial moral of this example is that the precise details of the semantics of basic causation terms are determined only by the submappings of the metaphors. The inferences we make about causal situations come from the metaphorical structure of our causation concepts. *You cannot grasp the meaning of the causal terms, nor can you do appropriate causal reasoning, without the metaphors.*

Moreover, the case of causation is even more complicated than it at first appears, because there turn out to be many different metaphorical conceptions of types of causation. Analyses to date reveal upward of twenty distinct metaphors that express twenty kinds of causation (see Lakoff and Johnson 1999, chap. 11). A brief survey of just a few of these additional metaphors is highly instructive. It smashes the illusion of core literal concepts of causation and of any objectivist philosophy that purports to be founded on such concepts.

Consider, for instance, a second major metaphor system for certain types of causation, one that conceives of change of state or having an attribute (or property) as the acquisition of a possession.

The OBJECT EVENT-STRUCTURE Metaphor

Source domain (transfer of possessions) | *Target domain (change of state)*
| |
Possession | → Attribute
Movement Of Possession | → Change Of State
Transfer Of Possession | → Causation
Desired Objects | → Purposes

The submapping Causation Is Transfer Of Possession is evident in expressions such as "Professor Johnson's lecture on causation *gave* me a headache, but the aspirin *took* it *away*," "Mary *gave* her cold to Janice," and "Janice *caught* Mary's cold." Even our common philosophical notion of a property is based on this metaphorical mapping. What does it mean for an object to *possess* a property? To possess something is to stand in a certain relationship to that object so that it becomes associated with you. So, metaphorically, to *have* or *possess* a certain property defines a certain relation between you and that abstract property. When something *loses* a property, it no longer manifests the features appropriate to that property. Additionally, there are many other submappings within this causation metaphor that specify various ways of acquiring a desired object, which equates metaphorically with acquiring a certain property or attribute and thus achieving a purpose. For example, there is the submapping Achieving A Purpose Is Getting Food, as in "I'm *hungry* for advancement," "All the best jobs were *gobbled up* early on," and "It was a *mouth-watering* opportunity." Each of the various ways we acquire food, such as hunting, fishing, and agriculture, show up in the language of our purposeful action:

- Trying To Achieve A Purpose Is Hunting
  I'm still job *hunting*. She is *aiming* for rapid advancement in the firm. Larry *bagged* a promotion. That idea *won't hunt*.
- Trying To Achieve A Purpose Is Fishing
  Ann *landed* a big promotion. Before that, she *had a line out* for a new job. My boss is always *fishing* for compliments. Every night he's out *trolling* for a date.
- Trying To Achieve A Purpose Is Agriculture
  Every worker should *reap the fruits* of his or her labor. That promotion is *ripe for the picking*. Harry's been *cultivating* several job prospects.

Metaphorically based expressions like these are not just colloquialisms, used loosely in ordinary talk. Once again, the submappings of the metaphor specify the precise details of the semantics of causation and determine what types of inferences we will make. Some people harbor the illusion that good science would merely avoid such expressions in causal explanations. But, as it turns out, there is *no way* to avoid the use of one or another basic causal metaphor in science, and scientists reason on the basis of the entailments of the submappings of these metaphors.

In the social sciences, for example, there are a number of quite specific metaphors that can be used for the types of causal explanation appropriate for the science of those fields. One especially common case is the Causal Path metaphor.

The CAUSAL PATH Metaphor

Source domain (motion along a path)		Target domain (events)
Self-Propelled Motion	→	Action
Traveler	→	Actor
Locations	→	States
A Lone Path	→	A Natural Course Of Action
Being On The Path	→	Natural Causation
Leading To	→	Results In
End Of The Path	→	Resulting Final State

This metaphor underlies such expressions as "Pot smoking leads *to* drug addiction," "As a nation, we're *careening* wildly *down the road* to destruction," "That *path* will *get you nowhere*," and "You're *heading for* catastrophe."

The CAUSAL PATH metaphor plays a key role in certain types of causal explanation for human actions. It utilizes our common knowledge about motion through space to some destination: if you start down a certain path, you will naturally end up where that path leads you, unless something intervenes to retard or block your progress. Metaphorically, then, if you start down a certain "path" of action, it will typically lead you to a certain destination (end), unless something intervenes to retard or block your metaphorical movement. This argument is used by those who believe that certain actions or behaviors will necessitate a certain specific outcome in the ordinary course of events (a colorful example would be the 1950s song lyrics "Son, you're gonna drive me to drinkin', if you don't stop drivin' that hot rod Lincoln"). In politics, the CAUSAL PATH metaphor can have decisive impacts. In recent U.S. history, we have often heard the argument that a particular third-world country is "on the road to democracy [read: capitalism]," so that if we will just eliminate any potential obstacles (i.e., if we intervene politically, economically, militarily, or covertly), then that country will naturally and inevitably continue along the path to the desired end state (namely, democracy). Billions of dollars and sometimes even the lives of citizens are sacrificed to supposedly ensure the smooth, unrestricted motion of some metaphorical entity (a country, an economy, or a political institution) along a metaphorical causal path to a metaphorically defined destination.[4]

4. The tight logic of this metaphor has been the dominant argument of the Bush administration for "staying the course" in Iraq, at a cost (so far) of hundreds of billions of dollars, thousands of lives, and many times more maimings and injuries to coalition soldiers and Iraqi citizens.

Another important metaphor in political and economic debate is the PLATE TECTONICS metaphor for social, political, and economic change, which is appropriated from the geological theory of plate tectonics. According to the logic of this metaphor, continuous, long-term application of "pressure" to a system, institution, or state will eventually result in a rapid, massive causal consequence. The surprisingly swift disintegration of the Soviet Union in 1991 is supposed by some to be a classic example of this process. In U.S. political debate, when large, sustained infusions of funds or other resources do not appear to be producing the desired change in a government or economy (usually both), the PLATE TECTONICS metaphor is frequently invoked to argue for the continued commitment of public resources, on the assumption that we need just a little bit more pressure to produce an eventual massive transformation.

A thorough analysis of the full range of causation metaphors could be continued along similar lines. In *Philosophy in the Flesh* (1999), George Lakoff and I summarized the mappings and entailments of nearly twenty different causal metaphors, showing how several of them are employed within various sciences. A number of key philosophical points emerge from these analyses.

(1) An adequate conceptual analysis (in this case, of causation concepts) must provide generalizations that explain the precise details of the semantics of the terms and must explain the inferences we make concerning those concepts. The details of the semantics of each causal concept are provided by the submappings that jointly constitute the metaphor, whereas the inferential structure is drawn from our shared knowledge of the source domain.

(2) All of the basic causation concepts we studied are metaphoric.

(3) There appears to be what we called a "literal skeleton" shared by all causation concepts, namely, that a cause is a determining factor in a situation. However, this bare skeleton is far too underspecified to generate any serious causal reasoning in the sciences. It is the metaphors that give rise to the relevant conceptual structure and that constrain the appropriate causal inferences.

(4) Several of the main causation metaphors are mutually inconsistent. In other words, there are significant metaphors that have incompatible ontologies. For example, in the LOCATION EVENT-STRUCTURE metaphor, we have the submapping States Are (stationary) Locations, and the object or agent changes by moving to a particular (metaphorical) location. In contrast, in the OBJECT EVENT-STRUCTURE metaphor, a state is an object that moves, rather than being a stationary location. Consequently, these two metaphors cannot be reduced to a consistent literal concept.

(5) *Causation* is thus a massive radial category. At the center of the category is the closest thing to a literal conception—something like the application of physical force to an object that results in a change in its state or location. One example of this is what we call "billiard-ball causation." Farther out from these prototypical causes are extended cases, such as indirect causes, action at a distance, and agent causation. Other, less prototypical kinds of causation are metaphorically defined.

If we take stock of the argument so far, the results are devastating for any objectivist and literalist philosophy. At least with respect to causation, there is no single literal concept of *cause* that captures the semantics and inference structure of all the different concepts of causation, nor are there even two or three basic literal concepts. There is no set of necessary and sufficient conditions that define all causes. Instead, there are twenty or more metaphorical concepts used by ordinary people, scientists, and philosophers in their reasoning about causation. This conclusion does not undermine science at all. It only reminds us that different scientific approaches rely on different metaphorical concepts, concepts that can be more or less appropriate in different situations and that dictate what counts as evidence and argument within a given science. What these analyses do undermine are objectivist philosophies that accept a classical theory of literal meaning, a classical objectivist metaphysics, and a classical correspondence theory of truth.

Moreover, it appears that what is true of our causal concepts holds for all of our most important abstract philosophical concepts. There does not now exist, and there probably never will exist, an exhaustive metaphorical analysis of the full range of perennial philosophical concepts and arguments. Such an analysis would be a daunting task. However, a surprisingly large number of philosophical concepts have been subjected to conceptual metaphor analysis over the past decade and a half. Some of the more prominent concepts for which we have at least a preliminary metaphorical analysis are *event, cause, action, state, property, purpose, mind, thought, concepts, reason, emotions, knowledge, being, attention, communication, self, will, moral rule, rights, justice, duty, good, happiness, society, democracy, love, marriage, number, set, infinity, addition* (and *subtraction, multiplication,* etc.), *the Cartesian plane,* and a host of other mathematical concepts.

The most extensive survey to date of the foundational metaphors of Western philosophy is found in Lakoff and Johnson 1999. The number of key concepts analyzed so far, and the depth of those analyses, strongly supports the prospect that *all* our abstract concepts, not just our philosophical ideas, are defined by conceptual metaphor and metonymy. If this is so, then philosophical analysis is primarily metaphor analysis—working out the logic and inferential structure of the metaphors that ground our basic philosophical understanding of experience. Philosophical theories, like all theoretical constructions, are elaborations of conceptual metaphors. In a very strong sense, philosophy *is* metaphor.

Metaphor and Contemporary Philosophy of Language

The reality of conceptual metaphor and its central role in abstract conceptualization and reasoning call into question large parts of traditional Western philosophical theories of meaning and truth, and also challenge some parts of contemporary philosophy of mind and language. If our abstract concepts are metaphorically structured, then the classical objectivist and literalist view must be false. According to objectivist metaphysics and objectivist theories of knowledge, the world consists of objects, properties, and relations that exist in themselves, independent of human conceptual systems and human agency (Putnam 1981). Meaning is a matter of how our concepts map onto or pick out aspects of this mind-independent objective reality. Literal concepts are the direct connection between what we think (or what is in our mind) and how the world is, and this connection (called variously "reference" and "intentionality") is the basis for the possibility of truth, which is taken to be a correspondence relation between propositions and states of affairs in the world. There cannot be any significant role for metaphor in this picture of mind and world, because the cognitive content of a metaphor would need to be reducible to some set of literal concepts or propositions if it were to have any meaning and play a role in truth claims.

Quite obviously, if conceptual metaphor is essential for abstract thought, then the objectivist and literalist picture cannot be correct. Conceptual metaphor is a structure of human understanding, and the source domains of the metaphors come from our bodily, sensorimotor experience, which becomes the basis for abstract conceptualization and reasoning. From this perspective, truth is a matter of how our body-based understanding of a sentence fits, or fails to fit, our body-based understanding of a situation. And when we are thinking with abstract concepts, that understanding involves conceptual metaphor. There is a form of "correspondence" here—a fitting of our understanding of a statement and our understanding of a situation. But this is not the classic correspondence of literal propositions to objective states of affairs in the world. Instead, the correspondence is mediated by embodied understanding of both the sentence and the situation.

In spite of the growing body of empirical research on conceptual meta-phor that has emerged over the past two and a half decades, contemporary analytic philosophy of language has, for the most part, refused to recognize the existence of conceptual metaphor. This is not surprising, considering that to do so would undermine certain fundamental assumptions of some parts of analytic philosophy. I want to briefly examine two of the most popular contemporary views of metaphor within analytic philosophy of language—that of John Searle and the view shared by Donald Davidson and Richard Rorty—in order to show why these views cannot accept the reality of conceptual metaphor and how they are done in by its existence.

Searle (1979) approaches metaphor from a speech-act perspective, and he regards the activity of speaking a language as a highly conventionalized, rule-governed form of behavior. Searle is also a literalist. He believes that the possibility of truth claims and a robust realism require that all meaning be reducible to literal concepts and propositions that can, in the last analysis, correspond to states of affairs in the world. According to Searle's account, various types of illocutionary speech acts would be rule-governed functions on these basic propositional contents. So, the problem of metaphor within Searle's philosophy of language is to state the rules by which the literal sentence meaning "S is P" can, when used for a meta-phorical utterance, come to be interpreted by a hearer as a different literal utterance meaning "S is R". On Searle's view, the hearer must recognize that the speaker cannot be intending to convey the literal meaning of the utterance; the hearer must then calculate the alternate meanings that the speaker might possibly be intending and must, finally, determine which is the most appropriate literal meaning in the present context.

The problem with this objectivist and literalist version of the speech-act approach is that it simply cannot explain how metaphors actually work. Searle correctly sees that most metaphors are *not* based on an underlying set of literal similarities that might explain how P (in "S is P") calls up R (in "S is R") when we hear the metaphorical utterance. Searle uses the example "Sally is a block of ice" to show that there are no literal similarities between Sally and a block of ice that could be the basis for the meaning of the metaphor. But Searle has no alternative specification of the rules for cases that cannot be based on similarities. He must surely recognize that his final attempt to formulate a rule for certain types of metaphors is *no explanation at all!* "Things which are P are not R, nor are they like R things, nor are they believed to be R; nonetheless it is a fact about our sensibility, whether culturally or naturally determined, that we just do perceive a connection" (Searle 1979, 108). Saying that it just "is a fact about our sensibility" that we do make certain connections does not explain anything. When a literalist is forced to admit that certain metaphors are not based on any literal similarities between the source and target domains, then his literalism leaves him without resources to explain where the meaning comes from or how it is possible.

Conceptual metaphor theory, however, solves this problem by rejecting literalism and by recognizing the pervasive structuring of our abstract concepts by metaphor. On this view, metaphors are based on experiential correlations, not on similarities. Conceptual metaphor theory can explain why "Sally is a block of ice" means what it means, once we recognize it as an instance of Joseph Grady's primary metaphor AFFECTION IS WARMTH. Grady hypothesizes that this metaphor is based not on similarities between warmth and affection, but rather on our experience, from infancy, of being held affectionately and at the same time feeling warmth from the other person's body. Multiple experiences of this sort in childhood would involve a neuronal co-activation of brain areas tied to the experience of bodily warmth and those tied to the subjective experience of affection and nurturance. This co-activation later becomes the basis for the primary metaphor AFFECTION IS WARMTH. The reason that Searle's example works as an argument against the similarity theory of metaphor is that there are, indeed, no literal similarities between a person named Sally and a block of ice that could explain the meaning of the metaphorical expression. This expression is not based on similarities; if anything, the similarities are a result of the experienced correlation. However, Searle cannot accept this alternative theory, because his literalism does not permit him to recognize that metaphoric source-to-target mappings could be as basic to our thought as are literal concepts. Searle's theory is constrained by his traditional objectivist views of meaning, knowledge, and truth.

Another extremely popular view of metaphor is Donald Davidson's deflationary rejection of metaphoric meaning. In his 1978 article "What Metaphors Mean," Davidson provocatively answers that they do not *mean* anything at all, or at least nothing beyond the ordinary literal meaning of the utterance used in the metaphor. In short, Davidson simply denies that metaphor is a semantic phenomenon, and he thus denies that metaphor has anything to do with making truth claims: "We must give up the idea that a metaphor carries a message, that it has a content or meaning (except, of course, its literal meaning)" (Davidson 1978, 45). Metaphor is only a pragmatic effect achieved by using a certain literal utterance to induce the hearer to notice something. Davidson says that a metaphorical utterance uses its literal meaning to "intimate" or "suggest" some nonpropositional insight: "Seeing as is not seeing that. Metaphor makes us see one thing as another by making some literal statement that inspires or prompts the insight" (ibid., 47).

Richard Rorty has become the flamboyant spokesman for Davidson's nonsemantic theory of metaphor. Seizing on Davidson's claim that metaphor is not about propositional content or meaning of any kind, Rorty describes metaphors as linguistic flares that catch and redirect the hearer's attention:

> Tossing a metaphor into a conversation is like suddenly breaking off the conversation long enough to make a face, or pulling a photograph out of your pocket and displaying it, or pointing at a feature of the surroundings, or slapping your interlocutor's face, or kissing him. Tossing a metaphor into a text is like using italics, or illustrations, or odd punctuation or formats.
>
> All these are ways of producing effects on your interlocutor or your reader, but not ways of conveying a message. (Rorty 1989, 18)

This view of metaphor as a nonsemantic use of language for certain attention-getting or other pragmatic purposes has an important implication that Rorty is quick to note. The distinction between the "literal" and the "metaphorical" is seen not as one "between two sorts of meaning, nor a distinction between two sorts of interpretation, but as a distinction between familiar and unfamiliar uses of noises and marks" (Rorty 1989, 17). According to Rorty, these "unfamiliar" marks and noises *somehow* get us searching for new vocabularies in which they are no longer unfamiliar, but he has no account whatsoever of how this process is supposed to work.

The considerable popularity of both Searle's view and the Davidson-Rorty view is easily understandable within the framework of analytic philosophy of language. Different as these two views may appear to be on the surface, they share a set of grounding assumptions about meaning and truth that are foundational for analytic philosophy. In particular, they agree (1) that meaning is conceptual and propositional in nature, (2) that meaning is truth-conditional (along with other illocutionary-act conditions), and (3) that only literal concepts can be the bearers of meaning. Searle thinks that metaphors can have a semantic content of sorts, but he is at a loss as to how to explain that possibility, since he sees that metaphors typically are not based on literal similarities and do not seem to be literal propositions. Davidson and Rorty think that metaphors have no semantic content, are not propositional, and so cannot be bearers of truth.

Both theories are badly mistaken. Both theories are at odds with the growing body of empirical research on conceptual metaphor as a basic operation of abstract thinking. It should come as no surprise that neither Searle nor Davidson pays any serious attention to the work of cognitive linguists on the semantics of natural languages. If they did, they would have acknowledged the pervasive role of conceptual metaphor in abstract conceptualization and reasoning. How could Searle, or especially Davidson, explain analyses of the semantics and inference structure of metaphors for causation? Their literalist views have no resources whatsoever to explain the polysemy and inference generalizations that are explained in cognitive linguistics by the source-to-target mappings. Rorty sees quite clearly that his view has nothing at all to say about the meaning and motivation for basic metaphors in science and philosophy:

> For all we know, or should care, Aristotle's metaphorical use of *ousia,* Saint Paul's metaphorical use of *agapē,* and Newton's metaphorical use of *gravitas,* were the results of cosmic rays scrambling the fine structure of some crucial neurons in their respective brains. Or, more plausibly, they were the result of some odd episodes in infancy—some obsessional kinks left in these brains by idiosyncratic traumata. It hardly matters how the trick was done. The results were marvelous. (Rorty 1989, 17)

This is extremely clever, and beautifully expressed, but it is quite wrongheaded. For it *does* matter "how the trick was done." It *does* matter where these metaphors came from—that is, why we have the ones we do, how they are grounded experientially, and how they shape our thought. Moreover, there are (at least partial) answers to such questions—answers provided by conceptual metaphor theory, ones that challenge some of the basic assumptions of contemporary analytic philosophy of language.

Rorty is probably right that we aren't going to explain why St. Paul came up with precisely the metaphor for love that he did. But that does not mean that his metaphor was an irrational, unmotivated miracle, or a chance occurrence. Our inability to predict what novel metaphors will emerge does not entail the opposite extreme—that metaphors just happen, irrationally. On the contrary, there is a great deal that we can say about what St. Paul's metaphor means, about how it connects with the other conceptual metaphors for love that were common in his time (and in ours), and about how his metaphor extends or creatively blends aspects of these other metaphors. Conceptual metaphor theory can explain how this new metaphor could possibly make sense to people and how they could draw inferences about its implications for how they should live their lives. Within cognitive linguistics, there already exist extensive analyses of the mappings for the key metaphors for love in our culture (Lakoff and Johnson 1980; Kovecses 1988, 2000). Nor did the Aristotelian conception of *ousia* spring fully armed from the head of Aristotle. Lakoff and I (1999) have traced some of the main steps in the development of the metaphorical understanding of Being that begins with the Presocratic philosophers, blossoms in Plato, and is transformed in Aristotle. The idea of Being (including Aristotle's conception of it) is a construction from various folk theories and conceptual metaphors concerning the nature of categories and entities in the world. Aristotle's *ousia* is a remarkable achievement, but it is not a miracle.

If, like Davidson and Rorty, you don't see that metaphor is a semantic phenomenon, then it should come as no surprise that, like them, you will regard metaphor merely as a nonrational rupture in a conceptual system (or, to use Rorty's favorite term, a "vocabulary") that inexplicably gives rise to a new way of talking. If you miss the experiential grounding of primary metaphors, you will, like Rorty, think that metaphor change is relatively arbitrary and not rationally motivated. Moreover, you will not recognize the crucial role of metaphor in shaping and constraining inference in ordinary thinking, scientific research, and philosophical theorizing. Davidson and Rorty are literalists. Because they are oblivious to the pervasive workings of conceptual metaphor in shaping our conceptual systems, they cannot see how metaphor lies at the heart of human understanding and reasoning.

Philosophy as Metaphor

Virtually all of our abstract concepts appear to be structured by multiple, typically inconsistent conceptual metaphors. If this is true, then philosophical theories are not systems of foundational literal truths about reality, but rather elaborations of particular complex, intertwining sets of metaphors that support inferences and forms of reasoning. Humanizing and embodying philosophy in this manner does not devalue it in any way. On the contrary, it reveals why we have the philosophies we do, explains why and how they can make sense of our experience, and traces out their implications for our lives.

In *Philosophy in the Flesh* (1999), Lakoff and I analyzed several philosophical orientations to reveal their underlying metaphors. That analysis included Presocratic metaphysics, Platonic and Aristotelian doctrines of

Being, Cartesian views of mind and thought, eighteenth-century faculty psychology, Kantian moral theory, and some of the founding assumptions of analytic philosophy of mind and language. As an example of how a metaphorical analysis of this kind might proceed and how it might be useful in analyzing any philosophical view or system, I want to consider Jerry Fodor's "language of thought" metaphor for mind, because it has been so influential in recent philosophy of mind.

Fodor wants to defend what he regards as a scientifically sophisticated version of the widespread folk theory that to have a mind is to have mental states (e.g., beliefs, wants, fears, hopes) that purport to be "about" aspects of our world. Thinking, as he sees it, must consist of chains of inner mental states that are somehow connected to each other (i.e., one thought leads to another) and that are also somehow connected to aspects of our experience (i.e., things in the world "cause" us to have the specific mental representations that we have). There are thus two major parts to Fodor's theory: (1) how the mental states are related, and (2) how those mental states are connected to the world (or how they are caused).

The first part of his theory consists of the claim that these mental states form a "language of thought": "A train of thoughts . . . is a causal sequence of tokenings of mental representations which express propositions that are the objects of the thoughts" (Fodor 1987, 17). The language of thought is purely computational:

> Mental states are relations between organisms and internal representations, and causally interrelated mental states succeed one another according to computational principles which apply formally *to the representations*. This is the sense in which internal representations provide the domains for such data processes as inform the mental life. It is, in short, of the essence of cognitive theories that they seek to interpret physical (causal) transformations as transformations of information, with the effect of exhibiting the rationality of mental processes. (Fodor 1975, 198)

Fodor's language of thought (sometimes called "mentalese") consists of symbols that in themselves are completely meaningless but that can be given meaning by the ways in which they are caused or "tokened" by certain events in the world. The mental representations in this language of thought are precisely like the arbitrary, meaningless symbols in computer programs. Within a computational program, operations are performed entirely on the formal (syntactic) features of the symbols, and Fodor believes that such features can "mimic" what we think of as semantic relations between our various mental representations: "Within certain famous limits, the semantic relation that holds between two symbols when the proposition expressed by the one is entailed by the proposition expressed by the other can be mimicked by syntactic relations in virtue of which one of the symbols is derivable from the other" (Fodor 1987, 19).

The second key part of Fodor's theory concerns the causal grounding of the internal representations. His claim is that these symbols are mental *representations* by virtue of the way they are caused by aspects of the world. Fodor summarizes this aspect of his theory thus: "I want a *naturalized* theory of meaning: a theory that articulates, in nonsemantic and nonintentional terms, sufficient conditions for one bit of the world to *be about* (to express, represent, or be true of) another bit" (Fodor 1987, 98).

Fodor and his followers believe that the language of thought hypothesis expresses literal truths about the nature of mind, namely, that the mind is a computational functional program, that thinking is governed by syntactic rules, and that the meaningless symbols of mentalese are given meaning through their relation to aspects of our experience that cause them to be tokened in our minds. There exists a large body of empirical research in the cognitive sciences that shows why this view of mind cannot be correct, but that is not my focus here. Rather, my point is to show that Fodor's entire model of mind, thought, and language is composed of a series of interwoven complex metaphors that give rise to specific entailments about the nature of mind and the operations of thought.

Fodor's key claim that all human thinking has the form of a language is an idea (a false idea) deeply rooted in our ordinary and philosophical ways of thinking. Because we so often express our thoughts in language, we are easily seduced into believing that human thinking has the form of a language. In other words, we presuppose the THOUGHT AS LANGUAGE metaphor.

The THOUGHT AS LANGUAGE Metaphor

Source domain (linguistic acts)	Target domain (thinking)
Linguistic Activity (Speaking/Writing)	→ Thinking
Words	→ Ideas
Sentences	→ Complex Ideas
Spelling	→ Communicating A Sequence Of Thoughts
Writing	→ Memorization

Our ordinary ways of thinking about the operations of mind and thought draw massively on our conception of written and spoken language. The idea that thoughts are linguistic forms written in the mind is the basis for expressions such as "Let me make a *mental note* of that," "She's an *open book* to me—I can *read* her every thought," "The public *misread* the president's intentions," and "Do you think I'm some kind of mind-*reader*?" Spoken language also provides a rich source domain for our conception of thinking as speaking, as in "She doesn't *listen to* her conscience," "I can barely *hear* myself think," and "That *sounds* like a good idea." The THOUGHT AS LANGUAGE metaphor covers all types of intellectual activity, as in "Liberals and conservatives don't *speak the same language*," "He can't *translate* his good ideas into practice," "What is the *vocabulary* of basic philosophical ideas?" and "I wouldn't *read* too much into what he's saying." Notice also that according to this mapping, careful, step-by-step thinking is conceived as careful spelling, as when we say "Our theory of embodied meaning is *spelled out* in chapter 3," "Do I have to *spell it out* for you?" and "He always *follows the letter* of the law."

Fodor's LANGUAGE OF THOUGHT metaphor makes intuitive sense to many people precisely because most of us assume that a purely formal language can be meaningful in the same way that a natural language is meaningful. That is, we assume the FORMAL LANGUAGE metaphor.

The FORMAL LANGUAGE Metaphor

Source domain (natural language)		*Target domain (formal language)*
Written Signs	→	Abstract Formal Symbols
A Natural Language	→	A Formal Language
Sentences	→	Well-Formed Symbol Sequences
Syntax	→	Principles For Combining Formal Symbols

Fodor correctly understands that a truly computational theory of mind requires that the language of thought be a formal language (akin to a computer language), and that a formal language cannot be modeled on a natural language. A formal language is an artificial language that, unlike natural languages, consists entirely of arbitrary, meaningless symbols, each of which has specific formal (syntactic) features that play a role in formal operations specified for the language.

The key problem with the FORMAL LANGUAGE metaphor is that actual formal languages do not and cannot possess the key features that make it possible for natural languages to be meaningful.[5] Consequently, if mind is a computational program (as in the MIND AS COMPUTER metaphor), then the language of thought will not, in itself, be meaningful in any way. As a result, Fodor must officially reject the FORMAL LANGUAGE metaphor. But then he is left with the problem of how an intrinsically meaningless language of thought can somehow acquire meaning.

Fodor's answer, as noted above, is that "tokenings" of particular mental symbols must become "representations" by being "caused" by objects and events that we experience. In other words, the "inner" mental symbols must be causally connected to things outside the mind. In his book *Psychosemantics* (1987), Fodor tries to develop a causal theory of how the symbols in mentalese can become meaningful—that is, how the symbols can come to be related to things "outside" the mind. Although I cannot argue this here, Fodor is ultimately unable to explain how there is a determinate connection between being in a certain situation and having certain specific symbols tokened in the mind. He cannot establish such relations for the reasons that W. V. O. Quine (1951) earlier articulated; namely, the "input" is always subject to multiple interpretations, so there is seldom or never a one-to-one correspondence between a mental symbol and an aspect of the "world" fixed uniquely by alleged causal relations.

Philosophy's Debt to Metaphor

My interest here is not to evaluate the adequacy of Fodor's theory of mind and language. It is, rather, to show that his theory is based on a set of intertwined conceptual metaphors that operate (mostly unconsciously) in our culture. It is no criticism of a philosophical or scientific theory to show the underlying metaphors on which it rests. Indeed, it is the metaphors that make it possible for the theories to make sense of our experience. *All* theories are based on metaphors, because all our abstract concepts are metaphorically defined. Understanding the constitutive metaphors allows us to grasp the logic and entailments of the theory. However, once one understands the underlying metaphors and how they are supposedly related, this can often be the basis for mounting a critique of one or more parts of a theory. In general, our analyses will often reveal various common meta-

---

5. Putnam (1981, 1987, 1988) has surveyed the chief arguments against functionalist views of mind and against attempts to think of formal languages as possessing the same characteristics (for meaning) that natural languages have. See also Lakoff and Johnson 1999, chapter 21.

phors that persist within a coherent philosophical tradition. For example, there are some recurring conceptual metaphors that underlie theories ranging from Presocratic notions of Being and *physis,* to ideas about God in medieval theology, to Cartesian doctrines of mind, and up to twenty-first-century neurocomputational theories of cognition.

It would be impractical to try to survey the metaphorical foundations of all our philosophical theories. But it is a task that can and should be undertaken if we want to understand the inner workings of any particular theory in philosophy or science. This task will always include a metaphorical analysis of concepts such as cause, being, reality, and event, but also of all aspects of mind and thought themselves, such as the grounding metaphors for concepts, reason, mind, thought, knowledge, logical relations, and values that lie at the heart of a specific theory. Even the theories of metaphor themselves must be analyzed. The theory of conceptual metaphor, for example, employs metaphors of "mapping" and "projection" to conceptualize the nature of metaphor itself. Such a conception could never be absolute—could never tell the whole story or cover all of the data—and so we must always be self-reflectively aware of our own metaphorical assumptions and their limitations.

I have argued that the biggest single reason that most traditional and contemporary philosophy cannot recognize the pervasive, theory-constituting role of metaphor in philosophy is the failure of philosophers to acknowledge the existence of deep, systematic conceptual metaphor and its grounding in embodied meaning. They cannot recognize it, because to do so would require a fairly substantial revision of some of the founding assumptions of their philosophies. It would require them to abandon some of their founding metaphorical conceptions in favor of other metaphors. If you acknowledge conceptual metaphor, then you have to give up literalism. If you give up literalism, you must abandon objectivist theories of knowledge. If you reject objectivist metaphysics and epistemology, you must abandon the classical correspondence theory of truth. Eventually, you will have to rethink even your most basic conception of what cognition consists in.

The hold that objectivist and literalist views have on us is so strong that we are sorely tempted to go to great lengths to salvage our traditional theories of mind, thought, and language. Searle ultimately falls back on a form of literalism. Davidson retains his literalism by denying that metaphors have meaning beyond their literal sense. Rorty doesn't appear to be a literalist, since he sees that metaphors are very important in the history of philosophy, but he has no theoretical resources to explain such phenomena as anything more than contingent, irrational, inexplicable, random events.

In sharp contrast, once you understand how conceptual metaphors lie at the heart of our abstract conceptualization and reasoning, you acquire a new set of tools for analyzing, explaining, and criticizing philosophical theories. Philosophies are built out of conceptual metaphors. We need not be slaves operating blindly under the strict influence of our metaphors. We can learn what our founding metaphors are and how they work. We can analyze the metaphors underlying other cultures and philosophical systems, too. Our ability to do this type of analysis is, admittedly, always itself shaped by metaphorical conceptions of which we are hardly ever aware. However, we *can* become aware of those metaphors; we can subject them to critical evaluation; and we can creatively elaborate them in developing new philosophies to help us deal with the problems that confront us in our daily lives.

PLATE I. Giorgio de Chirico, *Melancholy and Mystery of a Street* (1914). © 2006 Artists Rights Society (ARS), New York / SIAE, Rome.

PLATE 2. Henri Matisse, *Harmony in Red* (1908). © 2006 Succession H. Matisse, Paris /Artists Rights Society (ARS), New York.

PART III

Embodied Meaning, Aesthetics, and Art

Contemporary Anglo-American philosophers recognize that the nature of meaning is a pivotal philosophical issue, but they almost never regard either art or aesthetics as relevant to this topic. They labor under the illusion of the cognitivist view that meaning is properly only a linguistic phenomenon—a matter of words and sentences. Moreover, they tend to think of meaning as involving the truth conditions of sentences. They wouldn't dream of starting their analysis with a discussion of how we experience and understand art, because they will only grudgingly grant meaning to art (if they do so at all), on the basis of their analogy of art as a form of language. We thus hear people say that music can only have meaning if it is seen to be a type of language, with elements akin to words, phrases, and sentences, and with elements that refer beyond themselves to extramusical things, events, or ideas. Meaning in painting gets reduced to representational elements, and occasionally to visual "gestures." According to this language-centered view, music, painting, architecture, dance, and so on do not have meaning in its "proper" sense, and poetry has meaning only to the extent that it can be likened to prose.

As we have seen, the idea that only words can have meanings ignores vast stretches on the landscape of human meaning-making. It leaves out anything that cannot be linguistically encoded, and it denies the status of *meaning* to most of the meaning-making that occurs beneath our conscious awareness and beneath representational structures. On this view, the last place one would look for meaning is in the arts.

In sharp contrast with this traditional philosophical disparagement of the arts, most people turn to art not just because of its entertainment value, but precisely because it *is* meaningful and because it helps us to understand our human condition. We all want to be entertained, but beyond that, we want meaning in art. We are not mistaken when we look for meaning in music, poetry, painting, sculpture, dance, drama, and architecture.

Part 3 thus turns to art for insight into the nature of meaning. It holds up examples of images, image schemas, qualities, metaphors, and emotional contours in artworks that make those works meaningful to us. These chapters consist of what we might call existence proofs of meaning in art. Rather than supplying rigorous argument, I simply try to show some of the ways that the arts make use of the very same ordinary, everyday elements and dimensions of meaning that operate at the heart of our more prototypical meaning-making in language. I seek to bring aesthetics into the center of human meaning. Aesthetics is the stone that was cast out by philosophers who thought they were constructing large metaphysical, epistemological, and logical monuments. On my view, however, the very stone that was cast out shall become the cornerstone of a theory of meaning.

In this way I am, once again, following in the footsteps of John Dewey, who argued in *Art as Experience* (1934) that art matters because it provides heightened, intensified, and highly integrated experiences of meaning, using all of our ordinary resources of meaning-making. To discover how meaning works, we should turn first to gesture, social interaction, ritual, and art, and only later to linguistic communication. In chapter 10, I treat a few brief examples from poetry, fiction, and painting. Chapter 11 turns to music—the felt flow of musical meaning and our use of image schemas and metaphors to understand musical motion. I pursue Dewey's insight that the arts are a primary means by which we grasp, criticize, and transform meanings. In the final chapter, I summarize the view of meaning, thought, and language that arises from my exploration of embodied meaning. I also reflect on what the term *body* means for our nondualistic, naturalistic conception of mind. I end with the idea that philosophy will matter to people only to the extent that it is built on a visceral connection to our world.

CHAPTER 10

Art as an Exemplar of Meaning-Making

One of the greatest impediments to an appreciation of the full scope of embodied meaning is the way philosophers of language focus almost exclusively on *language* (i.e., spoken and written words and sentences) as the bearer of meaning. Anything that doesn't conform to this linguistic model is defined, by fiat, as not part of meaning proper. This language-centered prejudice leads many philosophers to overlook the deepest roots of meaning. The best way to avoid this blindness is to look beyond linguistic meaning and into the processes of meaning in the arts, where immanent bodily meaning is paramount. In the next two chapters, I want to make a brief survey of some of the ways embodied meaning operates in various arts. My hypothesis is twofold: (1) aesthetics is not just art theory, but rather should be regarded broadly as the study of how humans make and experience meaning, because (2) the processes of embodied meaning in the arts are the very same ones that make linguistic meaning possible. I thus seek to continue my expansion of the notion of meaning far beyond the confines of words and sentences.

THE DEVALUATION OF AESTHETICS
IN THE WESTERN TRADITION

Today, we are the inheritors of views about art that were first consolidated in Enlightenment Europe. The rise of the sciences of human nature during the seventeenth and eighteenth centuries prompted philosophers interested in the arts to change their focus from the nature of art to an almost exclusive concern with how the mind works in aesthetic judgment. By focusing primarily on the faculties of the mind that give rise to judgments about beauty—especially the faculties known as imagination and feeling—these philosophers ceased to regard art as a way of worldmaking. Even worse, their faculty psychology relegated feelings and emotions to the secondary status of noncognitive and merely subjective bodily states, unfitted to ground genuine understanding and knowledge.

From the very beginning of Western philosophy, art was never taken seriously as an essential mode of human engagement with and understanding of the world. The Platonic notion that art was *mimesis,* a form of imitation of the real, consigned it to a derivative and dependent status as a source of images and second-rate understanding, not a direct presentation of reality. This can be seen in, for example, Plato's notorious skepticism about whether certain types of poetic mimesis could provide any appropriate kind of intellectual or moral guidance. In his *Republic* (books 3 and 10), Plato ends up regretting that he must banish imitative poetry from his ideal state, because it "stirs and waters the passions" while simultaneously misleading us with third-rate copies of what is real.

By the end of the eighteenth century, the status of art had deteriorated from bad to worse. Things of beauty in nature and art had come to be dissociated from our engagement with the practical affairs of life. The sources of this deterioration are many, but two stand out. First, seventeenth- and eighteenth-century faculty psychology posited distinct "faculties" or "powers" of the mind, each having its unique function in generating human experience and cognition. The various faculties of *sensation* apprehended sense data—sights, sounds, tastes, smells, and tactile sensations. The faculty of *feeling* generated feelings of pleasure and pain in response to sense perceptions. The faculty of *imagination* composed unified sense images and, in its creative mode, generated novel images. The faculty of *understanding* produced concepts by which to organize and conceptualize experience. The faculty of *reason* combined conceptual propositions into larger forms of knowledge. This differentiation of cognitive functions reinforced a pervasive mind/body dualism and generated a series of foundational dichotomies between the "higher" faculties and functions and the "lower" ones—understanding versus sensation, cognition versus feeling, reason versus emotion. The "higher" faculties were intellectual and cognitive, capable of generating objective experience and knowledge.

The "lower" faculties were noncognitive and bodily, and they could only produce subjective mental states.

The second fateful assumption contributing to the deterioration of the status of art and aesthetic experience was that the principal office of art is to be beautiful and that beauty is primarily a matter of *feeling* rather than a matter of *thinking*. Eighteenth-century philosophers of art recognized, correctly, that beauty in nature and art can be a source of strong feeling that moves us. However, from this truth they erroneously concluded, on the basis of the dichotomies implicit in their faculty psychology, that aesthetics cannot be about cognitive understanding or knowledge or truth. If beauty is merely a feeling response to characteristics of objects or scenes, they argued, then it is not, properly, thinking based on concepts.

Nowhere is this derogation of the aesthetic more pronounced than in the impressive aesthetic theory of Immanuel Kant. I have elsewhere (Johnson 1987, chap. 6) celebrated Kant's profound treatment of imagination, suggesting how his views might be substantially revised to place imagination at the core of all experience, understanding, and reasoning. In his *Critique of Judgment* (1790), Kant toyed with the pervasiveness of blended imaginative-feeling-thinking processes in how we experience meaning, but he was never able to give up his architectonic of cognitive functions, and so he always pulls back from acknowledging the embodiment of mind, thought, and language. His adherence to a faculty psychology that rigidly demarcates cognitive from noncognitive mental acts made it impossible for him to ever fully embrace imagination (and feeling) as the key to meaning and understanding. As we will see, in spite of Kant's often brilliant remarks on the nature of imagination and its role in our ability to remake reality, and in spite of his glowing praise for the power of "aesthetic ideas" to engender rich thought, his reduction of the aesthetic to feeling alone and his exclusion of feeling from cognition and knowledge were carried forward most fatefully into twentieth-century aesthetic theory. Kant's influential idea that the experience of beauty requires a form of "disinterested" judgment that suspends one's practical, ethical, and political engagements persists even today in the guise of the conditions for genuine aesthetic contemplation of art.

Nineteenth-century romanticism's enthusiasm for poetry as the key to overcoming our alienation from nature, our innermost selves, and other people brought art temporarily back into the limelight, but mostly as a bearer of strong feelings rather than of rational thoughts. It turned out to be the Kantian legacy that persisted most forcefully into the twentieth century, underwriting popular formalist theories of art, aesthetic-attitude theories of art perception, and theories of aesthetic (as opposed to theoretical or practical) judgment and criticism.

It was precisely John Dewey's mission, in his 1934 book *Art as Experience,* to lead us to a rediscovery of art as a condition of life and meaning. He saw that art and the aesthetic had become marginalized in our lives, and he saw this marginalization as one of several poignant manifestations of the failure of our common philosophical heritage to help us address our problems in the modern world. Dewey argued that art is an exemplary form of human meaning-making. From this, it followed that understanding the nature of the arts could give us profound insight into how humans experience and construct meaning in their lives. He even went so far as to claim that art is experience in its most consummated, fully realized form. Dewey was essentially arguing that the stone (of aesthetics) that had been cast out by traditional philosophy must now become the cornerstone of the new philosophy of experience—a philosophy fitted to human problems and their solution: "I have tried to show in these chapters that the esthetic is no intruder in experience from without, whether by way of idle luxury or transcendent ideality, but that it is the clarified and intensified development of traits that belong to every normally complete experience" (Dewey 1934/1987, 52–53).

We need a Dewey for the twenty-first century. That is, *we need a philosophy that sees aesthetics as not just about art, beauty, and taste, but rather as about how human beings experience and make meaning. Aesthetics concerns all of the things that go into meaning—form, expression, communication, qualities, emotion, feeling, value, purpose, and more.* Instead of isolating the "aesthetic" as merely one autonomous dimension of experience, or merely one form of judgment, we must realize that aesthetics is about the conditions of experience as such, and art is a culmination of the possibility of meaning in experience. Dewey thus concludes that

> art—the mode of activity that is charged with meanings capable of immediately enjoyed possession—is the complete culmination of nature, and that "science" is properly a handmaiden that conducts natural events to this happy issue. . . .
>
> . . . The doings and sufferings that form experience are, in the degree in which experience is intelligent or charged with meanings, a union of the precarious, novel, irregular with the settled, assured and uniform—a union which also defines the artistic and the esthetic. (Dewey 1925/1981, 269)

Insofar as aesthetics concerns the very conditions of meaningful experience and thought, philosophy must be grounded in aesthetics. Hans-Georg Gadamer reiterates this revolutionary view:

> Thus at the end of our conceptual analysis of experience we can see what affinity there exists between the structure of experience as such and the mode of being of the aesthetic. The aesthetic experience is not just one kind of experience among others, but represents the essence of experience itself. . . . In the experience of art there is present a fullness of meaning which belongs not only to this particular content or object but rather stands for the meaningful whole of life. . . . The work of art is understood as the perfecting of the symbolic representation of life, towards which every experience tends. (Gadamer 1960/1975, 63)

This privileging of the aesthetic and its culmination in art as the basis for understanding experience is the exact opposite of the current mainstream view that the heart of philosophy is epistemology, logic, and metaphysics, with the "value fields" (ethics, social and political philosophy, and aesthetics) occupying, at best, only a secondary status. If Dewey and Gadamer are right, then one cannot do epistemology, logic, metaphysics, or any other philosophical undertaking adequately without first exploring aesthetics—the aesthetics of human experience and meaning.

In this chapter and the next, I hope to gesture toward what it would mean to recover Dewey's project for our new century. I want to provide some exemplary cases that show how the structures, processes, and qualities that make art possible and valuable are exactly the same ones that constitute *all* meaning, thought, and understanding. I will be emphasizing that these aspects of embodied meaning are not, for the most part, propositional, and it therefore follows that meaning cannot be primarily linguaform and propositional. In earlier chapters, I surveyed some of these key elements of embodied meaning. I now want to make the somewhat obvious, though underappreciated, point that the meaning of art depends on just these embodied elements and that in art they realize their fullest potential. The principal consequence of this, I shall argue, is the necessity of grounding philosophy in aesthetics—basing philosophy on an account of the origin and growth of embodied meaning and value.

KANT'S SUBJECTIVIZING OF AESTHETICS

It is important to see how things went wrong with aesthetics—that is, how it came to be regarded as one small branch of philosophy, and a relatively unimportant one at that.[1] The story of this progressive decline is long and philosophically interesting, but I will focus on just one fateful stage in this fall, namely, the culmination of what Gadamer calls the "subjectivization of the aesthetic" in Kant's philosophy of beauty. I pick this decisive episode in philosophy because it represents the clearest statement of the two alleged characteristics of the aesthetic—that it is subjective and based on feeling—that are traditionally cited as the reasons for its secondary, devalued status.

Immanuel Kant's *Critique of Judgment* is universally recognized as the classic statement of this dominant conception of aesthetics. Kant argues that the fundamental act of human cognition is judgment, by which he means the act of uniting a multiplicity of sensations, images, or concepts into larger, synthetic unities of thought. In Kant's three great *Critiques,* he identifies three different forms of judgment—scientific, moral, and aesthetic—that each lay claim to universal validity, and he then asks how each of these types of judgment is possible. In other words, he asks what activity of mind can give rise to each type of judgment. In the *Critique of Pure Reason* (1781), he seeks to explain the possibility and universal applicability of scientific knowledge (especially in its Newtonian forms). In the *Critique of Practical Reason* (1788), he asks how moral judgments can be universally binding on rational creatures. And in the *Critique of Judgment* (1790), he struggles to explain how certain types of aesthetic judgment—judgments based on feelings—can yet claim universal validity.

Notice Kant's fateful strategy from the very start. He distinguishes several types of judgments and then inquires how each type, with its peculiar characteristics, is possible. But this strategy already skews our entire understanding of mind, for it breaks thought into discrete types of judgments, each with its own conditions and field of application. It thus accepts the dominant faculty psychology of the Enlightenment. The "aesthetic"

---

1. When I was in graduate school in the mid-1970s, it was a commonplace prejudice of the culture of analytic philosophy to assume that the smartest, most serious students would do the intellectually rigorous work of logic, epistemology, and metaphysics, while those who weren't up to this exalted task could entertain themselves with the mushier, subjective "value fields." Moreover, even within these value fields there was a definite hierarchy of cognitive virtues, with metaethics at the top, normative ethical theory (and social and political theory) a step lower, applied ethics next, and aesthetics at the bottom. In sharp contrast with this marginalizing of aesthetics, I had the good fortune to study with Ted Cohen, for whom the arts were a profound source of insight into all things human and for whom aesthetic theory was a primary means of explaining those processes of human meaning.

will pertain only to a certain range of judgments grounded on feeling, and therefore, on Kant's view, it would make no sense to claim that the aesthetic is a matter of *thought*—let alone the basis of all thought, as I am claiming. In fact, Kant typically contrasts these feeling-based aesthetic judgments with cognitive (conceptual) judgments that can give rise to knowledge. In reference to aesthetic judgments of taste (judgments concerning beauty in nature and art), Kant insists that they are noncognitive and therefore can never claim the status of conceptual knowledge:

> If we wish to decide whether something is beautiful or not, we do not use understanding to refer the presentation to the object so as to give rise to cognition; rather, we use imagination (perhaps in connection with the understanding) to refer the presentation to the subject and his feeling of pleasure or displeasure. Hence a judgment of taste is not a cognitive judgment and so is not a logical judgment but an aesthetic one, by which we mean a judgment whose determining basis *cannot be other* than *subjective*. (Kant 1790/1987, § 1, p. 203)

Kant's assumption that judgments about beauty in nature and art are based on feelings of pleasure or displeasure arising from the formal dimensions of certain objects raises the staggering problem of the *Critique of Judgment*, which is how anything supposedly private and subjective like feelings could ever possibly give rise to demands for universal validity. Kant insists that whenever someone judges a thing to be beautiful, they are *not* merely expressing their subjective preference.

> Many things may be charming and agreeable to him; no one cares about that. But if he proclaims something to be beautiful, then he requires the same liking from others; he then judges not just for himself but for everyone, and speaks of beauty as if it were a property of things. That is why he says: The *thing* is beautiful, and does not count on other people to agree with his judgment of liking on the ground that he has repeatedly found them agreeing with him; rather, he *demands* that they agree. He reproaches them if they judge differently, and denies that they have taste, which he nevertheless demands of them, as something they ought to have. (Kant 1790/1987, § 7, pp. 55–56)

But how can judgments of taste claim universal validity if they are merely a matter of feelings? Kant finds himself in a fix, because he usually claims that *concepts* alone can give rise to universal validity of judgments, since concepts have a formal character that can in principle be shared by all rational creatures. Feelings, on the other hand, are regarded as being merely subjective, noncognitive, and private. Following the spirit of his time, Kant says that judgments of taste (as aesthetic) cannot be based on concepts, for otherwise there could be rules or criteria for judging whether or not a thing is beautiful, and everyone agrees that no such rules are possible. Experiencing the beauty of a natural scene or an artwork is not a matter of judging whether the scene or artwork possesses a set of beauty-constituting properties. But then what *is* the basis for such a judgment—a basis that isn't particular to the individual person and could therefore support a claim to universal validity?

The source of Kant's problem is a fundamental dualism that runs through his entire philosophical system. Here it is manifested as a dualism of concepts (as part of thought) versus feelings (as tied to the body). Concepts are supposedly formal and not intrinsically related to the body, whereas feelings are obviously and inescapably perturbations of the body. I emphasize this thought/feeling dualism because of the profound impact it has had on the shape of contemporary analytic philosophy. The dichotomy of concept versus feeling is not just a Kantian problem; it pervades our contemporary understanding of mind. On one side of the dualistic gap we have concepts, thought, reason, and knowledge. On the other side we have sensations, feelings, emotions, and imagination. What has been so fateful about this dualism for contemporary philosophy is the way it *aligns meaning with the cognitive and thus dismisses quality, feeling, and emotion from any account of meaning.* Therefore, according to analytic philosophy of mind and language, everything I've been presenting in this book as part of the bodily basis of meaning is denied any role in so-called cognitive meaning.

I do not wish to become mired in the intricate and highly technical details of Kant's struggles to explain how judgments of taste are possible. To oversimplify, Kant's explanation of the possibility of judgments of taste (of the form "This X is beautiful") is that even though such judgments are aesthetic and therefore based on feelings, they are distinguished by a certain intellectual dimension that other types of aesthetic judgment lack. For example, Kant argues that "aesthetic sensory judgments"—we could use "Bratwurst and beans are yummy" as an example—are mere subjective judgments based on the way certain objects immediately please a person's palate. There can be no claim to universality about bratwurst and beans pleasing everyone. However, "aesthetic reflective judgments" (judgments of taste, concerning the beautiful) have an intellectual (almost cognitive) dimension that supposedly raises them above the status of reports of private pleasure or displeasure. Kant claims that judgments of taste concern the *form* of some object, scene, or experience, and this formal characteristic is what makes the universality of a judgment of taste possible. He argues that we all share the ability to perceive formal structures in the same way, and this supposedly introduces a ground for our judging that is alleged to be more than mere private sensation and feeling: "A *pure judgment of taste* is one that is not influenced by charm or emotion (though these may be connected with a liking for the beautiful), and whose determining basis is therefore merely the purposiveness of the form" (Kant 1790/1987, § 13, p. 69). This "purposiveness of the form" means that the formal characteristics of some object give rise in us to an interplay of our imagination and understanding so that they harmonize in a way that is felt by us as ordered, rational, and pleasurable. In short, the feeling that *appears* to be the basis for a judgment that something is beautiful is actually our felt awareness of the free harmonizing of our imagination and understanding.

Because Kant could only think of feelings as subjective, he had to find some other basis for the possibility of the universal validity of a judgment of taste. So, we are not surprised when we learn that Kant finally comes clean and does, indeed, claim that the universality of a judgment of taste is based on a concept! This alleged underlying concept is not a "determinate" one that might have been the basis for a rule of beauty and might therefore constitute knowledge; instead, it is an "indeterminate" concept—the "indeterminate concept of the supersensible substrate of appearances" (Kant 1790/1987, § 57, p. 341). It is an indeterminate notion of the ground of nature *as if* natural forms were purposively created to freely harmonize our cognitive faculties, even in the absence of any determinate, controlling concept.

We need not venture any further into these metaphysically obscure territories of the supersensible substrate. My goal is not to explain in detail how Kant purports to solve the problem of taste. Rather, I want to indicate how, via Kant's influential formulation, the "aesthetic" came to be associated with art (through beauty) and then, because it was tied to feeling, dismissed from any role in conceptualization, meaning, reasoning, and knowledge. We see all of these strands woven together in Kant:

1. According to Kant, aesthetics is about how certain objects produce feelings of pleasure or displeasure in us.
2. He accepted Enlightenment faculty psychology, in which feeling (a bodily occurrence) is contrasted with thought (an intellectual, cognitive process).

3. Within this psychology, feeling is held to be subjective and nonconceptual; thought is conceptual and, thereby, at least potentially objective and capable of universal validity.

4. Therefore, because feeling is noncognitive, it cannot give rise to knowledge.

5. It follows, for Kant, that art and what is today called "aesthetic experience" are not primarily sources of knowledge; rather, they are sources of a certain refined, intellectual kind of feeling. Nothing pertaining to taste can ever be the basis for universal concepts, propositions, or knowledge.

Let us ask what this pervasive devaluation of the aesthetic (as being merely subjective and limited to a very specific type of feeling-based judgment), a view that is so characteristic of modern philosophy, entails for the philosophy of mind and language today. The answer is obvious and stunning: because of its alleged noncognitive character, nothing connected with the aesthetic can have any role in meaning, conceptualization, and reasoning! Consequently, because everything I have been discussing in previous chapters as being part of embodied meaning concerns the aesthetic dimensions of experience and thought, traditional philosophy of language tends to exclude it from consideration, claiming that it is not conceptual and propositional in the "approved" sense.

Ignoring the aesthetic basis of meaning eviscerates philosophy of mind and language (and much other philosophy as well) and makes it less relevant to life. Following Dewey's lead, my project is to rediscover the aesthetics of meaning as the key to the recovery of philosophy. Dewey was certainly not the only philosopher to pursue such an endeavor, either in his day or in ours, but he stands out for his explicit framing of the hypothesis of the central role of aesthetics in all experience. Dewey's claim, to reiterate, is that meaning-making in art is the exemplary or even paradigmatic case of all human meaning-making. Since much of art makes meaning without words or linguistic symbols, art reminds us that meaning is not the exclusive purview of language. Indeed, linguistic meaning is parasitic on the primordial structures and processes of embodied interaction, quality, and feeling.

Let us now, therefore, consider some brief examples of artistic meaning-making that reveal the embodied structures that have been the subject of this book: images, image schemas, qualities, feelings, emotions, and the flow of life. Let us see that they are indeed relevant to meaning, even though they are not "cognitive" or "conceptual" in the traditional senses of those terms. Let us see how these body-based meanings affect our understanding, even without the mediation of "high-level" conceptualization and reasoning.

MEANING BEYOND THE WORDS
IN POETRY AND LITERATURE

Polonius asks Prince Hamlet, "What do you read, my lord?" Hamlet answers, "Words, words, words" (Shakespeare, *Hamlet,* 2.2). It is true that when we read, we read words. But words have meanings, and meanings go far beyond the words. Meanings, as Eugene Gendlin (1991, 1997) argues, reach deep down into situations, into "that ....." out of which the meanings emerge and grow, carried forward in relation to what is made explicit in the words (see chapter 4). All of the poetry ever written stands as a testimony to this fact of embodied meaning. Beneath and within what is *said* is the vast richness of what is *meant,* and this meaning pulsates with corporeal significance. As exhibit A, consider Pablo Neruda's "Gentleman without Company."

GENTLEMAN WITHOUT COMPANY

The homosexual young men and the love-mad girls,
and the long widows who suffer from a delirious inability to sleep,
and the young wives who have been pregnant for thirty hours,
and the hoarse cats that cross my garden in the dark,
these, like a necklace of throbbing sexual oysters,
surround my solitary house,
like enemies set up against my soul,
like members of a conspiracy dressed in sleeping clothes
who give each other as passwords long and profound kisses.

The shining summer leads out the lovers
in low-spirited regiments that are all alike,
made up of fat and thin and cheerful and sullen pairs;
under the elegant coconut palms, near the sea and the moon,
there is a steady movement of trousers and petticoats,
and a hum from the stroking of silk stockings,
and women's breasts sparkling like eyes.

The small-time employee, after many things,
after the boredom of the week, and the novels read in bed at night,
has once and for all seduced the woman next door
and now he escorts her to the miserable movies,

where the heroes are either colts or passionate princes,
and he strokes her legs sheathed in their sweet down
with his warm and damp hands that smell of cigarettes.

The evenings of the woman-chaser and the nights of the husbands
come together like two bed-sheets and bury me,
and the hours after lunch, when the young male students
and the young women students, and the priests are masturbating,
and the animals are riding each other frankly,
and the bees have an odor of blood, and the flies buzz in anger,
and cousins play strange games with their girl-cousins,
and doctors look with rage at the husband of the young patient,
and the morning hours, when the professor, as if absentminded,
performs his marital duty, and has breakfast,
and still more, the adulterers, who love each other with true love
of beds high and huge as ocean liners,
this immense forest, entangled and breathing,
hedges me around firmly on all sides forever
with huge flowers like mouths and rows of teeth
and black roots that look like fingernails and shoes.

This poem is a crescendo of intense and troubling images that pulsate with the visions, smells, textures, and feelings of life, sex, and death. Simply put, it is "about" the anguish and frustration of those solitary people who feel themselves to be surrounded and smothered by raw sexuality but who can find no sexual fulfillment. Quite obviously, Neruda's poem does not merely develop its theme conceptually, in the thin air of intellectual connections. Rather, it digs down into what Gendlin called the implicit meaning of a situation and lets itself be carried forward by the palpable images, rhythms, and contours of felt experience. The first four lines pile up images of sexual desire that can go on, seemingly forever, in a desperate, mushrooming frustration: "The homosexual young men . . . / and the long widows . . . / and the young wives . . . / and the hoarse cats . . ." On and on it goes, never letting up, never releasing the pressure and suffering. All of this builds to that amazing image: "these, like a necklace of throbbing sexual oysters, / surround my solitary house." One hesitates to comment on this image, for fear of diminishing its incarnate realization of sexual longing. The meaning that is "working" here, as Gendlin would say, is the meaning of the body, developed through various senses (sight, hearing, smell, taste), and dependent on the precise rhythm of the images, sounds, pauses, and intensifications that define what is inadequately known as the "form" of the poem. Wherever that remarkable image came from, it was from somewhere deep within Neruda's unconscious, implicit understanding of sexuality. However, it is not just *his* private image, for it resonates with all of us, animating parts of our corporeal understanding—even though it is no doubt an entirely new concatenation of words (and meanings), one that never before existed.[2]

Neruda is absolutely relentless. He will not let up, will never release you, from this stream of corporeal images and feelings. The stream grows and grows and grows until it floods your imagination, carrying you forward on a tsunami of felt images. The lonely gentleman is overwhelmed and made to feel inconsequential. He is small and reduced to nothing in "beds high and huge as ocean liners"—completely engulfed and lost. And then, in a cascade of images that would give Freud a field day of psychoanalytic bliss, the poem ends with vaginal symbols (flowers, mouths, rows of teeth, shoes?) and phallic symbols (roots, fingernails, shoes?) interwoven in a squirming mass of sexual eroticism ("this immense forest, entangled and breathing") that is at once exhilarating and utterly threatening.

My descriptions of what the poem does and how it does it are unremarkable, the standard fare of poetry analysis that any bright undergraduate could carry off. The reason that nothing I've said is surprising is that we usually don't think of poems primarily as vehicles of *propositional* meaning and insight. We understand that, in addition to their propositional content, they use images, metaphors, image schemas, felt qualities, rhythm, meter, pitch contours, and other devices to construct a rich, moving experience. Because most people think they can clearly distinguish "poetic language" and "poetic devices" from the mechanisms of meaning in ordinary language, they tend not to see that the dimensions of meaning in poetry are the very same ones that underlie *all* our thought and symbolic interaction.

This in no way denies that there are typically characteristic differences between poetry and standard prose. However, they are not significant differences in meaning resources. They tend, rather, to be differences of meter, rhythm, and syntax, although not always. For example, some poetry has the advantage of the ways it breaks lines on the page, thereby ordering the flow of thought in ways that would be difficult to achieve in ordinary prose form. Some poetry relies on the careful alignment, repetition, and

---

2. The idea of oysters as an aphrodisiac is, of course, a common one. But that is only a very small part of what is working in the marvelous phrase "necklace of throbbing sexual oysters."

transformation of images. Other poetry emphasizes the sound quality of words and phrases. But these techniques are merely a matter of degree, not of kind, relative to how meaning operates in ordinary discourse.

Many philosophers have no trouble acknowledging the way poetry works with what I am calling immanent, embodied meaning, but they are quite reluctant to extend embodiment to all meaning. They are captivated by the dream of a pristine language—a language of carefully defined literal concepts free from the alleged taint of bodily processes. They want to deny that all meaning is embodied. For this reason, they treat poetry as a special, albeit cognitively diminished, form of writing and speaking. Such a view led C. K. Ogden and I. A. Richards, for example, to proclaim in *The Meaning of Meaning* (1923) that poetry has "emotive meaning," whereas science and philosophy (and all conveyors of knowledge) have "descriptive" or "cognitive" meaning. If you assume that the meaning of poetry is not true "cognitive" meaning, then you can ignore the pervasive workings of embodied meaning in all forms of symbolic interaction. One can then persist in the illusion that concepts are disembodied and that thought is strictly conceptual and propositional in the traditional senses of those terms.

However, even in so-called prose writing, we find all of the same meaning resources as those utilized in the Neruda poem. This can be seen in a passage from Albert Camus' short novel *The Stranger*. Camus' protagonist, Meursault, is notoriously a person who steadfastly refuses to read meaning into events or relationships. He says repeatedly that "nothing matters" and that all our illusions of eternity, God, freedom, love, marriage, friendship, and justice are negated and brought to nothing by the "dark wind" of death that is forever blowing toward us all, leveling everything in its path. Consequently, throughout most of the novel, Camus writes with an almost Hemingway-like conciseness and sparseness that matches Meursault's experience and understanding of the world and human affairs as devoid of any larger significance.

Yet Meursault is a man who experiences natural forces and the embodied qualities of situations. He is almost abnormally sensitive to light and heat, which stop his thought processes and reduce him to his animal engagement with the situation. On the day of his mother's funeral, he is physically exhausted after spending the night awake before her coffin. He is profoundly and oppressively affected by the sunlight and heat. In the following scene, he is walking in the blazing sun behind the hearse down to the church for the funeral. His dead mother's former companion, Thomas Pérez, is struggling to keep up with the funeral procession in the searing heat.

The procession seemed to me to be moving a little faster. All around me there was still the same glowing countryside flooded with sunlight. The glare from the sky was unbearable. At one point, we went over a section of the road that had just been repaved. The tar had burst open in the sun. Our feet sank into it, leaving its shiny pulp exposed. Sticking up above the top of the hearse, the coachman's hard leather hat looked as if it had been molded out of the same black mud. I felt a little lost between the blue and white of the sky and the monotony of the colors around me—the sticky black of the tar, the dull black of all the clothes, and the shiny black of the hearse. All of it—the sun, the smell of leather and horse dung from the hearse, the smell of varnish and incense, and my fatigue after a night without sleep—was making it hard for me to see or think straight. I turned around again: Pérez seemed to be way back there, fading in the shimmering heat. (Camus 1942/1988, 16–17)

The hearse finally enters the village below where the cemetery is located, and everything whirls out of control in a flood of images, sounds, colors, heat:

There was no way out. Several other images from that day have stuck in my mind: for instance, Pérez's face when he caught up with us for the last time, just outside the village. Big tears of frustration and exhaustion were streaming down his cheeks. But because of all the wrinkles, they weren't dripping off. They spread out and ran together again, leaving a watery film over his ruined face. Then there was the church and the villagers on the sidewalks, the red geraniums on the graves in the cemetery, Pérez fainting (he crumpled like a rag doll), the blood-red earth spilling over Maman's casket, the white flesh of the roots mixed in with it, more people, voices, the village, waiting in front of a café, the incessant drone of the motor, and my joy when the bus entered the nest of lights that was Algiers and I knew I was going to go to bed and sleep for twelve hours. (Camus 1942/1988, 17)

This powerful passage is a mass of liquid, flowing, embodied meaning. Images, sensations, rhythms, pulsations all carry the reader along by evoking a vast sea of unconscious, or barely conscious, connections and feelings. The shiny black pulp of burst-open tar that swallows the procession as it struggles along, a shiny black hearse (bearer of death), the mud-leather blackness of the coachman's hat, the oppressive, cruel sun burning the eyes and scorching the head, smells of horses and sticky lacquer—all are stirred together in a nauseating, overwhelming blend of sights, odors, and palpable sensations. Salty, warm, smothering sweat that blinds the eyes. Red geraniums, blood-red earth with flesh-white roots—like fingers and limbs—mixed inseparably into it. The passage develops its own distinctive rhythm as it courses forward. Camus' typically short, choppy sentences are replaced by ever-expanding masses of images and feelings and blended qualities that carry us forward in a rush of confusion, spinning us out of control in a buzz and hum of heat, odors, and stunning images. The very syntax of these long sentences creates the increasing momentum of everything that oppresses and smothers Meursault.

We do not really *think* about what is transpiring as we read this passage so much as we *feel* and *experience* the qualitative whole that pervades and unifies the entire scene. And then, as we read it more carefully, we experience the flow of images and qualities that draw us into the situation that is developing as the passage progresses. The parallel between how Neruda's poem does what it does and how Camus' novel does what it does is so strong that it challenges the notion that poetry is intrinsically different from prose. It undermines the notion of a distinctively "poetic language," just as it undermines the philosopher's dream of a pristine conceptual language. There are, instead, only the ways we humans make and experience meaning, no matter what the subject matter, literary form, or style might be. Different types of poetry marshal the syntactic, semantic, and pragmatic resources of a language in different ways, sometimes developing the potential of those resources in ways that far surpass ordinary prose. But this is only an intensification and heightening of our ability to find and to make meaning, rather than any radical difference in kind between poetry and our more mundane linguistic practices. Camus' description of the funeral procession evokes powerful visual, tactile, olfactory, and kinesthetic images that come alive for us as we read, images that are suffused with meaning, import, and feeling. This richly imagistic understanding of the funeral procession is characteristic of the ways we experience meaning in all of the arts and in all experience generally.

EMBODIED VISUAL MEANING

A thorough investigation into visual meaning would be a vast and highly complex undertaking. It would require looking into research in perceptual psychology, physiology, neuroscience, cognitive psychology, and aesthetics. Since I can do no more here than to scratch the surface, I propose to provide a few suggestive and representative examples of how we experience visual meaning. My chief goal, once again, is to show how we can

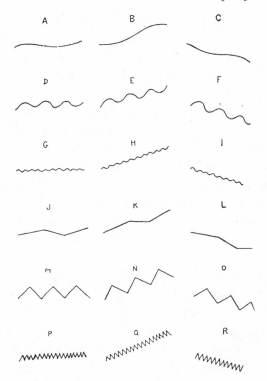

FIGURE 2. Lines matched to affective adjectives. (A. T. Poffenberger and B. E. Barrows, "The Feeling Value of Lines," *Journal of Applied Psychology* 8 (1924): 192, reprinted in Aiken 1998)

grasp the embodied meaning of a visual scene without the use of propositions or language.

Let us begin with a simple observation about how we routinely experience certain recurring forms or patterns as associated with certain feeling values. It is now well known that organic, curvilinear forms generate a very different visceral response in us than do linear, rectilinear, and jagged lines. In her book *The Biological Origins of Art,* Nancy Aiken presents the results of a 1924 study by A. T. Poffenberger and B. E. Barrows in which five hundred subjects were shown a set of curved or jagged lines (figure 2) and were asked to match these forms to a set of adjectives for different kinds of feelings, such as sad, quiet, lazy, merry, agitating, furious, dead, playful, weak, gentle, and harsh.

Anyone looking at these patterns of lines will know immediately which types of feelings were associated with which types of pattern. Curved lines are gentle, smooth, and flowing. Jagged lines are harsh, agitated, and intense. We feel in our body the gentleness of a smoothly curving line. If we were to dramatically increase the amplitude of the curves, we would experience more of a surge of feeling with each movement upward to the apex of the curve, followed by an accelerating downward rush to the bottom of the next curve. As we will see in the next chapter, Susanne Langer (1953) recognized a similar association of pattern and feeling in her claim that certain musical patterns are "tonal analogues" of the felt flow of our experience. Rising pitches, increases in volume, and a quickening tempo can create in us a heightening of tension and expectation that we experience as longing anticipation, or intensification of feeling, depending on the context. The same thing occurs with visual patterns. Poffenberger and Barrows found that "sad" and "quiet" are associated with big curves, while small and medium curves are associated with "merry" and "playful." As one would expect, small and medium angles are typically experienced as agitating and/or furious. Jagged forms and zigzagging lines create tension, heightened arousal, and even anxiety (Aiken 1998).

Following the lead of Rudolf Arnheim's famous analyses of linear and angular shapes versus curved shapes in paintings, Aiken has drawn a linear abstraction of one of Cézanne's Small Bathers paintings in order to contrast it with the line structure in Picasso's Les Demoiselles d'Avignon (see figure 3). Both paintings involve female nudes, but their similarities end there. Picasso's women are angular and pointed, aggressively so. Some of them stare confrontationally right at you. Aiken makes a great deal of the fact that in the animal kingdom, direct eye contact is a sign of confrontation, so that the submissive animal always looks away and down in a gesture of subservience. Picasso's women assault you with their piercing gaze. In strong contrast, Cézanne's bathers (and the entire painting) are drawn with organic curves. There is an admirable balance and harmony among them. Two standing figures balance each other and separate, in a symmetrical fashion, the three seated or squatting figures. There is no confrontational stare. Things are harmoniously integrated in the overall setting; humans and wild nature abide comfortably together as one.

Rudolf Arnheim, our greatest psychologist of art of the twentieth century, has devoted much of his research and writing to an exploration of the intimate connection of perception and thought. To avoid the false distinction between perceiving and thinking, Arnheim prefers to speak of "perceptual thinking," in order to emphasize that perception is an activity of thinking and that what we call abstract thought is closely tied to and grounded upon patterns of perceptual experience. His classic book, Visual Thinking, is a sustained and massively supported argument for the view that

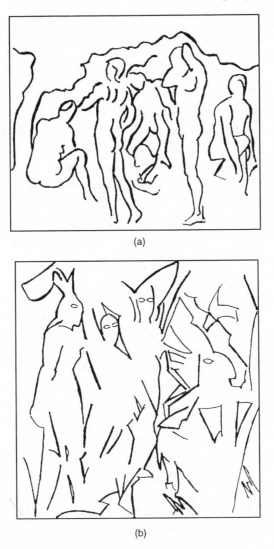

FIGURE 3. Nancy Aiken's line drawings of Cézanne's *Small Bathers* (top) and Picasso's *Les Demoiselles d'Avignon* (bottom). From chapter 7 (p. 120), "Threat Stimuli Used in Art," *The Biological Origins of Art,* by Nancy Aiken. Copyright © 1998. Reprinted with permission of Greenwood Publishing Group, Inc., Westport, CT.

the cognitive operations called thinking are not the privilege of mental processes above and beyond perception but the essential ingredients of perception itself. I am referring to such operations as active exploration, selection, grasping of essentials, simplification, abstraction, analysis and synthesis, completion, correction, comparison, problem solving, as well as combining, separating, putting in context. These operations are not the prerogative of any one mental function; they are the manner in which the minds of both man and animal treat cognitive material at any level. There is no basic difference in this respect between what happens when a person looks at the world directly and when he sits with his eyes closed and "thinks." (Arnheim 1969, 13)

Arnheim's work is one vast celebration of the embodiment of meaning and thought. It gives extensive support to Dewey's continuity principle, which, you will recall, holds that the operations of "mind" emerge through increasingly complex sensorimotor activity, so that there is no radical ontological or epistemological gap separating perceiving from thinking. Perceiving is a mode of thinking, just as much as thinking appropriates the resources and mechanisms of perception. In chapter after chapter of *Visual Thinking* (1969) and *Art and Visual Perception* (1954), Arnheim examines in exquisite detail how we experience the embodied meaning of shape, form, color, balance, harmony, light, space, growth, and a host of perceptual forces that shape how we *see* and how we *think*.

Seeing, Arnheim argues, is a matter of what we "take" from experience: "In organic development perception starts with the grasping of striking structural features" (1954, 34); and the structures we perceive are shaped by the nature of our bodies and brains, the nature of our environments, and our values and interests. What we *see* are certain salient features, structures, and qualities of a situation: "Seeing means grasping a few outstanding features of the object—the blueness of the sky, the curve of the swan's neck, the rectangularity of the book, the sheen of metal, the straightness of the cigarette" (ibid., 33). Arnheim is here challenging the traditional dualistic theory of generalization and abstraction, which holds that we begin by perceiving a number of individual cases from which we abstract, via a "higher-level" conceptual operation, the shared features or similarities present in the various individuals. Against this, Arnheim argues that "it became evident that over-all structural features are the primary data of perception, so that triangularity is not a late product of intellectual abstraction but a direct and more elementary experience than the recording of individual detail. The young child sees 'doggishness' before he is able to distinguish one dog from another" (ibid., 35). Moreover, since every act of perception already involves a capacity for abstraction—that is, an ability to select significant structure—it follows that visual perception is, at its heart, a form of thinking: "In the perception of shape lies the beginnings of concept formation" (Arnheim 1969, 27).

If perception is based on the discernment of significant patterns and structures, then one is led to ask whether there are general principles gov-

FIGURE 4. Pattern perception based on simplicity. (Arnheim 1969)

erning the perceptual process. Arnheim cites extensive evidence for such principles, many of which he appropriates from the gestalt psychology that was so popular in the mid-twentieth century. Let us consider a few representative examples.

One of the most fundamental principles of gestalt perception is simplicity, which means that our experience of a complex object or scene will be organized by the smallest possible number of structural features. For example, consider the eight black dots in figure 4a. The simplest recognizable pattern is one of either a circle or an octagon, as in 4a. Although the two intersecting squares (4b) are a possible pattern, they involve more structural features (i.e., two squares) than the simpler circle. Figure 4c is another possible perceptual arrangement, but it is a far more complex and highly unusual way of parsing the patterns. Notice that in figure 4d, the principle of simplicity leads us to perceive a circle with a single outlying black dot. Figure 4e is, and can only be perceived simply as, a solid circle.

FIGURE 5. Perceptual sorting by size. (Arnheim 1969)

Figure 4f is perceived as a star, but it is also possible to see one equilateral triangle superimposed on another that is rotated 180 degrees. However, figure 4g, after perhaps a modest amount of inspection, stands out clearly as a triangle and a rectangle superimposed, evidencing the simplicity of two overlapping basic geometric figures over against the more complex pattern of an unusual polygonal configuration with many outside edges for the eye to trace.

Other principles of perceptual organization involve the grouping of items according to similarity of shape, color, size, relative position, orientation, or vector direction. Arnheim explains that "the degree to which parts of a pattern resemble each other in some perceptual quality will help determine the degree to which they are seen as belonging together" (954, 67). In figure 5, for instance, we see six objects of the same shape and orientation, but we group them according to the differentiating factor of size, so that we experience the objects as two large squares and four small squares.

In figure 6 top, we have variations of size and orientation, but we group the triangles together and the circles together (i.e., according to shape). In figure 6 bottom, we see the colored (black) circles as forming one group and the white circles as forming another. In figure 7 top, the differentiating factor is spatial contiguity or proximity. In figure 7 bottom, similarity of orientation causes us to perceive the vertical lines as one group and the oblique lines as a second group. Another obvious principle, which emerges when we add motion to the scene, is that objects moving in the same direction are perceived together—as with a group of dancers such as the Sharks and the Jets in the film version of *West Side Story,* charging each other from opposite sides of the playground in the final rumble scene.

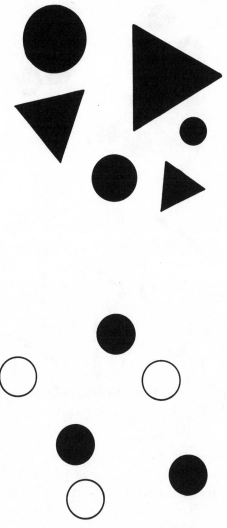

FIGURE 6. Perceptual sorting by shape (above) and by color (below). (Arnheim 1969)

Moreover, if some dancers moved slowly in a scene while others moved faster, we would see them as moving together according to similarity of speed.

Arnheim gives hundreds of examples of structural principles for visual perception that operate, usually unconsciously, to construct how a given scene makes sense to us. As a more complex example, consider Giorgio de Chirico's painting *Melancholy and Mystery of a Street* (plate 1). Like so many of de Chirico's works, this one leaves you feeling uneasy and anxious. There is a foreboding sense that something is wrong here, and it is not to

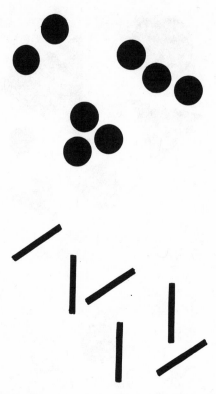

FIGURE 7. Perceptual sorting by spatial contiguity (above) and by orientation (below). (Arnheim 1969)

be explained merely by the innocent, playful little girl who is unaware of the figure she is about to encounter around the corner of the colonnade on the right. A large part of our dis-ease with this painting is the result of a profound spatial disharmony that we experience, if only unconsciously. Arnheim explains how there are two incompatible horizons in conflict in the painting.

> A roughly isometric solid—the wagon—denounces the convergences of the buildings as actual distortions. Furthermore, the perspectives of the two colonnades negate each other. If the one to the left, which confirms the horizon as lying high up, is taken as the basis of the spatial organization, the one to the right pierces the ground. Under the opposite condition the horizon lies invisibly somewhere below the center of the picture, and the rising street with the bright colonnade is only a treacherous mirage guiding the child to a plunge into nothingness. (Arnheim 1954, 289)

In the world created by this painting, the center does not hold; something does not make sense, does not hang together, in a profoundly disturbing way. This is not a world you can comfortably inhabit. You cannot escape the anxiety and metaphysical rupture of this world. And the fact of two incompatible horizon points is only part of what makes you feel yourself a stranger in the work.

Now contrast the uneasy, foreboding, menacing sense of de Chirico's painting with the harmonious, living world of Matisse's *Harmony in Red* (plate 2). Although it doesn't make much sense to say that this painting (or any painting) has a specific, definite meaning, it is perfectly appropriate to say that Matisse's painting is redolent with meaning. It does not get its meaning primarily by being "about" something (e.g., about a woman at a table in a red room), although this is certainly part of what matters in the work. The deeper meaning of the work comes from the way it activates certain neural patterns that are significant for creatures with brains and bodies like ours, dwelling and acting in certain kinds of environments.

Our encounter with Matisse's great painting begins with our experience of the "pervasive unifying quality" (in Dewey's words) of *that particular work* and the world it invites us to inhabit. This is the level at which the painting captures our attention, claims us, and draws us in. Only then do we begin to explore it. Only then do our eyes begin to move around the painting, guided by the underlying perceptual forces (what Arnheim calls the "perceptual skeleton") that determine where our attention goes, how it moves, and how we experience the structure of the work.

A major part of the effect of this painting is its preponderance of organic forms emanating from everywhere in the work. The painting is held together by the repetition and interconnectedness of the living forms—flowers, stems, and vines—that tie the tablecloth together with the wall and with nature "outside." The tablecloth merges almost seamlessly with the painted wall, as though everything in the room were blended together in one living, pulsing, organic whole. Your eye moves in a free-flowing transition from the organic interior of the room to the organic world of nature outside the window, with its trees, flowers, and bushes. Interior and exterior blend and fuse, almost to the point of erasing the split between inside and outside. Everywhere there are natural curves, from the woman's figure to the tablecloth design to the walls to nature beyond. This is a world in which all things are part of one interconnected, living whole, and where everything is freely ordered, balanced, and harmonious. This harmony is achieved not by rigid measure and symmetry, but by the gentle perceptual forces balanced in the composition. The two bottles sit comfortably on opposite sides of the elevated dish of fruit and flowers, all their lines curved and flowing. The figure of the woman is a strong center of attention. The imposing black of her blouse carries considerable perceptual weight, but the caned chair across the table has enough perceptual weight to balance that of the female figure, or nearly so. Furthermore, to emphasize the connectedness and continuity of all things, Matisse blends the foreground and background almost seamlessly together by continuing the rich, luscious red of the tablecloth onto the wall. In this marvelous work, everything is alive, everything flows, everything is connected, humans and nature are in harmony, indoors and outdoors share the feeling of organism and life. This is truly a "harmony in red."

★   ★   ★

The point of this chapter has been to show how the arts are exemplary cases of embodied, immanent meaning. We must recover the embodied meaning that Kant's formalism left behind. In poetry and prose, there is much meaning beneath and beyond concepts and propositions. In the visual arts, it is images, patterns, qualities, colors, and perceptual rhythms that are the principal bearers of meaning. The obvious fact that we usually cannot put into words what we have experienced in our encounter with an artwork does not make the embodied, perceptual meaning any less a type of meaning. When we turn to music, and especially music without reference to lyrics, we will see just how much this embodied meaning is operating below the level of words and propositional content.

CHAPTER 11

Music and the Flow of Meaning

The question of whether there is "meaning" in music has a long, troubled, and inconclusive career in the philosophy of art. One of the principal obstacles to answering this question in the affirmative is the widespread prejudice that only language (i.e., words) can properly be said to have meaning. From this, it is concluded that if there is musical meaning, then music must be some kind of language. According to the MUSIC AS LANGUAGE metaphor, passages in music are conceived as sentences, with individual notes or clusters of notes taken to be the equivalent of words. This metaphor thus gives rise to terms like *musical ideas, musical sentences, propositions, punctuation, musical questions,* and other quasi-linguistic phrases.

However, if you start with the popular assumption that only language has meaning and that meaning is primarily referential, then music comes off looking semantically impoverished, since it is not typically regarded as having substantial referential meaning.[1] Anyone who has perused some of the vast literature on meaning in music will be painfully aware of how music always appears to be a second-class citizen on the issue of its status with respect to meaning. One always has the sense that the key terms of linguistic theory get twisted and stretched, sometimes to the point of breaking, as theorists try to make the MUSIC AS LANGUAGE metaphor work. This strategy of trying to force music into the MUSIC AS

---

1. I do not mean to deny that there are referential elements in certain musical works. However, the way music means cannot be explained principally via referential content.

LANGUAGE mode notoriously ends up satisfying the concerns of nobody, neither those of analytic philosophers of art nor those of music composers and theorists. If you subscribe to a classical analytic philosophy of mind and language, then your view of language will end up excluding most of the nonverbal meaning of music. On the other side, if you are a believer in music as immanent meaning, you will probably find the vocabulary and basic assumptions of contemporary philosophy of language (especially the MUSIC AS LANGUAGE metaphor) to be inadequate to describe the full range of ways that music is vitally meaningful to most people.

MUSIC AS THE EMBODIED FLOW OF LIFE

This perceived inadequacy of the MUSIC AS LANGUAGE metaphor suggests two possible solutions: either abandon the metaphor, or else show that linguistic meaning employs the same semantic resources as music. I am not a fan of the MUSIC AS LANGUAGE metaphor, chiefly because of most people's impoverished views about linguistic meaning. I prefer to focus on enriching our appreciation of the vast array of embodied structures that make meaning possible. Therefore, the central thesis of this chapter is that music is meaningful because it can present the flow of human experience, feeling, and thinking in concrete, embodied forms—and this is meaning in its deepest sense. A fundamental fact about music is that it appeals to our felt sense of life. Granted, music theorists can listen to music for analytical purposes, focusing on key changes, rhythm patterns, pitch contours, and harmonic progressions, but most of us are simply imaginatively and emotionally drawn into the music, without any theoretical knowledge of what is happening. We are moved by it, and we are moved because music orders our experience using tone quality, pitch, meter, rhythm, and other processes that we feel in our bodies.[2] We are moved bodily and emotionally and qualitatively. The experience of sitting quietly in a chair and listening to music is almost unnatural, for our *bodies* want to move with the music. That is why music and dance are so closely and happily intertwined.

2. Whenever I teach a course on the philosophy of art, I always include a section on music, and the main question I ask is "How does music do what it does to us?" Inevitably, after a couple of weeks of discussing texts in musical aesthetics, I find myself having to remind my students that music is a body-mind experience, something *felt*. I tell them that they need to stop analyzing and remember what they know implicitly when they listen to their CDs, which is that they are powerfully moved by their music—moved in their bodies.

Music captures us, carries us along on a sensuous, rhythmic tonal adventure, and then deposits us, changed, in a different place from where we started.

The composer Roger Sessions fully understood the grounding of music in the living, moving, feeling body. I know of no clearer statement of the bodily basis of several key elements of musical meaning and experience than that presented by Sessions in his essay "The Composer and His Message," from which I quote at length:

It seems to me that the essential medium of music, the basis of its expressive powers and the element which gives it its unique quality among the arts, is *time,* made living for us through its expressive essence, *movement.* . . .

Time becomes real to us primarily through movement, which I have called its expressive essence; and it is easy to trace our primary musical responses to the most primitive movement of our being—to those movements which are indeed at the very basis of animate existence. The feeling for tempo, so often derived from the dance, has in reality a much more primitive basis in the involuntary movements of the nervous system and the body in the beating of the heart, and more consciously in breathing, later in walking. Accelerated movement is, from these very obvious causes, inevitably associated with excitement, retarded movement with a lessening of dynamic tension. The experience of meter has the most obvious and essential of its origins in the movements of breathing, with its alternation of upward and downward movements. The sense of effort, preparation, suspense, which is the psychological equivalent of the up-beat, finds its prototype in the act of inhalation, and the sense of weight, release, and finality produced by the down-beat corresponds most intimately to the act of exhalation. . . .

The other primary elements of music—melody and rhythm—derive from more complicated but only slightly less essential muscular movements, which it has been fairly well demonstrated, are reproduced in miniature by the human nervous system in response to musical impressions. If we instinctively respond to a rising melodic pitch by a feeling of increased tension and hence of heightened expression, or a falling pitch by the opposite sensation; if an increase in intensity of sound intensifies our dynamic response to the music, and vice versa, it is because we have already in our vocal experiences—the earliest and most primitive as well as later and more complicated ones—lived intimately through exactly the same effects. A raising of pitch or an increase in volume is the result of an intensification of effort, energy, and emotional power in the crying child just as truly as in the highly-evolved artistry of a Chaliapin or an Anderson.

Similarly, our feeling for rhythm in the stricter sense, derives from the subtle and more expressive nervous and muscular movements, such as occur in speech, song, gesture, and the dance. (Sessions 1941, 105, 108–9)

This remarkable passage is a primer for our understanding of the power of music to move us, to give rise to feelings, and to enact changes in our body-mind. It resonates deeply with our earlier discussion of what Daniel Stern calls vitality-affect contours—the patterns of process and flow of our felt experience, such as the buildup of tension and its release, the sense of drifting, the energetic pursuit of a goal, the anxious anticipation of some coming event, and the starting and stopping of a process. Stern sums up vitality affects as "those dynamic, kinetic qualities of feeling that distinguish animate from inanimate and that correspond to the momentary changes in feeling states involved in the organic processes of being alive" (Stern 1985, 156). Stern's account of the role of vitality affects in dance applies directly to music, too: "Dance reveals to the viewer-listener multiple vitality affects and their variations, without resorting to plot or categorical affect signals from which the vitality affects can be derived. The choreographer is most often trying to express a way of feeling, not a specific content of feeling" (ibid., 56).

The meaning of music is precisely this kind of embodied meaning. Music does not typically *re-present* anything, even though there may occasionally be a few representative elements in a particular musical work. Music's function is, instead, *presentation* and *enactment* of felt experience. Susanne Langer captured this dimension when she said that

> a work of art is an expressive form created for our perception through sense or imagination, and what it expresses is human feeling. The word "feeling" must be taken here in its broadest sense, meaning *everything that can be felt,* from physical sensation, pain and comfort, excitement and repose, to the most complex emotions, intellectual tensions, or the steady feeling-tones of a conscious human life. (Langer 1947, 15)

An expressive form is "any perceptible or imaginable whole that exhibits relationships of parts, or points, or even qualities or aspects within the whole, so that it may be taken to represent some other whole whose elements have analogous relations" (Langer 1947, 20). In any musical work, for example, there is a structure and pattern of temporal flow, pitch contours, and intensity (loudness/softness) that is analogous to felt patterns of the flow of human experience. When a listener becomes imaginatively engaged in the development of these musical contours, that person's *experience* has the felt qualities of the music. That is, if the music builds to a climax of high drama and tension, the engaged listener experiences (in their own feeling body-mind) that dramatic tension.

When Langer says that an expressive form "represents" something, she does *not* mean that the music gets its meaning by referring beyond itself to some other object, event, or experience that is its meaning. On the contrary, the meaning of the music is immanent: "But a work of art does not point us to a meaning beyond its own presence. What is expressed cannot be grasped apart from the sensuous or poetic form that expresses it. In a work of art we have the direct presentation of a feeling, not a sign that points to it" (Langer 1947, 133–34).

The feeling is presented—enacted—in the felt experience of the listener. To hear the music is just to be moved and to feel in the precise way that is defined by the patterns of the musical motion. Those feelings are meaningful in the same way that any pattern of emotional flow is meaningful to us at a pre-reflective level of awareness.

Langer is saying that when we are actively listening to music, we imaginatively enter into its "motion," experiencing all of the ways it moves, swells, hops, rushes, floats, trips along, drags, soars, and falls. This *musical* soaring, floating, or falling is experienced by us as *our felt flow* of experience. We feel it in our vital, tactile-kinesthetic bodies. When the music builds up tension (for example, as it moves pitchwise from the lower through the middle to a high range), *we* experience that tension *in ourselves*. If we didn't, music would never move us. Langer sums this up: "A work of art presents feeling (in the broad sense I mentioned before, as everything that can be felt) for our contemplation, making it visible or audible or in some way perceivable through a symbol, not inferable from a symptom. Artistic form is congruent with the dynamic forms of our direct sensuous, mental, and emotional life" (Langer 1947, 25).

As an example of this process of musical meaning-making—of the musical presentation of forms of feeling and the meaning that is intrinsic to those forms—let us briefly consider the song "Over the Rainbow," from the 1939 film *The Wizard of Oz*.[3] This is one of the best-known songs ever written, and it comes inextricably intertwined with the events of *The*

---

3. "Over the Rainbow," music by Harold Arlen and words by E. Y. Harburg, EMI Feist Catalog, 1939; from *The Wizard of Oz,* Metro-Goldwyn-Mayer, 1939. "Over the Rainbow" was recently voted the number one song from a motion-picture soundtrack in the American Film Institute's top 100 songs.

Some - where   o - ver the rain - bow   way   up   high,

there's   a   land that I heard of   once in a lull - a - by.

EXAMPLE 1. Arlen and Harburg, "Over the Rainbow," opening

Wizard of Oz; it is always measured relative to Judy Garland's famous first rendition of the song. It is thus difficult, and somewhat artificial, to talk about what and how the song means, independent of the lyrics. However, we can highlight some of the embodied structures of meaning and see how perfectly they mesh with the lyrics.

"Over the Rainbow" is a simple song, as simple as the longing that it expresses (Dorothy's longing and ours). The form of the chorus, which constitutes most of the song, is roughly AABBAABBC. The chorus starts with the famous A section, "Some-where o-ver the rain-bow way up high" (example 1).

The movement in the first two notes (E-flat moving up an octave to E-flat) is already dramatic. The slide from "some" (E-flat) up to "where" (the octave) creates a tension, the felt tension as we move from the lower pitch to the higher pitch and feel the strain and increased energy required to reach the higher note. The second measure ("o-ver the rain-bow") sustains this tension and expectation by sliding slightly downward and then tensively upward to high E-flat again. The next two measures ("way up high") resolve this tension somewhat, but not completely, finally settling into B-flat. Some of the tension remains, since the pitch never returns to the range of the initial lower E-flat. The next four measures ("there's a land that I heard of once in a lull-a-by") start with two measures that structurally mirror the pattern of the opening two measures ("Some-where o-ver the rain-bow"), although in a lower pitch register, and then the subsequent two measures resolve most of the tension by eventually moving back to the initial lower E-flat from which the chorus began. So, there was a buildup of tension, a longing that points you toward some as-yet-unrealized state but then brings you gradually back home. Immediately, however, this entire section is repeated, thereby reinstituting the longing, sustaining it briefly, and then resolving it in a move back down to the starting pitch.

With this longing tension still in the air, we then turn to the more active B section (example 2), which speeds up, surges forward, and jumps rapidly up and down, ever driving toward some anticipated future event. The speeding up is a definite change in the character of the song. Something new is happening. Excitement and anticipation build.

The first four measures ("Some day I'll wish up-on a star and wake up where the clouds are far be-hind me") are a series of middle-range, rapidly alternating eighth notes that create a strong sense of anticipation and anxious, energetic forward movement. In the first two measures, we jump from G to B-flat four times in quick succession, jerking us up and down emotionally. But then in the next measure, simply by the move up a half step from G to A-flat, our agitated expectation is heightened even more: the rapidly alternating eighth notes jump from A-flat to B-flat, instead of the previous G to B-flat. This modest, almost imperceptible change ratchets up the sense that something is about to happen, that we are "going somewhere" via this half-step upward pitch change. And indeed we *do* go somewhere—we are carried right on up to C. Two measures later, we are back again to the alternating G to B-flat leaps; but in the next measure, instead of rising just a half step to A-flat (as before), we now go even a half step higher, to A-natural. The result is an even greater heightening of anticipation, which carries us on up to a high F that resolves downward slightly to a middle C. This is the passage "where you'll find me," and it slows down considerably from the rapidly jumping eighth notes to reduce some of the sense of forward movement and give the listener a feeling of temporary rest.

In short, we have moved from a soft, dreamy longing that seeks fulfillment in something yet to come, musically, to a sense of rapid oscillation up

EXAMPLE 2. Arlen and Harburg, "Over the Rainbow," middle section

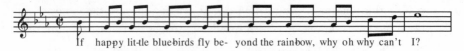

If   happy lit-tle bluebirds fly be- yond the rainbow, why oh why can't I?

EXAMPLE 3. Arlen and Harburg, "Over the Rainbow," ending

and down with increased agitation and a strong sense of moving toward some unrealized goal. Then the song brings us back to the original patterns of longing and expectation. In the final section (example 3), there is that anxious return to the earlier pattern of alternating eighth notes (four alternations from G to B-flat) stepping up the tension to a higher-pitched alternating movement (three alternations from A to B-flat), ending in a continuing ascent up to the sustained high E-flat.

The final effect is a feeling of rising up in longing and eventually drifting, without any final resolution of tension, at a high level of desire for a hoped-for state ("why oh why can't I"). The last three measures gradually slow down and wane into a barely audible pianissimo. The effect is as though we were carried up and away, drifting off into the space of another place or world.

It is quite difficult to describe the dynamics of this melody without interpreting them from the perspective of the lyrics. For example, I spoke of the sense of longing that accompanies the rise in tension as the pitch moves upward into a higher range, pulling up and away from the starting point, which we are tempted to call "home." Perhaps we are enticed into reading "longing" into this passage because we hear Judy Garland (Dorothy) longing for some place far, far away, where things will be better and her hopes will be realized (in Technicolor). Should you take exception to the finding of "longing" in the musical passage, you will at least know the felt sense that the rising notes convey, a feeling pattern that fits perfectly with the pattern of Dorothy's longing.

THE NATURE OF MUSICAL MEANING

The meaning in and of the music is not verbal or linguistic, but rather bodily and felt. We understand the meaning of longing, desire, expectation for better things to come, and so on. We cannot convey it verbally, but it is nonetheless meaningful, and it is enacted via our active engagement with the music. Antonio Damasio correctly describes meaning of this sort as consisting of series of related, interwoven images. Images in this sense are not merely, or even primarily, visual; rather, they are patterns of neural activation that result from the ongoing interaction of organism and environment. Damasio explains that

> by *image* I mean a mental pattern in any of the sensory modalities, e.g., a sound image, a tactile image, the image of a state of well-being. Such images convey aspects of the physical characteristics of the object and they may also convey the reaction of like or dislike one may have for an object, the plans one may formulate for it, or the web of relationships of that object among other objects. (Damasio 1999, 9)

> By the term images I mean mental patterns with a structure built with the tokens of each of the sensory modalities—visual, auditory, olfactory, gustatory, and somatosensory. The somatosensory modality (the words comes from the Greek soma which means "body") includes varied forms of sense: touch, muscular, temperature, pain, visceral, and vestibular. The word image does not refer to "visual" image alone, and there is nothing static about images either. The word also refers to sound images such as those caused by music or the wind, and to the somatosensory images that Einstein used in his mental problem solving—in his insightful account, he called those patterns "muscular" images. (Damasio 1999, 318)

Meaningful images of this sort are thus not representations in the classical sense, for they typically are not "about" some extramental content that would constitute their meaning. Instead, they are (often unconscious) patterns by which the contours of our understanding take shape and undergo transformation. They do not so much "picture" or "represent" objects and events as they simply *are* the patterns of our experience of those objects and events. Consequently, when we talk about meaning in music, it will be in terms of the way auditory images and their relations evoke feeling-thinking responses in us. It will be the contours of those images and the way they flow and connect with each other that will define our experience of the music and the meaning it has for us.

CONCEPTUAL METAPHOR AND MUSICAL MOTION: THE BODILY GROUNDING OF MUSICAL MEANING

Strong evidence for the embodied nature of musical meaning comes from the fact that virtually all of our conceptualization and description of music uses metaphors whose source domains are drawn from sensorimotor experience. For example, since music is a tonal and temporal art, we experience and understand a musical piece as an extended motion, via the

MOVING OBSERVER metaphor for temporal change. We cannot help but understand "Over the Rainbow" as starting somewhere, moving on a musical journey toward some other place, and finally arriving at some metaphorical destination. Nor can we help but experience this metaphorical motion as a striving—an endeavor to reach a goal. Thus, Heinrich Schenker describes the succession of tones as a felt sense of inner motion: "Since it is a melodic succession of definite steps of a second, the fundamental line signifies motion, striving toward a goal, and ultimately the completion of this course. In this sense we perceive our own life-impulse in the motion of the fundamental line, a full analogy to our inner life" (Schenker 1979, 4).

Steve Larson and I (Johnson and Larson 2003) have provided an extensive analysis of the metaphors of musical motion by which musical progression is understood, showing how each of the main metaphors is grounded in some aspect of our bodily experience of motion. We claim that people have no robust way of conceptualizing musical motion without metaphors, and that all our reasoning about musical motion and musical space inherits the internal logic of such body-based metaphors. I want to take a close look at these metaphors for musical motion, because they show some of the ways that our experience and understanding of music is tied to our bodily sense of moving, desiring, and striving.

What Is Musical Motion?

If we try to explain how the opening line of the Beatles' "Something" captures the meaning and sound of the words "Something in the way she moves," we immediately encounter two metaphorical senses of motion, one related to pitch and the other to rhythm.[4] First, the pitches move. Before the word "moves," every note is sung to the same pitch; when we reach "moves," the pitch *moves* (down from C to B). Second, the rhythm moves. It moves in the same way that speech rhythms do, so that accented words are musically accented. Moreover, the words that are the most important to the song's message ("something," "way," and "moves") are emphasized through agogic and metric accents. To better appreciate this, consider the musical notation given in example 4. If one sings each of the words with notes of equal duration, as in example 4a, the result is stiff, unmusical, and at odds with the rhythms and accents of speech—it does not *flow*. Putting the main words on the main beats, as in example 4b, is an improvement,

---

4. George Harrison, "Something," on *Abbey Road* (London: Apple, 1969).

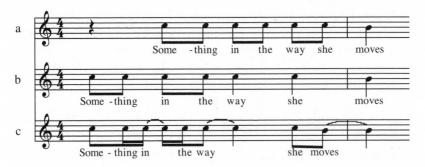

EXAMPLE 4. Harrison, "Something," opening lyric compared to two alternate settings

because it produces a more speech-like prosody. But the Beatles' setting, example 4c, is even better. Each of these three notes receives a different kind of accent, and those differences create an overall shape that leads to the word "moves" ("Some-" is a downbeat; "way" is an anticipated long note; and "moves" is both, which gives it special emphasis). To appreciate the "motion quality" of this overall shape, sing this melody and stop "up in the air" on the word "way." Suspended on the long note "way," we feel a strong anticipation of movement to the next downbeat ("moves"), to complete both the musical and the semantic sense of the passage.

In these ways, the music reflects the meaning of the words. But notice that the musical meaning does not depend on the words. Even without the lyrics, we would still speak of the melody *moving* from C to B, or of the rhythm *moving* ahead. There is immanent meaning here. This one brief musical passage is enough to suggest two of the many senses of musical motion that we use all the time for thinking and talking about our musical experience. But while our discourse about music is filled with such references to motion, the idea of musical motion is a profound enigma. Victor Zuckerkandl (1969) reminded us that we know almost nothing about melodic motion. He surveys a number of received ideas we have about tonal motion and then shows that they appear to have little to do with our ordinary literal understanding of motion. A typical passage conveys just one of the many enigmas of melodic motion. Zuckerkandl asks whether tones move, and he answers:

Actually, they stand still! In the *Marseillaise,* for example, we hear the first tone E—it does not move; then comes A, another static tone; this one is repeated; then comes B; and so on. No tone, as long as it sounds, moves from its place. What has happened to the motion? . . . Motion is the process that *conveys* the thing from here to there, in a continuous and never suspended traversal of the interval. If it stops anywhere, the motion is instantly abolished. But in a melody we have nothing but this, nothing but stops, a stringing together of static tones, and, between tone and tone, *no* connection, *no* transition, *no* filling up of intervals, nothing. It is the exact opposite of motion. (Zuckerkandl 1969, 83)

Many writers, such as Donald Ferguson (1960) and Stephen Davies (1994) have tried to address the problem of musical motion, but we still lack a clear answer to the question posed by Zuckerkandl.

So the concepts of musical motion that all of us use unreflectively to describe our musical experience turn out, under scrutiny, to be anything but clear, literal, and unproblematic. Musical motion must be some kind of metaphorical motion that takes place within a metaphorical space. That "space" must be "in" our experience, because the notes or pitches don't move in themselves. The "movement" comes from our ability to hear progressions that constitute unities within the musical piece. My project here is to explain the metaphoric structure and logic of such motion and to ask what this means for how we experience and understand musical meaning. Just as the Beatles emphasize different words in turn in the lyric "*Something* in the *way* she *moves*," I will begin with the observation that something in the music *moves*. I will next consider the question of what the *something* is that moves, and I will then go on to look at the *way* music moves.

Temporal Motion as a Basis for Musical Motion

Our metaphorical concepts of tonal motion are based on our two metaphorical models of time. Robert Morgan (1980) has noted the inseparability of musical space and musical time, and Philip Alperson observes that our experience of musical motion depends upon "the familiar habit of regarding the properties of time as analogous to those of space" (Alperson 1980, 409). Alperson cites Henri Bergson's claim that "we set our states of consciousness side by side in such a way as to perceive them simultaneously, no longer in one another, but alongside one another; in a word we project time into space, we express duration in terms of extensity, and succession thus takes the form of a continuous line or chain, the parts of which touch without penetrating one another" (Bergson 1910, 100).

In chapter 1, I summarized recent research in cognitive linguistics on the internal structure of two of the most important metaphorical spatializations of time: the MOVING TIMES metaphor, in which times are moving objects (with fronts and backs) moving toward and past a stationary observer; and the MOVING OBSERVER metaphor, in which times are extended locations on a landscape over which the observer moves. Recall that in both of these metaphors, the future is in front of the observer, the past is behind her, and the present is at her location. These two metaphor systems define most of our spatialization of time and supply the basis for our metaphorical understanding of musical motion. That is, we understand music as *moving,* and we understand ourselves as *being moved* by music. Now, if the source domain for musical motion is motion in space, then the ways we learn about space and physical motion should be crucial to how we experience and think about musical motion. To see this, let us begin by considering three of the most important ways we experience and learn about motion:

1. We *see objects move.*[5]
2. We *move our bodies.*
3. We *feel our bodies being moved by forces.*

Notice that all of these fundamental and pervasive experiences of motion are, for the most part, nonconceptual and pre-reflective, yet they give rise to a large body of knowledge that we have about motion. For example, we experience objects and we experience ourselves moving from one point to another along some path, and so we develop our sense of *loco*motion: movement from one place (*locus*) to another. We experience moving objects changing speed through the application of physical forces. We know, in an immediate bodily way, what it feels like to be moved by something else and to move ourselves. It is this source-domain knowledge of physical motion that is carried over into the target domain (musical motion) via systematic metaphoric mappings.

My central claim is that these three basic experiences of physical motion give rise, via metaphor, to three of the chief ways we conceptualize musical motion. Let us examine each of these three types of experience of motion, along with the metaphors based on them. I offer this analysis as an example of how both our understanding *and* experience of music are tied to body-based meaning.

5. For most people, our perception of moving objects is based principally on vision. However, other sensory modalities, such as the auditory system, give important information on motion. In blind people, for example, auditory cues will play the critical role of determining the direction, speed, and distance of moving objects.

The Moving Music Metaphor

"*Here comes* the recapitulation." "The strings *slow down* now." "The music *goes faster* here." In these ways, we describe the metaphorical motion of a musical event as moving toward and then past us. According to this orientation, which incorporates the MOVING TIMES metaphor (i.e., the metaphor of TIMES AS MOVING OBJECTS), a musical event is conceptualized as an object that moves past the stationary hearer from front to back. A future musical event—something that's "coming" in a piece of music we're listening to—exists in a musical space in front of the hearer and moves toward the hearer. When it reaches the stationary observer, it is experienced (heard), because it now exists in the present moment. Once the musical event has occurred for us, it exists only in memory in the past, that is, in the metaphorical space behind the observer.

Since music is both a temporal and a tonal art, the MOVING MUSIC metaphor is a complex set of mappings that combine a notion of physical contours of motion with the MOVING TIMES metaphor.

The MOVING MUSIC Metaphor

Source domain (physical motion)		Target domain (musical motion)
Physical Object	→	Musical Event
Physical Motion	→	Musical Motion
Speed Of Motion	→	Tempo
Location Of Observer	→	Present Musical Event
Objects In Front Of Observer	→	Future Musical Events
Objects Behind Observer	→	Past Musical Events
Path Of Motion	→	Musical Passage
Starting/Ending Point Of Motion	→	Beginning/End Of Passage
Temporary Cessation Of Motion	→	Rest, Caesura
Motion Over Same Path Again	→	Recapitulation, Repeat
Physical Forces (e.g., Inertia, Gravity, Magnetism)	→	"Musical Forces" (e.g., Inertia, Gravity, Magnetism)

This mapping defines one of our most influential and pervasive ways of experiencing and thinking about musical motion, as we import some of the logical entailments of the source domain into our experience of the target domain. Thus, the metaphorical logic of musical motion is based upon the spatial logic of physical motion. To test this claim, let us consider three of the most important kinds of inferences we draw about physical motion: (1) that motion requires an *object* that moves, (2) that motion will take place along a *path,* and (3) that motion will have a *manner.* We can then ask how those same structures of reasoning are present in our understanding of musical motion.[6]

First, the logic of physical motion (here, the fact that there must be something that moves) generates a corresponding question about music, namely, what is it that "moves" in music? This is a deeply perplexing and, I will suggest, misleading question. When we speak of music in terms of the MOVING MUSIC metaphor, we mean that our experience of a bit of music shares something with our experience of seeing objects move in physical space. The metaphor leads us to speak as if there must be musical objects. Notice that we have this same problem in the MOVING TIMES metaphor, according to which we conceptualize times as moving objects, even though times are not objects in any physical sense.

Second, moving objects trace out an imaginary *path* of motion. In music, segments of a musical path are thus called *passages.*

Third, physical motion will have a *manner;* there will be something in the *way* the music moves. Objects can move quickly or slowly, abruptly or smoothly, forcefully or gently. Via the MOVING MUSIC metaphor, this logic carries over into our understanding of the music as moving at a particular speed. That metaphorical speed is the *tempo.* We describe music as *fast* or *slow.* The "manner" of the motion is marked by words like *creep, crawl, rush, fly, slow down, speed up, walk, float, stumble,* etc. The music can proceed *by steps,* or it can make *leaps* of various lengths. Virtually any concept of a particular manner of physical motion can be applied to music.

Notice that the word *way* is polysemous—it has multiple related meanings. *Way* can mean the literal *path* one takes to a destination (as in "The Roman legions marched along the Appian *Way*"). It can also mean the *manner* (metaphorically understood) in which something is done (as in "Play the piece this *way,* with vibrato"). Or it can mean the metaphorical

6. The analysis that follows explores how our experience and understanding of musical motion relies on our more basic experience and understanding of physical motion. The analysis begins with a relatively simple view of physical motion. Of course, a similar analysis could explore our concepts of physical motion and space. For example, Eric Pederson and colleagues (1998) argue that some concepts of space and orientation that we might expect to be universal are in fact culturally shaped in that they systematically reflect the structures of that culture's language. Such an exploration would further illuminate the ways in which metaphor structures all of our concepts. But such an analysis lies beyond the scope of this book.

path one takes to achieve an end (as in "That's the best *way* to solve this equation"). So when we say, for example, "The tune *goes this way*," the *way* is the metaphorical path the music takes.

The MUSICAL LANDSCAPE Metaphor

A second basic experience of physical motion is our ability to move our bodies through a spatial landscape. We have the experience of moving from a starting point through a series of intermediate steps to a destination. Such experiences are the basis for a second major conception of a musical work, as an extended three-dimensional landscape through which the hearer moves. The listener takes a journey over the path that defines the particular piece of music being heard. In the MOVING OBSERVER metaphor, the present moment is wherever the moving observer is; likewise, in the music the present moment is where the listener is at, a particular point along their journey. In other words, *where* the musical traveler is in the music landscape is *what* the listener hears at that moment. Consequently, what has already been heard is conceptualized as points in the landscape that are behind the listener-traveler, while parts of the music not yet heard are future points on the path that one will encounter later. This explains expressions like the following: "We're *coming to* the coda." "When we *get to* measure 57, we'll see how the dissonance is resolved." "Let's see, *where are we* in the second movement?" "The melody *rises up ahead*." "At measure 4, the horns *enter*." "Once you *reach* the refrain, the dissonant part is *behind* you." "We're *going faster here*" (said in reference to a point in the score). "Two voices *start,* but soon a third *enters* (*joins in*)." "The soloist is waiting to *come in* seven measures *from here*."

Musical events are thus locations on a musical landscape, according to the following conceptual mapping.

The MUSICAL LANDSCAPE Metaphor

Source domain (physical space)	*Target domain (musical space)*
Traveler	→ Listener
Path Traversed	→ Musical Work
Traveler's Present Location	→ Present Musical Event
Path Already Traveled	→ Music Already Heard
Path In Front Of Traveler	→ Music Not Yet Heard
Segments Of The Path	→ Elements Of Musical Form
Speed Of Traveler's Motion	→ Tempo

One can take two perspectives on the musical landscape: that of the participant and that of the observer. In the *participant perspective,* you, the listener, are moving over the musical landscape. As listener, you are metaphorically *in* the piece—that is, you are traveling over the path that defines a particular musical piece, and you are actually hearing it (either in a live performance or on a recording). Imagine yourself, for example, listening to a Mozart string quartet and saying, "The cello comes in right *here!*" (where the word "here" is uttered just as the cello enters). The "here" is the place on the musical landscape where you are at the present moment. Many people have a strong tendency to use a pointing gesture to accompany their uttering of the word "here," indicating the exact "location" at which the cello enters.

As you, the hearer, move through a musical space, you can stand in various spatial relations to different musical events (as locations), and you can notice various things along your journey. You can *approach* the refrain, *come to* a resolution, *look ahead* to measure 21, *pass* the dissonant part, and *see* where the melody stops.

Within this landscape framework, repetition is tracing out the same trajectory of motion again. In music, one can repeat the same path of motion, but always *at a different time* from the original musical event. However, the experience of tracing the *same* musical path over again is so powerful that it can actually make you feel as though you are experiencing the *same time* over again. Such metaphorically understood experiences are not limited to music. We say, for example, "Oh no, it's Monday again," or "Here comes the weekend again!" with the sense that there is something about Monday (or the weekend) that is experienced as *the same* every time it occurs. In music, this effect appears to be even stronger. Some of the most striking effects in music come from its ability to make us feel like we're experiencing the *same time* over again, as though we are "back home" (and back *now*) again.[7]

A second perspective on the musical landscape is the *observer perspective.* It is conceived as a distant standpoint from which you can observe the path through a musical landscape that defines a particular work. This is the per-

---

7. The 1986 film *Peggy Sue Got Married* draws powerfully on this desire we have to live through certain moments and experiences one more time—to be able to return to what happened before and to relive it. In music, when you hear a certain motif once again, it may not merely be that something that occurred before is returning at a different time. Rather, you may feel that the *same time* is returning.

spective utilized most often by musicians and music theorists who are analyzing a score. The score is one metaphorical representation of the imaginary path through an abstract musical space. Every expression that can be used when speaking from the *participant* perspective can also be used from the *observer* perspective, just as though observers were making the musical journey in their imagination (in an imaginary space). The advantage that the allegedly objective observer perspective supplies is that one can see the entire musical piece at once, since it is an abstract object that can be viewed from afar. By contrast, from the participant perspective you ordinarily cannot see everything that is up ahead, because according to the logic of the MUSICAL LANDSCAPE metaphor, from a particular standpoint within the music, you may not be able to see the entire path ahead.

The observer perspective on the musical landscape is typically the preferred metaphor for music analysis, since it allows one to treat the entire musical work as an abstract object and to study its features. Those features can supposedly be measured, analyzed, and looked at from various perspectives—precisely what the "objective" music theorist is regarded as doing.

I have argued that it is primarily our experience of seeing objects move that gives rise to the MOVING MUSIC metaphor and that it is primarily our experience of moving our own bodies from one place to another that gives rise to the MUSICAL LANDSCAPE metaphor.[8] My central claim has been that it is the specific spatial logic of each particular sensorimotor source domain that controls the entailments of our metaphors of musical motion. For example, when music is viewed as a moving object, its status as metaphorical object gives it an aura of permanence. Also, taking the participant perspective within the musical landscape introduces strong notions of intentional action within a piece of music. The music can *strive, seek, want to resolve, push ahead,* and so forth.

Another important entailment shared by both of the central metaphors discussed so far is that motions are shaped by forces. Whether we are experiencing the physical motion of our bodies or of other objects, we learn that this motion is influenced by physical "forces" like gravity, magnetism, and inertia. Recent work on "musical forces" makes this set of metaphorical entailments explicit. Rudolf Arnheim (1986), Candace Brower

---

8. Ray Gibbs has suggested (personal communication) that our experience of moving our own bodies may also provide a basis for the MOVING MUSIC metaphor. Although I do not deny this possibility, I have not found either polysemy or inferential evidence that supports this hypothesis.

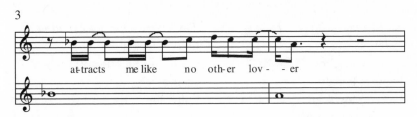

EXAMPLE 5. Harrison, "Something," opening lyric compared to underlying whole-note melodic skeleton

(1997–98, 2000), Robert Hurwitz (Hurwitz and Larson 1994), Steve Larson (1993a, 1993b, 1994a, 1994b, 1997, 1997–98, 1999, 2002, forthcoming), Fred Lerdahl (1996, 2001), William Pelto (1994), and Leigh VanHandel (Larson and VanHandel 2005) have used the idea of musical forces to illuminate issues of theory, analysis, cognition, and pedagogy.

Musical forces often pull us in different directions. But at one point in the Beatles' "Something," these forces all agree in a way that elegantly illustrates the meaning of the text "attracts me like no other lover." The line "Something in the way she moves" (example 5a, beginning) may be heard as an embellishment of the simpler, whole-note melody given in example 5b (i.e., a C-B that begins a descending motion in half steps).

Musical inertia, the tendency of a pattern to continue in the *same* fashion, suggests that this whole-note motion will continue descending in half steps, as in example 5b (i.e., C-B-Bflat-A). Musical gravity—the tendency of a melody to *descend*—suggests that this whole-note motion will continue by going down. And musical magnetism, the tendency of an unstable pitch to resolve to the *closest* stable pitch, suggests that B-flat will resolve to A. Thus, all three musical forces here reinforce each other to powerfully "attract" the B-flat of "attract" to the A of "lover."

The Music As Moving Force Metaphor

The third major way we experience physical motion is when physical substances and entities like wind, water, and large objects move us from one point to another. In music, the metaphorical force is the music itself, moving the hearer from one location (state) to another (different state). If music is a force, then it has causal effects. This idea of musical forces is thus a special case of the LOCATION EVENT-STRUCTURE metaphor.

The MUSIC AS MOVING FORCE Metaphor

Source domain (physical motion)		*Target domain (musical experience)*
Locations	→	Emotional States
Movement (From Place To Place)	→	Change of Emotional State
Physical Forces	→	Causes
Forced Movement	→	Causation
Intensity Of Force	→	Intensity Of Musical Impact

On the basis of this generic metaphor for causation, musical forces are conceived as acting on listeners to move them from one state-location to another along some path of metaphorical motion. You can actually feel yourself being *pushed, pulled,* and generally *moved* by the music. When music is a *moving* experience, it can *bowl you over, blow you away, carry you along, transport you, give you a lift,* and *take you on a roller-coaster ride.* It can make you *float along* or it can *drag you down.* When the music *swings,* you *swing.* "Something in the way she moves, attracts me like no other lover," can be as much about music as it is about love.

So when we say that music moves and that music moves us, we do more than make a pun. This is another important instance of polysemy. Just as *way* has multiple metaphorically related senses (as we saw above), so too does *move* in its application to musical experience. The MUSIC AS MOVING FORCE metaphor helps to explain why we use the word *move* to mean these different but related things.

To summarize: Our three major ways of experiencing physical motion, coupled with our two primary metaphorical spatializations of time, give rise to our three most important metaphors for musical motion. This is only part of the story. A comprehensive account would have to include additional metaphors and metonymies based on additional ways we experience motion and causation. But this, I trust, is enough to show some of the sensorimotor basis for our experience, understanding, and conceptualization of musical space and motion. The *meaning* of this musical motion is grounded in our bodily encounter with the motion of objects in space that are subject to physical forces.

Is Musical Motion Real?

If most of what we can think and say about musical time and musical motion depends on metaphor and metonymy, then it might seem that there is no such thing as musical motion! Maybe it is just a fiction and a mere manner of speaking about music. Yet we do seem to *experience* movement in music. So, is it real?[9]

My answer is that musical motion is just as real as temporal motion, and just as completely defined by metaphor. Music *moves*. We *experience* musical events as *fast* or *slow, rising* or *falling, creeping* or *leaping, pausing* and *stopping*. The reason that musical motion is "real" is that, as Eduard Hanslick (1854/1986) said more than 150 years ago, music exists only in our "aural imagination," that is, only as experienced by us. Music is not the notes on the scores. Nor is it merely the vibrations of air that we hear as sounds. It is, rather, our whole vast, rich experience of sounds synthesized into meaningful patterns that extend over time. This experience of musical motion is no less real for being a product of human imagination—which is our profound capacity to experience ordered, meaningful patterns of sensations. If there were no people like us, with bodies and brains like ours, then there would be no musical time and no musical motion. Music "exists" at the intersection of organized sounds with our sensorimotor apparatus, our bodies, our brains, our cultural values and practices, our music-historical conventions, our prior experiences, and a host of other social and cultural factors. Consequently, musical motion is really experienced by us, albeit via our imaginative structuring of sounds.

On the basis of the kinds of analyses and evidence given above, how strong a conclusion can we draw about the constitutive role of metaphor in our experience and understanding of music? The safer, although still controversial, claim is that our understanding and conceptualization of musical experience, and therefore our linguistic discourse about music, are in large measure irreducibly structured by deep conceptual metaphors.

---

9. Eric Clarke (n.d.) observes that music can give us clues about the motion of "fictional" or "virtual" sources. He argues that "the sense of motion and gesture in music is a truly perceptual phenomenon" and that "the perceptual information that specifies motion is broadly speaking the same as for the perception of motion in the everyday world." While he claims that the experience of musical motion "is neither real nor metaphorical," I believe that a close reading of his paper, rather than contradicting the arguments presented here, provides additional support for my argument. See also Gjerdingen 1994.

I am suggesting that there is a compelling body of empirical evidence for the correctness of this claim, some of which I have examined here.

However, I am inclined toward the even stronger, more polemical claim that our very *experience* of musical meaning is fundamentally shaped by conceptual metaphors that are grounded in our bodily experience. This clearly applies to mature listeners who have learned how to experience certain genres and styles of music. Infants, of course, can have a non-conceptual, prelinguistic bodily experience of music, and young children dance gleefully to various rhythms without knowing a thing about music history or having any developed conceptualization of music. But surely, each of us does *learn* how to listen as part of our cultural edification. At this level, there can be no robust experience of musical meaning without these conceptual metaphorical framings and their spatial and bodily logics. As relatively mature listeners, we do not merely experience a musical work and *then* understand and interpret it. Rather, our understanding is woven into the fabric of our experience. Our understanding is our way of being in and making sense of our experience. Thus, the way we *experience* a piece of music will depend importantly on how we *understand* it, via our sensorimotor capacities, our emotional systems, and the conceptual metaphors we have learned within our culture.

EMPIRICAL EVIDENCE FOR EMBODIED MUSICAL MEANING

The evidence given so far for the existence of at least three major metaphors for musical motion takes the following form: I have shown that people's bodily experience of, and reasoning about, various types of physical motion provides the basis for metaphors of musical events. This explains why we use the terms of space (and motion through space) for conceptualizing musical events, and it explains the inferences we make about musical motion.

Recent work on "musical forces" offers some additional empirical support for the assertion that our experience of physical forces shapes our experience of musical motion. The evidence, to date, is of three kinds: (1) the distribution of patterns within compositions, improvisations, and analyses; (2) the behavior of computer models of melodic expectation; and (3) the responses of participants in psychological experiments.

As an example of the first sort of evidence, Steve Larson (1997–98) used his account of the musical forces of "gravity," "magnetism," and "inertia" to generate a small, well-defined set of three-, five-, and seven-note patterns in which the musical forces are best represented, and he found these patterns to be nearly identical with those discussed in published accounts of "hidden repetition" in tonal music. Larson (2002) considered all possible patterns that fill a third within the seventh chords of selected jazz compositions and transcribed jazz improvisations, and he found that the musical forces could account well for the distribution of those patterns within his analyses of those pieces.

As an example of computer models of melodic expectation, Larson's computer models (1993a, 1994b, 1999, forthcoming) rely on an algorithm that quantifies the interaction of musical forces, and he found that this algorithm—as well as Fred Lerdahl's proposed revision (1996) of it—gave higher ratings to melodic continuations that were sung more often by participants in several different experiments.

Thirdly, Leigh VanHandel and Larson (2000) found that the musical forces could account well for listeners' judgments about the experienced "strength" of presented pattern completions, as well as the distribution of those same patterns within Heinrich Schenker's *Five Graphic Music Analyses* (1932/1969).

Evidence in each of these forms provides some support for the theory of musical forces that is consistent with my hypothesis that metaphors for musical motion are grounded in experiences of physical forces and physical motion. But the ideas advanced here may suggest other hypotheses to be tested. Perhaps the approach described by Raymond Gibbs (1994) for priming studies could be used to test whether certain metaphorical entailments shape descriptions of musical experience.

THE IMAGE-SCHEMATIC STRUCTURE OF MUSICAL MEANING

We have seen how the logic of physical motion structures our experience and understanding of musical motion.[10] Part of that logic involves the action of forces that aid or obstruct motion toward some destination. It should be expected, then, that all of the image schemas for force dynamics (e.g., COMPULSION, BLOCKAGE, ATTRACTION, ENABLEMENT, etc.) and all of the structural elements of paths (e.g., starting points, paths, steps along the path, destination, progress toward destination, etc.) will play a role in our experience and understanding of music. And so they

---

10. Parts of this paragraph and the next are taken from my essay "Embodied Musical Meaning," *Theory and Practice* 22–23 (1997–98): 95–102.

do. William Echard (1999) has analyzed the image schemas of balance and force dynamics that structure Neil Young's "Powderfinger." Janna Saslaw (1997–98) shows how the structural characteristics of certain prototypical image schemas for physical forces are present in our experience and conceptualization of music and, consequently, in our ordinary and theoretical discourse about music. Prototypical physical forces, for example, exhibit a path of motion, a directionality, a source and a goal of the motion, a structure of causality, and various degrees of intensity. Saslaw reveals these same structural features in music descriptions. Candace Brower (1997–98) gives several examples of some of the ways we automatically and unconsciously experience music as goal-directed movement, on the basis of image schemas such as SOURCE-PATH-GOAL. So structured, music is experienced as going *fast* or *slow, meeting obstacles, seeking goals, overcoming blockages, faltering, recovering,* and *surging ahead.* Brower quotes Schenker's description of this process of striving for a goal: "In the art of music, as in life, motion toward the goal encounters obstacles, reverses, disappointments, and involves great distances, detours, expansions, interpolations, and in short, retardations of all kinds. . . . Thus we hear in the middleground and foreground an almost dramatic course of events" (Schenker 1979, 16).

The longing, searching character of "Over the Rainbow" thus has a dramatic character realized via image schemas that structure our purposeful motion toward a destination, along a path that can be difficult and dangerous. We do not merely project (imaginatively) these image schemas onto music, any more than we project them onto our ordinary bodily experience of motion. Rather, such image schemas actually constitute the structure and define the quality of our musical experience. They are in and of the music as experienced; they *are* the structure of the music. And they have meaning because they are partly constitutive of our bodily experience and the meaning it gives rise to.

THE PLURALISTIC ONTOLOGY OF MUSICAL MOTION

A persistent worry about the idea that body-based conceptual metaphors can be constitutive of our experience stems from the fact that typically there are multiple inconsistent metaphors for any given phenomenon. For example, in the MOVING MUSIC metaphor, music moves and the perceiver is stationary, whereas in the MUSICAL LANDSCAPE metaphor, the musical landscape is stationary and the perceiver moves over and through it. In the first case, musical events are *objects* that move, while in the second case they are *locations* on a musical landscape (and thus don't move). Consequently, we have two different and incompatible ontologies underlying these two different metaphors.

To some people, this inescapable inconsistency among various metaphorical structurings of our basic concepts for musical motion will be taken as evidence that the metaphors cannot really be constitutive and must, rather, be nothing but figures of speech.

In arguing against this objection, we should begin by noting that what is true of musical motion is equally true of our incompatible conceptions of time. In the MOVING TIMES metaphor, times are moving objects, whereas in the MOVING OBSERVER metaphor, times are stationary locations on the time landscape. This inconsistency of multiple metaphorical structurings of a single concept is typical of a vast range of abstract concepts, including causation, morality, mind, self, love, ideas, thought, and knowledge (Lakoff and Johnson 1999). My claim is that each of these different, and often inconsistent, metaphorical structurings of a concept gives us the different logics that we need in order to understand the richness and complexity of our experience. However strong our desire for a monolithic, consistent ontology might be, the evidence does not support such a unified and simple view of human experience. The absence of any core literal concept of musical "events" should direct our attention to the ways we imaginatively conceive of the flow of our musical experience by means of multiple body-based metaphors that provide the relevant logics of our various conceptions of musical motion and space. There is no more a single, univocal notion of musical motion than there is of causation, and yet we have gotten along reasonably well by knowing when a specific metaphor for causation is appropriate for a specific context of inquiry.

The fact of multiple inconsistent metaphors for a single concept also sheds light on the important question of cultural difference and variation. The grounding of metaphors in bodily experience suggests possible universal structures (of bodily perception and movement) for understanding music. However, since there are multiple metaphors available, and since there may be differing cultural interpretations of bodily experience, metaphor provides one important avenue for exploring cultural and historical variation in significantly different conceptions of musical experience that might arise around the world.

THE PRIMACY OF EMBODIED MUSICAL MEANING

I would like to end my account of embodied musical meaning by highlighting one important insight that comes from an examination of the role of metaphor in our experience and understanding of music—namely, that the mechanisms of human meaning extend far beyond the capacity for language. As I mentioned earlier, philosophers reflecting on music have often assumed that music is some kind of "language" and that our primary experience of meaning is in language, so that whatever meaning music has must be measured relative to linguistic meaning. Moreover, these same theorists often adopt false views of linguistic meaning as being tied solely to reference and truth conditions. When music seems not to measure up to such mistaken conceptual and referential criteria of linguistic meaning, it is then erroneously concluded that music is a second-class citizen of the intellectual world.

The problem here lies not so much in the idea of music as language, but rather in overly narrow and restricted views of linguistic meaning as involving literal concepts and objective reference that is alleged to be completely independent of the nature of our bodies. What is left out are the embodied and affective dimensions of linguistic and musical meaning alike. Music is meaningful in specific ways that some language cannot be, but it shares in the general embodiment of meaning that underlies *all* forms of symbolic expressions, including gesture, body language, ritual, spoken words, visual communication, etc. Thinking about how music moves us is not going to explain everything we need to know about language, but it is an excellent place to begin to understand how all meaning emerges in the flesh, blood, and bone of our embodied experience.

This brings us back, finally, to our earlier discussion of the Beatles' music. We have already admired some of their intertwining of the lyrics and aspects of the music's motion. I would like to conclude by drawing your attention to another fine example of the lyrics and music working together that emphasizes my point about the embodiment of musical meaning. The passage of music in example 6 resembles a common musical pattern known as a sentence.

In a sentence, a short bit of music ("I don't want to leave her now") is followed by a similar short bit of music ("You know I believe, and how"), which is then typically completed, and answered, by a longer, balancing unit. But here the balancing unit is stated by the guitar alone. We expect a balancing unit of text to answer the two lines of text. In fact, we might expect words that will tell us, finally, what that "something in the way she moves" actually *is* that "attracts me like no other lover." By giving us that balancing unit only in the guitar, without words, the Beatles seem to be saying that in the end, only music can say what needs to be

I don't want to leave her now, you

know I be - lieve, and how,

(guitar)

EXAMPLE 6. Harrison, "Something," guitar line ending verse

said.[11] And they do it with a melodic line that not only retraces the path of what has gone before (the essential pitches of the guitar line, A-Bflat-B-C, reverse the essential pitches of the opening lines of text—see the whole notes in example 5), but also leads us back to the beginning of the piece. Where the text leaves off, embodied musical meaning answers.

WHAT ART REVEALS ABOUT MEANING

The principal point of this and the previous chapter is that by looking at how art affects us, we gain profound insights into the bodily basis of meaning and understanding. Art uses the very same syntactic, semantic, and pragmatic resources that underlie *all* meaning, but in art those resources are exploited in remarkable ways that give us a sense of the meaning of things that is typically not available in our day-to-day affairs. Although we sometimes go to the arts merely for entertainment, we sometimes also appreciate them as consummations of meaning. In art we seek an intensification, harmonizing, and fulfillment of the possibilities for meaning and growth of meaning.

11. Walter Everett reaches a related conclusion about "Something." Although speaking of a different section of the song, he suggests that "the structural core of the song's melody, a fully-supported ^3-^2-^1 descent heard only in the guitar solo, is best expressed in a musical fantasy. A poetic text here would only get in the way" (Everett 1999, 251).

Consequently, when you investigate the workings of various arts, you are investigating what meaning is, where it comes from, and how it can grow. In this chapter and the previous one, I have offered brief glimpses of some of the ways that various arts have meaning, and I have emphasized the nonconceptual, mostly unconscious, and embodied way that meaning arises in our experience. Even in poetry and prose, we saw how meaning exceeds conceptual form and expression. In music this is even more obvious, since we leave the realm of linguistic meaning when we focus exclusively on the music itself.

The reason that so many philosophers are unwilling to call these embodied structures part of meaning is that images, image schemas, affect contours, and metaphors cannot be satisfactorily put in propositional form. However, instead of concluding that music must therefore not have meaning in the proper sense, we ought rather to conclude that meaning, in the proper sense, goes far beyond conceptual and propositional content. We ought to realize that our human capacities for discerning meaning operate pervasively in all our experience, artistic and non-artistic alike, but in good art those capacities operate in an exemplary fashion, showing us how experience can be significant and meaningful. Art—at least art that is not overly enamored with postmodernism—is not an escape from meaning, but rather a pursuit of consummated meaning. That is part of what Dewey meant when he insisted that art is a condition of life.

CHAPTER 12

The Meaning of the Body

I fell for philosophy as an undergraduate student in the late 1960s because I believed that philosophy was about our human quest for meaning. This still seems right to me today, and if I ceased to believe it, philosophy would lose its relevance to my life. When philosophy fails to address our most basic existential concerns, it becomes merely an intellectual game, or an exercise of an eviscerated intelligence in solving narrowly defined, highly technical problems within specialized subfields. Such a conception of philosophy is not worthy of its calling. Therefore, it is time for me to tie together the threads of the previous chapters in order to say what meaning is, what the body is, and what the bodily basis of meaning entails for the nature of philosophy and for human wisdom.

The central theme of this book is that philosophy becomes relevant to human life only by reconnecting with, and grounding itself in, bodily dimensions of human meaning and value. Philosophy needs a visceral connection to lived experience. Unfortunately, much of the philosophy of mind and language of the past century lost this visceral engagement, chiefly because it focused on only a small and highly intellectualized part of meaning, leaving out much of what goes into actual human meaning-making. It is not the rigor of its methods that makes certain parts of Anglo-American analytic philosophy sterile; that rigor is a fine and important contribution to philosophical reflection. Rather, it is what that rigor is applied to (namely, conceptual and propositional structures alone) that leads people to overlook the visceral depths of meaning.

The necessary remedy for our current problematic state must be a non-dualistic, embodied view of meaning, concepts, mind, thought, language, and values. A new philosophy of this sort cannot emerge directly from mainstream analytic philosophy, because it is precisely some of the founding assumptions of that tradition that are the problem. We must challenge the assumptions of what Lakoff and I (1999) have called first-generation cognitive science, that is, cognitive science based on information-processing psychology, artificial intelligence, model theory, and analytic philosophy of mind and language.

We have seen that over the past two decades, many important developments have emerged that show promise for repairing the previous neglect of embodied human meaning. The new account of embodied meaning is developing in recent work coming from several sources: (1) the re-birth of interest in pragmatist views of experience, meaning, and value (e.g., present-day pragmatists);[1] (2) the phenomenology of the embodied mind, especially in the style of Merleau-Ponty and, to a lesser extent, parts of Heidegger and Husserl that focus on the lifeworld[2]; (3) second-generation cognitive science, which pursues empirical studies of embodied cognition (in psychology, neuroscience, linguistics, and anthropology); and (4) ecological philosophies that emphasize organism-environment processes of meaning-making and that acknowledge the human connection to other animal species and to the more-than-human world. Currently, we are just at the dawn of what might someday become a serious reconstruction of philosophy, but nobody can say for sure where this will ultimately lead.

In this final chapter, I want to summarize what I have been trying to say about the nature of meaning in light of the role of the body in its construction. A key part of this new view of meaning must necessarily be a revised view of what "the body" means. Finally, we need to ask what

1. Much exciting work is being carried out by many present-day pragmatist philosophers, such as John McDermott, John Lachs, Hilary Putnam, Tom Alexander, Charlene Haddock Siegfried, Richard Shusterman, Scott Pratt, Robert Innis, Douglas Anderson, and a host of others. A full listing would end up including a large proportion of the current membership of the Society for the Advancement of American Philosophy. I offer my apologies to the scores of people working out of the pragmatist tradition whom I have not mentioned.

2. Here I should mention a large number of contemporaries who focus on the bodily, intersubjective dimensions of our lived experience. I would note especially the work of Shaun Gallagher, Francisco Varela, Hubert Dreyfus, Beata Stawarska, David Levin, Eugene Gendlin, David Abrams, and most members of the Merleau-Ponty Circle.

the task of philosophy becomes once embodied meaning is restored to its rightful place at the center of human experience, thought, and practice.

THE MEANING OF MEANING

The view I have been developing in the previous chapters is that meaning is a matter of relations and connections grounded in bodily organism-environment coupling, or interaction. The meaning of something is its relations, actual and potential, to other qualities, things, events, and experiences. In pragmatist lingo, the meaning of something is a matter of how it connects to what has gone before and what it entails for present or future experiences and actions. Dewey expressed this conception of meaning as follows:

> A thing is more significantly what it makes possible than what it immediately is. The very conception of cognitive meaning, intellectual significance, is that things in their immediacy are subordinated to what they portend and give evidence of. An intellectual sign denotes that a thing is not taken immediately but is referred to something that may come in consequence of it. (Dewey 1925/1981, 105)

Things are felt or experienced in their immediate qualities. For instance, your whole present situation might be frightful, or anxious, or joyful, or doubtful. These objective qualities of situations are at first only minimally meaningful. If a situation is frightful, then minimally it means that danger is actually or potentially at hand. Something might hurt you and overpower you; or it might just reduce you to quivering pudding. If, on the other hand, a situation is joyful, it is expansive and vitalizing, opening out upon many possibilities for growth, enhancement of meaning, and fluid development. It is a situation in which your whole being wants to "affirm the Eternal Yes" (to steal a line from a love-smitten young man in the film *A Room with a View* who is shouting out his happiness from his perch in the boughs of an olive tree). The threatening or joyful characteristic of your situation takes on new meaning as the situation develops and as you engage in thought and action. Each stage of that situation's development opens up possibilities for further exploration of its fuller meaning. That will come only as you mark more distinctions, recognize more relations and connections, and take action. Your threatening situation becomes more meaningful when you notice *that desperate man* with *that gun* pointed at *you,* barking his demand for you to turn over your money.

Each new marking of connections and relations increases the meaning of the threatening situation. *Now* you see how the frightful, threatening, and doubtful dimensions of your situation are intimately connected—and so the meaning of what is happening emerges. Dewey emphasizes the role of qualities and consequences in this process of meaning-making:

> This state of things in which qualitatively different feelings are not just had but are significant of objective differences, is mind. Feelings are no longer just felt. They have and they make *sense;* record and prophesy.
>
> That is to say, difference in qualities (feelings) of acts when employed as indications of acts performed and to be performed and as signs of their consequences, *mean* something. And they mean it directly; the meaning is had as their own character. . . . Without language, the qualities or organic action that are feelings are pains, pleasures, odors, colors, noises, tones, only potentially and proleptically. With language they are discriminated and identified. They are then "objectified"; they are immediate traits of things. . . . The qualities were never "in" the organism; they always were qualities of interactions in which both extra-organic things and organisms partake. When named, they enable identification and discrimination of things to take place as means in a further course of inclusive interaction. (Dewey 1925/1981, 198)

Although I will not develop these themes here, Dewey proceeds to connect the emergence of meaning with the communicative use of language (symbolic interaction), and he regards this process as leading to the emergence of "mind" via shared meaning. Dewey observes that it is language and other forms of symbolic interaction that allow us to grasp most fully the meaning of things and to employ that meaning for inquiry and deliberation. It is crucial to recognize that the term *language,* as Dewey uses it, does not merely consist of spoken or written words; rather, it includes all forms of symbolic interaction by means of which we indicate significant qualities, patterns, and structures. Language in this rich sense is the basis of our ability to communicate with others, to coordinate actions, and to engage in fruitful inquiry through the employment of meaningful signs. Meaning is thus both (1) grounded in our bodily interactions—in the qualities and structures of objective situations; and (2) always social, because it would not exist in its fullness without communicative interactions and shared language, which give us the means of exploring the meaning of things.

Dewey notes the profound irony that language (in the broadest sense of symbolic communication in general) is both our great vehicle for the growth of meaning, inquiry, and knowledge and simultaneously the source of our all-too-frequent failure to capture the depth and richness of our experience, thereby limiting our ability to understand and reconstruct our experience. Language both enriches meaning and at the same time, as a result of its selective character, ensures that we are forever doomed to overlook large and important parts of meaning. This fact, as we saw, is the basis for Gendlin's entire project of recovering the deep processes of meaning, by looking beyond and beneath the formal, structural, conceptual, propositional, representational dimensions of meaning. It is not surprising, therefore, that one of the fundamental problems with traditional analytic philosophy of language is that it typically tries to account for all meaning in terms of just one very limited type of meaning relation—usually that of "reference" or, correspondingly, "truth conditions"—as if that single relation alone could embrace all of the ways in which something, even a word, can have meaning.

So-called truth-conditional semantics, made popular over the past thirty years especially by the writings of Donald Davidson (1967), assumes that only statements or utterances have meaning and that their meaning "cashes out" in terms of the conditions under which they would be true (or false). With meaning so narrowly and shallowly defined, most of what goes into human meaning is left out, typically by relegating it to background conditions, feelings, emotional coloring, or pragmatics. It was Dewey, once again, who presciently observed that meaning is a far broader notion than truth:

> But the realm of meanings is wider than that of true-and-false meanings; it is more urgent and more fertile. . . . Poetic meanings, moral meanings, a large part of the goods of life are matters of richness and freedom of meanings, rather than of truth; a large part of our life is carried on in a realm of meanings to which truth and falsity as such are irrelevant. And the claim of philosophy to rival or displace science as a purveyor of truth seems to be mostly a compensatory gesture for failure to perform its proper task of liberating and clarifying meanings, including those scientifically authenticated. (Dewey 1925/1981, 307)

In a similar vein, J. L. Austin famously observed that the philosophy of his own day had been etiolated, as he liked to say, by its slavish insistence that "the sole business, the sole interesting business, of any utterance—that is, of anything we say—is to be true or at least false" (Austin 1970, 233).

In the more expansive and comprehensive sense of meaning that I have been developing, meaning includes qualities, emotions, percepts, concepts, images, image schemas, metaphors, metonymies, and various other imaginative structures. Learning the meaning of something would thus include a growing sense of all the qualities, percepts, distinctions, recollections of what has gone before, and anticipations of possible future experience that follow from it. No isolated thing, percept, or quality has any meaning in itself. Things, qualities, events, and symbols have meaning *for us* because of how they connect with other aspects of our actual or possible experience. Meaning is relational and instrumental. According to the view I am developing, mere "redness" has no intrinsic meaning, no meaning in its immediacy and in itself, whereas the redness of blood, the redness of a swollen wound, the redness of a ripe bing cherry, the redness of my lover's lips, and the redness of an Oregon-coast sunset all have plenty of meaning, with each red having a different meaning, but one related in certain specific ways to the other reds. Another way of making this point is to say that the quality of redness means different things in different experienced situations. The redness of blood means life (or loss of life), the redness of a ripe bing cherry means the possibility of a certain exquisite taste and texture available to me if I eat that cherry, and the redness of a swollen wound means bodily insult, infection, danger, suffering, and the need for remedial therapeutic action. Any meaning that an isolated patch of red has for me will be parasitic on these other meanings of red—red lips, wounds, cherries, and sunsets.

Aspects of our experience take on meaning, then, insofar as they activate for us their relations to other actual or possible aspects of our experience. The redness of a wound becomes a sign of infection or inflammatory reaction. It portends pain and suffering and sometimes healing. It points to possible future medical complications if it is not treated. For those with medical knowledge, it might signify any of a number of possible causes and suggest any of a number of possible medical treatments. James and Dewey observed that once we recognize that one thing can point beyond itself and its immanent qualities to other qualities, structures, or experiences, our whole world is transformed from one in which we are mostly passive recipients of what happens to a quite different world, in which we can inquire, communicate with others, and coordinate our actions. Grasping meaning becomes a matter of selecting one or more qualities or patterns within a situation as pointing toward some different qualities or patterns, either in that same situation or in some other situation. For example, in Camus' *The Stranger,* there is a haunting image that is redolent with meaning precisely through its vast fund of connections to other scenes, images, qualities, and ideas in the world evoked within the novel. Having returned from his mother's funeral, Meursault goes to the beach, meets a woman he had earlier known at his office, and brings her back to his nearly empty flat to spend the night. After she leaves the next morning, a Sunday morning, Meursault spends the entire day observing the passing of life in the streets below his balcony, mostly disengaged from the lives of those people—young and old, alone and in groups, with families or friends—who bustle about to their various Sunday events, each of them carrying on with their own sense of purpose. Meursault is but a detached observer of this play of life, unable to engage the meaning of what is passing before his eyes. As evening falls, after an entire day of detached observation of life, he finally rises from his chair on the balcony and eats his dinner of spaghetti and bread, standing up, alone in the growing darkness.

> I wanted to smoke a cigarette at the window, but the air was getting colder and I felt a little chilled. I shut my windows, and as I was coming back I glanced at the mirror and saw a corner of my table with my alcohol lamp next to some pieces of bread. It occurred to me that anyway one more Sunday was over, that Maman was buried now, that I was going back to work, and that, really, nothing had changed. (Camus 1942/1988, 24)

Here is Meursault, alone in a mostly empty room, surrounded by the darkness. He sees, not directly but only in the mirror reflection, that haunting, sad, lonely image of a part of his table with only the dim light of a lamp and a few pieces of bread; these are images of alienation, loneliness, and emptiness. Meursault's situation reaches, via a wealth of both immediate and symbolic connections, back into the events of the burial of his mother and forward into the events about to unfold, in which his existence as a stranger—an alien in an alien world—leads to his undoing. But the power of this small scene is only an intensification of the way in which virtually any image or event we encounter can have meaning for us. Things and events have meaning by virtue of the way they call up something beyond them to which they are connected.

This "selection" or partial "taking" from the continuous flow of experience that lies at the heart of meaning is, on the one hand, the means of the very possibility of fruitful investigation, symbolic interaction, and communication; on the other hand, it simultaneously requires us to ignore the nonselected aspects of a situation. What we emphasize and, conversely, what we ignore will make all the difference in what "things" mean to us.

Abstraction is a great tool for the furtherance of human inquiry, but it is also responsible for much of the loss of meaning that is available to us in any given situation. As Dewey says,

> Enter upon this road (of abstraction) and the time is sure to come when the appropriate object-of-knowledge is stripped of all that is immediate and qualitative, of all that is final, self-sufficient. Then it becomes an anatomized epitome of just and only those traits which are of indicative and instrumental import. (Dewey 1925/1981, 106; parentheses added)

In other words, continued processes of abstraction—however well they serve various purposes of inquiry, and however revealing and necessary they may be—do not always bring us closer to the fullness of a situation; they may take us farther from its full meaning. Hence, our individual and collective habits of grasping the meaning of anything via abstraction will fatefully determine how our world stands forth for us. And if our philosophies—our most comprehensive accounts of the meaning of things—are grounded on the most partial or superficial aspects of experience, then our entire understanding of life will be drastically impoverished.

It thus makes all the difference whether we take experience in the limited sense, as meaning "things as known or conceptualized," or whether we take it in its fullness, as redolent with meaning that surpasses our undoubtedly useful abstractions from it. Part of philosophy's job is to help us recover the fullest possible meaning of our experience—the pulsating, lived world that transcends any conceptual specification of it.

Philosophy of language, the principal repository of the theory of meaning in contemporary analytic philosophy, cannot provide an adequate theory of meaning, because it has selected for its "objects" of study only concepts, sentences, propositions, and words. Influenced by a pervasive behaviorism and positivism that eschewed "meanings," "experiences," and "mental states," the philosophers who created the new field of "philosophy of language" during the 1940s and 1950s were restricted to taking only observable things, such as words and sentences (or utterances of them), to be the sole proper bearers of meaning. They treated words and sentences as quasi-objects that could be analyzed into their constituent parts. Even worse, they frequently accepted the logical empiricist division of utterances into those that were descriptive versus those that were expressive. The descriptive, truth-stating sentences were declared to be the rightful purveyors of cognitive meaning, their proper function being to make truth claims. The expressive function of language was just that—expressive, and supposedly lacking significant cognitive content. The rest is old, tired history, a history of propositional, truth-conditional theories of language and their correlative views of mind, thought, and knowledge. The capacity of a "sign" to point beyond itself to actual or potential experiences got reduced to the thin notion of reference. And so John Searle, whose clear writing has helped make the technical aspects of the philosophy of language available to a broader audience, confidently asserts that the fundamental question of the philosophy of language is how words can relate to the world (Searle 1969, 3). Philosophy of language was built around the questions of how words refer and how sentences can be true or false. For non-truth-stating speech acts, this became the question of what conditions must be satisfied to successfully carry off the particular speech act being performed.

It is not my intention to underestimate the many contributions to our understanding of language and meaning that have come out of Anglo-American analytic philosophy. The philosophical work that has emerged from this orientation has given us many insights into reference, truth, and speech-act structure. But the chief mistake that many philosophers have made, and that has virtually defined contemporary philosophy of language, is the assumption that this approach to language can provide the basis for understanding meaning in general. The real problem is this: more often than not, the aspects of meaning that I have been surveying here—such as image schemas, qualities, emotions, affect contours, and conceptual metaphor—are dismissed as falling outside the domain of meaning proper. This dismissal is catastrophic from the perspective of an adequate account of meaning, because it peremptorily eliminates from consideration most of what goes into human meaning-making, particularly all of the body-based dimensions. It radically distinguishes linguistic meaning from all other types of symbolic interaction, and it assumes that if any of these forms of expression (e.g., painting, music, sculpture, architecture, dance, sign languages) have meaning, then it must be in some second-rate sense, as being parasitic on linguistic meaning (where "linguistic" is already a severely limited selection from the full scope of actual linguistic meaning).

What follows from this is that the philosophies of mind and theories of knowledge that are based on these versions of analytic philosophy of language inherit (and then reinforce) all of the ontological and epistemological dualisms (e.g., mind/body, cognitive/emotive, fact/value, knowledge/imagination) that give us a picture of human thought as cut off from the world, thereby requiring criteria for determining whether and how sentences can be connected to things in the world. With this view, skepticism is never far behind, precisely because the meanings seem to get locked up within "mind" and then need to somehow get back in touch with "the world" from which they were originally separated.

Let me be more specific about the nature of the problem that I am claiming to identify in most mainstream, contemporary Anglo-American philosophy. It is the problem of the objectivist theory of meaning.

THE OBJECTIVIST THEORY OF MEANING

1. Words and sentences are the proper bearers of meaning.
2. The words from which meaningful sentences are built are regarded as conventional signs (which indeed they are).
3. We must then ask how those meaningless, conventional sign entities can ever come to acquire meaning. The answer is that they can be placed in relation to things, persons, and events in the world. So, we have words on the one hand and "the world" on the other, and the problem is how certain sequences of the first type of object (words) connect with certain sequences or concatenations of the second kind of objects (world). The meaning relation thus gets defined without any connection to the experience of the creature (i.e., the human) for whom the words are meaningful. Meanings end up being either "senses" grasped (Frege) or truth conditions (Davidson).
4. And if knowledge is to be objective, we will need literal terms (or literal concepts, in some versions) mapping directly onto parts of the world, at least at some points that will ground the web of belief. Otherwise, all our language could be an empty, meaningless tissue of mere sounds, signifying nothing. As Searle (1969) notes, since we "just know" that our language is meaningful and can sometimes give us knowledge of the world, then we'd better construct a theory of speech acts and reference that explains under what conditions this is possible.

What if, in direct opposition to the objectivist theory of meaning, we were to start (as I have in this book) with a mind that is not separate from, or out of ongoing contact with, its body and its world? What if we do not begin with arbitrary signs as exemplars of meaning, and what if we don't simply assume that truth conditions more or less roughly capture the full extent of meaning? The answer is that we get a very different conception of meaning—meaning as embodied—and, correspondingly, we get a very different conception of human thought and of the nature and purpose of philosophy.

AN EMBODIED, EXPERIENTIALIST VIEW OF MEANING

1. Meaning is embodied. It arises through embodied organism-environment interactions in which significant patterns are marked within the flow of experience. Meaning emerges as we engage the pervasive qualities of situations and note distinctions that make sense of our experience and carry it forward. The meaning of something is its connections to past, present, and future experiences, actual or possible.

2. The distinctions that we mark can be among qualities, affect contours, images, image schemas, or various kinds of connections within or across domains.

3. None of these aspects of meaning are necessarily conceptual or propositional in any traditional sense; so, as we saw in Gendlin's argument (in chapter 4), meaning involves the blending of the structural, formal, and conceptual dimensions on the one hand and the preconceptual, nonformal, felt dimensions on the other. Meaning resides in neither of these dimensions of experience alone, but only in their ongoing connectedness and interanimation.

4. The more cuts, or selections, we make within what we might call the flow of our thought-feeling, the greater the number of explicit connections we can make with other aspects of our experience. This is one type of growth of meaning, the growth that, according to Dewey, is made possible by language and all other types of symbolic communication.

5. What we call our "highest," or most abstract, concepts may not seem to be based on aspects of our sensorimotor experience, *but this is an illusion.* Concepts that we think of as utterly divorced from physical things and sensorimotor experiences (concepts such as justice, mind, knowledge, truth, and democracy) are never really independent of our embodiment, because the semantic and inferential structure of these abstract concepts is drawn from our sensorimotor interactions, typically by cross-domain mappings (conceptual metaphors). *This is the only way it could be for a creature with a body-mind who has neither a disembodied ego nor an eternal soul, for there is no nonbodily entity or process to perform the abstraction.* Our understanding of abstract notions is thus pervasively structured via systematic connections (neurally realized) among sensorimotor meanings and other, "higher" aspects of thought. Because these reentrant neural connections are activated automatically for us and operate for the most part beneath the level of our conscious awareness, we are fooled into believing that our abstract thoughts have nothing to do with our embodiment. However, it is precisely our embodiment that supports this illusion of disembodied thought.

6. The reason that the meaning of certain things can be so rich for us is that so many parts of our bodily experience are neurally connected and continually interact. Our sense of meanings that transcend the words available to us is nothing more than the richness and depth of connections that transcend any formalization, abstraction, or selection that we are able to make in a given situation.

7. The greatest mystery that remains for an embodied, experientialist theory of meaning is how creative imagination works—that is, how new meanings and new connections emerge. We have a partial understanding of some of the elements and processes involved here, such as Vittorio Gallese and George Lakoff's notion (2005) of cogs as the basic structures for extending sensorimotor meaning and inferences into abstract domains. Don Tucker (forthcoming) speculates on some of the neural architecture that makes imagining possible. We also have Gilles Fauconnier and Mark Turner's taxonomy (2002) of general patterns and strategies for conceptual blending. But we are really only beginning to see how something new can emerge that transcends and transforms what has gone before.

THE MEANING OF "THE BODY"

Up to this point, I have been focusing primarily on the *meaning* of the body—that is, on how meaning is grounded in the body. But what about the meaning of the term *body*? Just what do we mean by the idea of "body" when we say that meaning, thought, and mind are embodied? Any naturalistic view like the one I am developing cannot speak of "the body" and "the mind," for that would simply reinstate the mind/body dualism that I am going to such great lengths to deny. Hence, I have often used Dewey's term, "the body-mind," which is intended to capture the fact that what we call "mind" and "body" are not two separate and ontologically distinct entities or processes, but instead are aspects or abstractable dimensions of an interactive—or "transactive" (Dewey 1938/1991) or "enactive" (Varela, Thompson, and Rosch 1991)—process.

The chief problem with our commonsense notion of the body is that it makes the body out to be a *thing*. It seems so obvious to most people that the body must be just an organized collection of skin, bones, blood, organs, nerves, and fluids, made up of various chemicals, all interacting together. We have natural sciences for studying these physical things and processes, and so it would seem that the story of the body can be told, more or less reductively, by science. This makes it very difficult for most people to think of their mind (and identity) as thoroughly embodied, since they conceive of the body as a material thing—and they are utterly convinced that they most certainly cannot be a mere thing! Each of us believes, correctly, that he or she is surely *more than* a lump of pulsating flesh that will someday stop pulsating. Consequently, our commonsense view of the body as an object among other objects in the world leads many people to dismiss the idea that meaning, thought, and mind can be understood as inextricably tied to our bodies.

The challenge, of course, is to stop thinking of a human body as merely a thing. It was Merleau-Ponty's *Phenomenology of Perception* that helped us see why our bodies cannot be understood merely as objects interacting with other objects: "My body appears to me as an attitude directed towards a certain existing or possible task. And indeed its spatiality is not, like that of external objects or like that of 'spatial sensations', a *spatiality of position,* but a *spatiality of situation*" (Merleau-Ponty 1962, 100).

My body is never merely a thing; it is a *lived* body—what Merleau-Ponty called the "phenomenal body," the situation from which our world and experience flows: "It is never our objective body that we move, but our phenomenal body, and there is no mystery in that, since our body, as the potentiality of this or that part of the world, surges towards objects to be grasped and perceives them" (Merleau-Ponty 1962, 106).

Once we learn to give up our reductive, hypostatizing concepts of the body, we get a very much richer and more complex picture of how we are at once always embodied and yet also always more than a thing. In *Philosophy in the Flesh* (1999), George Lakoff and I expressed this by saying that any account of embodied mind that is even remotely adequate to the complexity of human nature will require multiple nonreductive levels of explanation. Meaning and mind are embodied at the very least at the following levels, without which there could not be a human body in its fullest manifestation.[3]

1. *The body as biological organism.* The principal physical locus of my being-in-the-world is the living, flesh-and-blood creature that I call "my body." My world extends out from and is oriented in relation to this body of mine. This body is a functioning biological organism that can perceive, move, respond to, and transform its environment. It is this whole body, with its various systems working in marvelous coordination, that makes

---

3. For other ways of carving up the levels or aspects of embodiment, see Rohrer, forthcoming; Gallagher 2005; and Anderson 2003.

possible the qualities, images, feelings, emotions, and thought patterns that constitute the ground of our meaning and understanding. It requires at least a minimally functioning brain and nervous system, which is a necessary condition of any living human body-mind. However, my body is quite obviously far more than just my brain and central nervous system. It includes the preconscious capacities for bodily posture and movement that Shaun Gallagher (2005) names the *body schema*. Nor is my body merely a representation in my brain. No human is, or could ever be, merely a "brain-in-a-vat." The extensive philosophical literature on the so-called brain-in-a-vat thought experiment, made famous by Putnam (1981), is interesting only insofar as it provides a way of thinking about what goes into meaning and selfhood. Otherwise, the brain-in-a-vat hypothesis is laughable, as Putnam showed, because it leaves out the critical role of our body-in-interaction-with-our-world that defines human meaning, reference, and truth.

2. *The ecological body.* There is no body without an environment, no body without the ongoing flow of organism-environment interaction that defines our realities. Once again, the trick is to avoid the dualism of organism *and* environment, a dualism that falsely assumes the existence of two independent entities, each bringing its own structure and preestablished identity into the interactions. Instead, we must think of organism (or body) and environment in the same way that we must think of mind and body, as aspects of one continuous process. As Gerald Edelman (1992) has shown, both the brain and its body develop into human corporeality only by virtue of the precise kinds of organism-environment couplings, with their precise temporal sequencing, that mold the neural development of our species. We are thus left with the somewhat counterintuitive idea that the body is not separate from its environment and that any boundaries we choose to mark between them are merely artifacts of our interests and forms of inquiry.

3. *The phenomenological body.* This is our body as we live it and experience it. There is a way that it feels to be embodied in the way that I am embodied. Maxine Sheets-Johnstone (1999) rightly calls this the "tactile-kinaesthetic body"—the living, moving, feeling, pulsing body of our being-in-the-world. We are aware of our own bodies through proprioception (our feeling of our bodily posture and orientation), through our kinesthetic sensations of bodily movement, and through our awareness of our internal bodily states via feeling and emotion, which constitute our felt sense of ourselves. Gallagher's term *body image* (2005) is meant to capture our reflexive and self-referential perceptions, attitudes, and beliefs about our bodies at this phenomenological level.

4. *The social body.* The human environment of which the body partakes is not just physical or biological. It is also composed of intersubjective relations and coordinations of experience. This was a central theme of chapter 2, in which I argued that we are all "big babies" and that this is not a bad thing at all. We are what we are only in and through others and by virtue of our intersubjective capacity to communicate shared meanings (Trevarthen 1993; Stern 1985; Stawarska 2003). Some of our bodily capacities are either evolutionarily selected for or merely adapted to the forms of social interactions that make us who we are.

5. *The cultural body.* Our environments are not only physical and social. They are constituted also by cultural artifacts, practices, institutions, rituals, and modes of interaction that transcend and shape any particular body and any particular bodily action. These cultural dimensions include gender, race, class (socioeconomic status), aesthetic values, and various modes of bodily posture and movement. There may well be commonalities of bodily comportment across cultures, but cultural differences in the shaping and understanding of the body are real and significant. If there is a way to "throw like a girl" (Young 1980), that is certainly not a biological or physiological essence, but rather a consequence of social and cultural conditioning. That is why it can change as attitudes and practices surrounding women change (an example is the recent dramatic increase in girls' and women's participation in sports). The ways people stand, walk, and hold themselves often vary noticeably across cultures and subcultures and at different times in history. Cultural institutions, practices, and values provide shared ("external") structures that influence the development of our bodily way of engaging our world. It is popular today in various circles to speak of culture as autonomous and independent of individual bodies. Culture has a *relative* stability and independence. But there is no culture without embodied creatures who enact it through customs, practices, actions, and rituals. Even though aspects of culture obviously transcend and outlive particular individuals, those artifacts and practices have *no* meaning without people who use the artifacts while engaging in complex social practices.

The principal problem with our commonsense or folk-theoretical concept of the body is that it is limited almost exclusively to the biological body. We see the body as that physical "thing," and we see everything else (environment, social relations, and culture) as standing outside of our bodies. This is the mistake that leads many to assume that "body" and "mind" must obviously be two different kinds of things. However, *the reduction of the body to the mere physical organism is just as misguided as the opposite error of claiming that the body is nothing but a cultural construction.* They are both reductions; the first leaves out large parts of what makes meaning and mind possible, and the second leaves out many of the sources of, and constraints on, meaning and mind that come from the character of our corporeal rootedness in the biological-ecological processes of life.

The human body has all five of the dimensions outlined above, and it cannot be reduced to any one (or two or three) of them. I do not object to colloquial uses of "my body," "the body," and "your body" to refer to an individual fleshy creature when we are talking about ourselves and others. Clearly, our most central sense of the term *human body* is the living, biological body, typically correlated with our felt sense of our phenomenological body. What I am objecting to, and where the danger arises, is when we take our commonsense or folk-theoretical notion of the body as the basis for our entire philosophical, psychological, and religious view of the body. The problem, to repeat, is that our simplistic, commonsense view tends to land us in a philosophically and scientifically untenable dualism of body and mind. It also tends to reduce the body to a mere object.

This complex view of multiple aspects of our embodiment thus requires us to always entertain multiple methods of inquiry and levels of explanation for anything pertaining to our body-mind. No single method of inquiry could ever capture everything we need to help us understand the tightly interwoven phenomena of body, meaning, and mind. For example, unless human beings as a species someday lose their capacity for consciousness, we are never going to give up the phenomenological level of explanation. At the very least, we are going to define many of the primary phenomena of mind on the basis of our felt experience of our bodies and our world. Consequently, the adequacy of explanations at other levels (such as accounts from cognitive neuroscience) is going to be judged, in part, by how well they help us understand the phenomena so described (i.e., the phenomenological body). What else could we expect, since all explanations are explanations *to* and *for* ourselves, geared to helping *us* understand our world? They are necessarily going to be evaluated by us relative to our body-based capacities for meaning-making, inquiry, and thought.

THE PHILOSOPHICAL IMPLICATIONS OF THE EMBODIED MIND

In the preface and introduction to this book, I suggested that a full appreciation of the aesthetics of meaning and thought as being tied to the body would require us to reconsider some of our most dearly held views about what it means to be human. We can now revisit some of those key implications with a greater appreciation of their significance. We can suggest why it should matter whether we take seriously the embodiment of mind and meaning.

1. *Mind and body are not two things.* A human being is not two ontologically different kinds of thing joined together. Mind is not a mysterious metaphysical guest that just happens to drop in for a temporary visit at the home of the body. The human mind is not contained in the body, but emerges from and co-evolves with the body. The language I have been using throughout this book to sum up this point is this: A human being is a body-mind, that is, an organic, continually developing process of events. Human mind and meaning require at least a partially functioning human brain within at least a partially functioning human body that is in ongoing interaction with complex environments that are at once physical, social, and cultural. These environments both *shape* and *are shaped by* the humans who inhabit them.

2. *Human meaning is embodied.* From the moment of our entrance into the world, and apparently even in the womb, we begin to learn the meaning of things at the most primordial bodily level. Things are meaningful by virtue of their relations to other actual or possible qualities, feelings, emotions, images, image schemas, and concepts. We begin our lives mostly by feeling or sensing this vast complex of meaning, and we never cease to access it via feeling, even when we make use of our culture's most remarkable tools of symbolic expression and interaction.

3. *Understanding and reasoning are embodied.* Our understanding, which is our way of making sense of our world, is embodied, precisely because our meaning-making capacities are embodied. Our resources for making sense of our world are based primarily on our sensorimotor capacities, which have neural connections to other parts of the brain responsible for planning, deliberating, and reasoning. Our brains recruit patterns of sensorimotor inference for the performance of what we regard as abstract inference, that is, reasoning about abstract entities and events. At present, the thesis of the embodiment of meaning and reason is only an explanatory hypothesis. There is so far only a modest amount of evidence for the embodiment-of-reason aspect of the hypothesis, but it is currently the most strongly supported hypothesis I am aware of that would articulate a nondualistic, naturalistic view of mind, thought, and language.

4. *Human beings are metaphorical creatures.* Conceptual metaphor is a nearly omnipresent part of the human capacity for abstract conceptualization and reasoning. There are other imaginative structures involved in

abstraction, but conceptual metaphor shows up in virtually all of our abstract thinking. The power of conceptual metaphor is that it permits us to use the semantics and inferential structure of our bodily experience as a primary way of making sense of abstract entities, relations, and events. It follows from this that literalism, which claims that all of our meaningful concepts can be spelled out literally, is false, misleading, and very dangerous. Literalism is false because you cannot find an adequate literal core for each abstract concept that can account for the semantics and inference structure of the concept. Literalism is misleading because it tempts you back into the traditional narrow focus on reference and truth conditions as the sole bases for meaning. Literalism is dangerous because it leads to the misguided quest for certainty and for absolute truth. Literalism lies at the heart of fundamentalism.

5. *There is no absolute truth, but there are plenty of human truths.* I have not argued this point in the present book, but it is elaborated by Lakoff and me in *Philosophy in the Flesh* (1999), and it is too important to overlook. I want only to point out here that *human life does not require absolute truths.* Neither science, nor morality, nor philosophy, nor politics, nor spirituality really need absolute truths, even though most of our traditional theories in these areas assume that they are founded on absolute (disembodied, universal, eternal) truths. Human truth, by contrast, arises in the context of human inquiry, relies on embodied meaning, and is relative to our values and interests. Finite, fallible, human truth is all the truth we have, and all we need. As Hilary Putnam is so fond of observing, the trail of the human serpent is everywhere.

6. *Human freedom.* In this book, I have provided no explicit arguments about the nature of freedom. However, the view that is most clearly at odds with the account of human nature developed here is the Kantian idea of radical freedom. This is the view that we are, or possess, a transcendent ego that is the locus of our capacity to negate any bodily, social, or cultural influence, habit, or tendency. This is the idea that we are forever free to choose who and what we shall become. The popularity of the idea of radical freedom no doubt stems from its compatibility with our cultural notions of moral responsibility and our religious aspirations for eternal life. By contrast, the concept of freedom that is supported by the naturalistic idea of the body-mind is a modest freedom to contribute to transformations of our situation, and thereby to self-transformations.

7. *The person you are cannot survive the death of your body.* As controversial and distressing as this claim might be, it follows directly from the embodiment of mind. Let us be quite clear about what precisely my claim

is: If there is anything that survives the death of your body, it could not be the *you* that we know and love. For *your* experience is made possible by the working of your (human) brain, within the workings of your (human) body, as it engages its (human-related) environments. Any *you* that survived bodily death would lack your memories, your experience, your emotions, and your grasp of the meaning of things. Notice that even popular films like *Heaven Can Wait, Ghost,* and *The Invasion of the Body Snatchers* are all predicated on some spirit's finding the requisite human body to inhabit so that it can be a person, whether for good or evil purposes.

8. *Embodied spirituality.* Spirituality has always been connected to the idea that we are either part of, or can stand in relation to, something that transcends our limited situation, perspective, or embodiment. But there are at least two plausible conceptions of transcendence. One is what I call *vertical transcendence,* the alleged capacity to rise above and shed our finite human form and to "plug into" the infinite. Throughout virtually all of human history, humanity's plight has been tied to our finiteness, which each of us experiences as limitation, weakness, dependence, alienation, loss of meaning, absence of love, and anxiety over sickness and death. If there were such a thing as vertical transcendence, it would indeed answer the dilemma of human finitude, at least if our identity could be carried over into the infinite. But there is a different notion of transcendence, which we might call *horizontal transcendence,* that recognizes the inescapability of human finitude and is compatible with the embodiment of meaning, mind, and personal identity. From this human perspective, transcendence consists in our happy ability to sometimes "go beyond" our present situation in transformative acts that change both our world and ourselves. This is tied to a sense of ourselves as part of a broader human and more-than-human ongoing process in which change, creativity, and growth of meaning are possible. Faith thus becomes faith in the possibility of genuine, positive transformation that increases richness of meanings, harmony among species, and flourishing, not just at the human level, but in the world as an ongoing creative development. Hope is commitment to the possibility of realizing some of this growth—not in some final eschatological transformation of the world, but rather *locally,* in our day-to-day struggles and joys. Grace is the undeserved experience of transformative growth even in spite of your individual or communal failures to do what would make things better. Love is a commitment to the well-being of others in a way that takes you at least partly beyond your ego-centered needs and desires and opens up your potential to respect and care for others and for your world. None of this is grounded in the infinite, but rather in the

creative possibilities of finite human experience. It gives each of us more good work to do than we can possibly realize within our lifetime.

9. *Philosophy as a search for meaning.* Finally, given the limitations of embodied human understanding, philosophy cannot be properly construed in the traditional ways—as, for instance, a quest for certain knowledge, the search for absolute truth, the pursuit of supreme moral principles, or the discovery of Being-Itself. Instead, as Dewey argued, philosophy is reflective inquiry into the fullest, richest, deepest meaning of experience, as a way of helping us deal with the real problems of human existence that define our existential condition. Philosophy needs to help us reestablish our visceral connection to ourselves, to other people, and to the world. It should help us rediscover the experiential depth of the situations we find ourselves in, so that we can base our inquiry and decisions on an appropriately complex understanding of the meaning of what we are encountering. And then philosophy must employ the capacities and tools of the embodied mind in an attempt to transform our situation for the better.

Critics of pragmatist philosophy have infamously, and mistakenly, claimed that pragmatism reduces to the view that what is true, good, and right is nothing more than whatever permits us to achieve our goals or to satisfy any interests we might have. This mischaracterization draws on our commonsense use of the term *pragmatic* to mean "practical"—conducive to problem-solving. By contrast, when genuine pragmatist philosophy talks about remaking experience, it recognizes that our concern must be not only determining the best means to some end, but also assessing the nature, the long-term adequacy, and the general appropriateness of the ends themselves. In light of this ongoing reflection, it recognizes that we may need to revise and reform those ends as experience develops. Pragmatism is about discerning the full meaning of experience and transforming experience for the better. What "the better" is must be the focus of careful reflection, and it is seldom either utterly clear, unproblematically given in advance, or monolithic in nature. Pragmatism's methods for transforming situations are modeled more on the creation and judging of the arts than on simplistic means-ends reasoning. So understood—as critical, constructive, and expansive inquiry—philosophy is the most meaningful and powerful way we have of trying to live rightly and well.

THE ART OF LIFE

The view I have been exploring in this book amounts, in its essentials, to this: We humans live in a human-related world, for even the more-than-human world can only be understood and engaged by us via the structures and processes of human understanding and action. Our meaning is human meaning—meaning grounded in our human bodies, in their humanly encountered environments. All of the meaning we can make and all of the values we hold grow out of our humanity-interacting-with-our-world.

Our humanity encompasses our animal needs, our personal relationships, our need and capacity for love, our social relations, our cultural institutions and practices, and our spirituality. We make sense of all of these dimensions of our being by means of body-based feeling, conceptualization, reasoning, and symbolic expressions. Our aspirations for transcendence must be realized not in attempts to escape our bodily habitation, but rather by employing it in our ongoing efforts to transform ourselves and our world for the better.

We are born into this world, make of it what we can while we live, and return to its earthiness when, at last, our functional integrity disintegrates forever. The art of our lives is the art of the meaning of the body. In some people, it is beautiful art.

Aiken, N. 1998. *The Biological Origins of Art*. Westport, CT: Praeger Publishers.

Alperson, P. 1980. "Musical Time" and Music as an "Art of Time." *Journal of Aesthetics and Art Criticism* 38:407–17.

Anderson, M. 2003. Embodied Cognition: A Field Guide. *Artificial Intelligence* 149, no. 1 (September): 91–130.

Arnheim, R. 1954. *Art and Visual Perception: A Psychology of the Creative Eye*. Berkeley and Los Angeles: University of California Press.

———. 1969. *Visual Thinking*. Berkeley and Los Angeles: University of California Press.

———. 1986. Perceptual Dynamics in Musical Expression. In *New Essays in the Psychology of Art*, 214–27. Berkeley and Los Angeles: University of California Press.

Austin, J. L. 1970. Performative Utterances. In *Philosophical Papers*, 233–52. Oxford: Oxford University Press.

Ayer, A. J. 1936. *Language, Truth, and Logic*. New York: Oxford University Press.

Bailey, D. 1997. *A Computational Model of Embodiment in the Acquisition of Action Verbs*. Ph.D. diss., Computer Science Division, EECS Department, University of California, Berkeley.

Baldwin, D. A., and J. A. Baird. 2001. Discerning Intentions in Dynamic Human Action. *Trends in Cognitive Sciences* 5:171–78.

Bateson, Mary Catherine. 1975. Mother-Infant Exchanges: The Epigenesis of Conversational Interaction. In *Developmental Psycholinguistics and Communicative Disorders*, edited by D. Aronson and R. W. Reiber, Annals of the New York Academy of Sciences, vol. 263. New York: New York Academy of Sciences.

Bechtel, W., A. Abrahamsen, and G. Graham. 1998. The Life of Cognitive Science. In *A Companion to Cognitive Science*, edited by W. Bechtel and G. Graham, 2–104. Oxford: Blackwell Publishers.

Bergson, H. 1910. *Time and Free Will.* Translated by F. L. Pogson. Reprint. Whitefish, MT: Kessinger Publishing Co.

Bjerre, C. 2005. Mental Capacity as Metaphor. *International Journal for the Semiotics of Law* 18:101–40.

Bowdle, B., and Gentner, D. 2005. The Career of Metaphor. *Psychological Review* 112, no. 1:193–216.

Brooks, R. A. 1991. Intelligence without Representation. *Artificial Intelligence Journal* 47:139–59.

Brooks, R. A., and A. M. Flynn. 1989. Fast, Cheap and Out of Control: A Robot Invasion of the Solar System. *Journal of the British Interplanetary Society,* 478–85.

Brooks, R. A., and L. A. Stein. 1994. Building Brains for Bodies. *Autonomous Robots* 1, no. 1:7–25.

Brower, C. 1997–98. Pathway, Blockage, and Containment in *Density 21.5. Theory and Practice* 22–23:35–54.

———. 2000. A Cognitive Theory of Musical Meaning. *Journal of Music Theory* 44:323–79.

Buccino, G., F. Binkofski, G. R. Fink, L. Fadiga, L. Fogassi, V. Gallese, R. J. Seitz, K. Zilles, G. Rizzolatti, and H. J. Freund. 2001. Action Observation Activates Premotor and Parietal Areas in a Somatotopic Manner: An fMRI Study. *European Journal of Neuroscience* 2:400–404.

Buonomano, D. V., and M. M. Merzenich. 1998. Cortical Plasticity: From Synapses to Maps. *Annual Review of Neuroscience* 21:149–86.

Butterworth, G., and L. Grover. 1990. Joint Visual Attention, Manual Pointing, and Pre-verbal Communication in Human Infancy. In *Attention and Performance,* vol. 13, *Motor Representation and Control,* edited by M. Jeannerod, 605–24. Hillsdale, NJ: LEA Associates.

Camus, A. 1942/1988. *The Stranger.* Translated by M. Ward. New York: Vintage Books.

Cienki, A. 1998. Metaphoric Gestures and Some of Their Relations to Verbal Metaphoric Expressions. In *Discourse and Cognition: Bridging the Gap,* edited by J. P. Koenig, 189–204. Stanford, CA: CSLI/Cambridge.

Clark, A. 1998. *Being There: Putting Brain, Body, and World Together Again.* Cambridge, MA: MIT Press.

Clarke, E. n.d. Meaning and the Specification of Motion in Music. Manuscript.

Collis, G., and H. Schaffer. 1975. Synchronization of Visual Attention in Mother-Infant Pairs. *Journal of Child Psychology and Psychiatry* 16:315–20.

Coslett, H. B., E. M. Saffran, and J. Schwoebel. 2002. Knowledge of the Human Body: A Distinct Semantic Domain. *Neurology* 59:357–63.

Cox, Arnie. 1999. *The Metaphorical Logic of Musical Motion and Space.* Doctoral diss., School of Music, University of Oregon.

Craig, D., N. Nersessian, and R. Catrambone. 2002. Perceptual Simulation in Analogical Problem Solving. In Magnani and Nersessian 2002, 167–89.

Damasio, A. 1994. *Descartes' Error: Emotion, Reason, and the Human Brain.* New York: G. P. Putnam's Sons.

————. 1999. *The Feeling of What Happens: Body and Emotion in the Making of Consciousness.* New York: Harcourt Brace.

————. 2003. *Looking for Spinoza: Joy, Sorrow, and the Feeling Brain.* Orlando, FL: Harcourt.

Damasio, A., T. Grabowski, A. Bechara, H. Damasio, L. Ponto, J. Parvizi, and R. Hichwa. 2000. Subcortical and Cortical Brain Activity during the Feeling of Self-Generated Emotions. *Nature Neuroscience* 3:1049–56.

Davidson, D. 1967. Truth and Meaning. *Synthese* 17:304–23.

————. 1978. What Metaphors Mean. *Critical Inquiry* 5, no. 1:31–47.

Davies, S. 1994. *Musical Meaning and Expression.* Ithaca, NY: Cornell University Press.

DeBello, W. M., D. E. Feldman, and E. I. Knudsen. 2001. Adaptive Axonal Remodeling in the Midbrain Auditory Space Map. *Journal of Neuroscience* 21, no. 9:3161–74.

Deneubourg, J. L, J. M. Pasteels, and J. C. Verhaeghe. 1983. Probabilistic Behavior in Ants: A Strategy of Errors. *Journal of Theoretical Biology* 105:259–71.

Descartes, René. 1641/1984. *Meditations on First Philosophy (with Objections and Replies).* In *The Philosophical Writings of Descartes,* vol. 2, translated by J. Cottingham, R. Stoothoff, and D. Murdoch. Cambridge: Cambridge University Press.

Dewey, J. 1925/1981. *Experience and Nature.* Vol. 1 of *The Later Works, 1925–1953,* edited by Jo Ann Boydston. Carbondale: Southern Illinois University Press, 1981.

————. 1930/1988. Qualitative Thought. In *The Later Works, 1925–1953,* vol. 5, edited by Jo Ann Boydston. Carbondale: Southern Illinois University Press, 1988.

————. 1934/1987. *Art as Experience.* Vol. 10 of *The Later Works, 1925–1953,* edited by Jo Ann Boydston. Carbondale: Southern Illinois University Press, 1987.

————. 1938/1991. *Logic: The Theory of Inquiry.* Vol. 12 of *The Later Works, 1925–1953,* edited by Jo Ann Boydston. Carbondale: Southern Illinois University Press, 1991.

Dodge, E., and G. Lakoff. 2005. Image Schemas: From Linguistic Analysis to Neural Grounding. In Hampe and Grady 2005, 57–91.

Duhamel, J.-R., C. L. Colby, and M. E. Goldberg. 1998. Ventral Intraparietal Areas of the Macaque: Congruent Visual and Somatic Response Properties. *Journal of Neurophysiology* 79:126–36.

Echard, W. 1999. An Analysis of Neil Young's "Powderfinger" Based on Mark Johnson's Image Schemata. *Popular Music* 18, no. 1:133–44.

————. 2005. *Neil Young and the Poetics of Energy.* Bloomington: Indiana University Press.

Edelman, G. 1987. *Neural Darwinism.* New York: Basic Books.

————. 1992. *Bright Air, Brilliant Fire: On the Matter of Mind.* New York: Basic Books.

Edelman, G., and G. Tononi. 2000. *A Universe of Consciousness: How Matter Becomes Imagination.* New York: Basic Books.

Erickson, H. P., D. W. Taylor, K. A. Taylor, and D. Bramhill. 1996. Bacterial Cell Division of Protein FtsZ Assembles into Protofilament Sheets and Minirings, Structural Homologs of Tubulin Polymers. *Proceedings of the National Academy of Sciences* 93, no. 1:519–23.

Esposito, T. 1996. *The New 50 Golden Movie Songs.* Miami: Warner Bros. Publications.

Everett, W. 1999. *The Beatles as Musicians.* New York: Oxford University Press.

Fadiga, L., et al. 1995. Motor Facilitation during Action Observation: A Magnetic Stimulation Study. *Journal of Neurophysiology* 73:2608–11.

Fauconnier, G., and M. Turner. 2002. *The Way We Think: Conceptual Blending and the Mind's Hidden Complexities.* New York: Basic Books.

Feldman, J., and S. Narayanan. 2004. Embodied Meaning in a Neural Theory of Language. *Brain and Language* 89, no. 2:385–92.

Ferguson, D. 1960. *Music as Metaphor: The Elements of Expression.* Minneapolis: University of Minnesota Press.

Fernandez-Duque, D., and M. Johnson. 1999. Attention Metaphors: How Metaphors Guide the Cognitive Psychology of Attention. *Cognitive Science* 23, no. 19:83–116.

———. 2002. Cause and Effect Theories of Attention: The Role of Conceptual Metaphors. *Review of General Psychology* 6, no. 2:153–65.

Fesmire, S. 2003. *John Dewey and Moral Imagination: Pragmatism in Ethics.* Bloomington: Indiana University Press.

Fodor, J. 1975. *The Language of Thought.* New York: Thomas Y. Crowell Co.

———. 1987. *Psychosemantics: The Problem of Meaning in the Philosophy of Mind.* Cambridge, MA: MIT Press.

Fogassi, L., V. Gallese, G. Buccino, L. Craighero, L. Fadiga, and G. Rizzolatti. 2001. Cortical Mechanism for the Visual Guidance of Hand Grasping Movements in the Monkey: A Reversible Inactivation Study. *Brain* 124, no. 3:571–86.

Forceville, C. 1994a. *Pictorial Metaphor in Advertising.* Amsterdam: Vrije Universiteit te Amsterdam.

———. 1994b. Pictorial Metaphor in Advertisements. *Metaphor and Symbolic Activity* 9, no. 1:1–29.

Fraser, S. E. 1985. Cell Interaction Involved in Neural Patterning: An Experimental and Theoretical Approach. In *Molecular Bases of Neural Development,* edited by Gerald Edelman, W. E. Gall, and W. M. Cowan, 481–507. New York: Wiley.

Frege, G. 1892/1970. On Sense and Reference. In *Translations from the Philosophical Writings of Gottlob Frege,* 56–78. Oxford: Basil Blackwell.

Gadamer, H.-G. 1960/1975. *Truth and Method.* Translated by G. Barden and J. Cumming. New York: Crossroad Publishing Co.

Gallagher, S. 2005. *How the Body Shapes the Mind.* Oxford: Oxford University Press.

Gallese, V. 2003. A Neuroscientific Grasp of Concepts: From Control to Representation. *Philosophical Transactions of the Royal Society of London* 358:1231–40.

Gallese, V., and A. Goldman. 1998. Mirror Neurons and the Simulation Theory of Mind-Reading. *Trends in Cognitive Science* 2, no. 2:493–501.

Gallese, V., and G. Lakoff. 2005. The Brain's Concepts: The Role of the Sensory-Motor System in Conceptual Knowledge. *Cognitive Neuropsychology* 22:455–79.

Gaze, R. M., and S. C. Sharma. 1970. Axial Differences in the Reenervation of the Goldfish Optic Tectum by Regenerating Optic Nerve Fibers. *Experimental Brain Research* 10:171–81.

Gendlin, E. 1991. Crossing and Dipping: Some Terms for Approaching the Interface between Natural Understanding and Logical Formulation. Manuscript, University of Chicago.

————. 1992. Thinking beyond Patterns: Body, Language, and Situations. In *The Presence of Feeling in Thought,* edited by B. den Ouden and M. Moen, 21–151. New York: Peter Lang.

————. 1997. How Philosophy Cannot Appeal to Experience, and How It Can. In *Language beyond Postmodernism: Saying and Thinking in Gendlin's Philosophy,* edited by M. Levin, 3–41. Evanston, IL: Northwestern University Press.

Gentner, D. 1983. Structure-Mapping: A Theoretical Framework for Analogy. *Cognitive Science* 7:155–70.

Gibbs, R. 1994. *The Poetics of Mind: Figurative Thought, Language, and Understanding.* Cambridge: Cambridge University Press.

————. 2003. Embodied Experience and Linguistic Meaning. *Brain and Language* 84, no. 1:1–15.

Gibbs, R., and G. Steen, eds. 1999. *Metaphor in Cognitive Linguistics.* Current Issues in Linguistic Theory, no. 175. Amsterdam: John Benjamins.

Gibson, E., and A. Pick. 2000. *An Ecological Approach to Perceptual Learning and Development.* Oxford: Oxford University Press.

Gibson, J. J. 1966. *The Senses Considered as Perceptual Systems.* Boston: Houghton-Mifflin.

————. 1979. *The Ecological Approach to Visual Perception.* Boston: Houghton-Mifflin.

Gjerdingen, R. O. 1994. Apparent Motion in Music? *Music Perception* 11:335–70.

Goldberg, J. L. 2003. How Does an Axon Grow? *Genes and Development* 17, no. 8:941–58.

Grady, J. 1997. Foundations of Meaning: Primary Metaphors and Primary Scenes. Ph. D. diss., University of California, Berkeley.

Guo, Y., and S. B. Udin. 2000. The Development of Abnormal Axon Trajectories after Rotation of One Eye in Xenopus. *Journal of Neuroscience* 20, no. 11:4189–97.

Hampe, B., and J. Grady, eds. 2005. *From Perception to Meaning: Image Schemas in Cognitive Linguistics.* Berlin: Mouton de Gruyter.

Hanslick, E. 1854/1986. *On the Musically Beautiful.* Translated by G. Payzant. Indianapolis, IN: Hackett Publishing Co.

Hauk, O., I. Johnsrude, and F. Pulvermüller. 2004. Somatotopic Representation of Action Words in Human Motor and Premotor Cortex. *Neuron* 41, no. 2:301–7.

Hodges, A. 1983. *Alan Turing: The Enigma.* New York: Walker and Co.

Hurwitz, R., and S. Larson. 1994. Step Collections in Aural Theory. Presentation to a special panel, Applying a Theory of Expressive Meaning in the Written- and Aural-Theory Classrooms, for the College Music Society.

Hutchins, E. 1995. *Cognition in the Wild.* Cambridge, MA: MIT Press.

Innis, R. 1994. *Consciousness and the Play of Signs.* Bloomington: Indiana University Press.

James, W. 1890/1950. *The Principles of Psychology.* 2 vols. New York: Dover.

————. 1900. *Psychology.* American Science Series, Briefer Course. New York: Henry Holt and Co.

————. 1911/1979. Percept and Concept. In *Some Problems of Philosophy,* 21–60. Cambridge, MA: Harvard University Press.

Jeannerod, M. 1994. The Representing Brain: Neural Correlates of Motor Intention and Imagery. *Behavioral and Brain Sciences* 17:187–245.

Johnson, C. 1997. Metaphor vs. Conflation in the Acquisition of Polysemy: The Case of *See*. In *Cultural, Typological and Psychological Issues in Cognitive Linguistics,* edited by M. K. Hiraga, C. Sinha, and S. Wilcox, Current Issues in Linguistic Theory, 155–69. Amsterdam: John Benjamins.

Johnson, M. 1981. Metaphor in the Philosophical Tradition. In *Philosophical Perspectives on Metaphor,* edited by M. Johnson, 3–47. Minneapolis: University of Minnesota Press.

———. 1987. *The Body in the Mind: The Bodily Basis of Meaning, Imagination, and Reason.* Chicago: University of Chicago Press.

———. 1993. *Moral Imagination: Implications of Cognitive Science for Ethics.* Chicago: University of Chicago Press.

———. 1997–98. Embodied Musical Meaning. *Theory and Practice* 22–23:95–102.

———. 2002. Architecture and the Embodied Mind. *OASE* 58:75–93.

———. 2005. The Philosophical Significance of Image Schemas. In Hampe and Grady 2005, 15–33.

Johnson, M., and S. Larson. 2003. "Something in the Way She Moves": Metaphors of Musical Motion. *Metaphor and Symbol* 18, no. 2:63–84.

Kant, I. 1790/1987. *Critique of Judgment.* Translated by W. Pluhar. Indianapolis, IN: Hackett Publishing Co.

Kawamura, S. 1959. The Process of Subculture Propagation among Japanese Macaques. *Primates* 2:43–60.

Kellman, P. J. 1984. Perception of Three-Dimensional Form by Human Infants. *Perception and Psychophysics* 36:353–58.

Knudsen, E. I. 1998. Capacity for Plasticity in the Adult Owl Auditory System Expanded by Juvenile Experience. *Science* 279, no. 5356:1531–33.

———. 2002. Instructed Learning in the Auditory Localization Pathway of the Barn Owl. *Nature* 417, no. 6886:322–28.

Kosslyn, S. M. 1994. *Image and Brain: The Resolution of the Imagery Debate.* Cambridge, MA: MIT Press.

Kovecses, Z. 1988. *The Language of Love: The Semantics of Passion in Conversational English.* Lewisburg, PA: Bucknell University Press.

———. 2000. *Metaphor and Emotion: Language, Culture, and Body in Human Feeling.* Cambridge: Cambridge University Press.

Lakoff, G. 1987. *Women, Fire, and Dangerous Things: What Categories Reveal about the Mind.* Chicago: University of Chicago Press.

———. 1996. *Moral Politics: What Conservatives Know That Liberals Don't.* Chicago: University of Chicago Press.

———. Forthcoming. The Neural Theory of Metaphor. In *The Cambridge Handbook of Metaphor and Thought,* edited by R. Gibbs. Cambridge: Cambridge University Press.

Lakoff, G., and M. Johnson. 1980. *Metaphors We Live By.* Chicago: University of Chicago Press.

———. 1999. *Philosophy in the Flesh: The Embodied Mind and Its Challenge to Western Thought.* New York: Basic Books.

Lakoff, G., and R. Núñez. 2000. *Where Mathematics Comes From: How the Embodied Mind Brings Mathematics into Being*. New York: Basic Books.

Lakoff, G., and M. Turner. 1989. *More Than Cool Reason: A Field-Guide to Poetic Metaphor*. Chicago: University of Chicago Press.

Langacker, R. 1986. *Foundations of Cognitive Grammar*. 2 vols. Stanford, CA: Stanford University Press.

Langer, S. 1947. *Problems of Art*. New York: Charles Scribner's Sons.

———. 1953. *Feeling and Form: A Theory of Art*. New York: Scribner.

———. 1967. *Mind: An Essay on Human Feeling*. Baltimore: Johns Hopkins University Press.

Larson, S. 1993a. Computer Models of Melodic Continuation and Key Determination. Presentation to the Society for Music Perception and Cognition in Philadelphia. Available from Center for Research on Concepts and Cognition, 510 North Fess, Bloomington, IN 47408, as CRCC Technical Report #77.

———. 1993b. Scale-Degree Function: A Theory of Expressive Meaning and Its Application to Aural-skills Pedagogy. *Journal of Music Theory Pedagogy* 7:69–84.

———. 1994a. Another Look at Schenker's Counterpoint. *Indiana Theory Review* 15, no. 1:35–52.

———. 1994b. Musical Forces, Step Collections, Tonal Pitch Space, and Melodic Expectation. In *Proceedings of the Third International Conference on Music Perception and Cognition*, 227–29. Liège, Belgium.

———. 1997. The Problem of Prolongation in Tonal Music: Terminology, Perception, and Expressive Meaning. *Journal of Music Theory* 41, no. 1:101–36.

———. 1997–98. Musical Forces and Melodic Patterns. *Theory and Practice* 22–23:55–71.

———. 1999. Swing and Motive in Three Performances by Oscar Peterson. *Journal of Music Theory* 43, no. 2:283–313.

———. 2002. Musical Forces, Melodic Expectation, and Jazz Melody. *Music Perception* 19, no. 3:351–85.

———. Forthcoming. Musical Forces and Melodic Expectation: Comparing Computer Models and Experimental Results. *Music Perception*.

Larson, S., and L. VanHandel. 2005. Measuring Musical Forces. *Music Perception* 23, no. 2:119–36.

Leder, D. 1990. *The Absent Body*. Chicago: University of Chicago Press.

LeDoux, J. 2002. *Synaptic Self: How Our Brains Become Who We Are*. New York: Viking.

Lee, D. N. 1993. Body-Environment Coupling. In *The Perceived Self: Ecological and Interpersonal Sources of Self-Knowledge*, edited by U. Neisser, 43–67. Cambridge: Cambridge University Press.

Lee, D. N., and E. Aronson. 1974. Visual Proprioceptive Control of Standing in Human Infants. *Perception and Psychophysics* 15:529–32.

Lerdahl, F. 1996. Calculating Tonal Tension. *Music Perception* 13, no. 3:319–63.

———. 2001. *Tonal Pitch Space*. New York: Oxford University Press.

Levins, R., and R. Lewontin. 1985. *The Dialectical Biologist*. Cambridge, MA: Harvard University Press.

Lewkowicz, D. J., and G. Turkewitz. 1981. Intersensory Interaction in Newborns: Modification of Visual Preferences Following Exposure to Sound. *Child Development* 52, no. 3:827–32.

Magnani, L., and N. Nersessian, eds. 2002. *Model-Based Reasoning: Science, Technology, Values.* New York: Kluwer Academic/Plenum Publishers.

Maring, B. 2003. *The Metaphorical Bases of Children's Developing Theories of Mind.* Ph.D. diss., Department of Psychology, University of Oregon.

Maturana, H. R., and F. J. Varela. 1998. *The Tree of Knowledge: The Biological Roots of Human Understanding.* Rev. ed. Translated by Robert Paolucci. Boston: Shambhala Press.

McGrew, W. C. 1998. Culture in Nonhuman Primates? *Annual Review of Anthropology* 27:301–28.

McNeill, D. 1992. *Hand and Mind: What Gestures Reveal about Thought.* Chicago: University of Chicago Press.

Meltzoff, A., and R. W. Borton. 1979. Intermodal Matching by Human Neonates. *Nature* 282, no. 5737:403–4.

Meltzoff, A., and M. Moore. 1977. Imitation of Facial and Manual Gestures by Human Neonates. *Science* 198:75–78.

———. 1983. Newborn Infants Imitate Adult Facial Gestures. *Child Development* 54:702–9.

———. 1989. Imitations in Newborn Infants: Exploring the Range of Gestures Imitated and the Underlying Mechanisms. *Developmental Psychology* 25:954–62.

———. 1995. Infants' Understanding of People and Things: From Body Imitation to Folk Psychology. In *The Body and the Self,* edited by J. Bermudez, A. Marcel, and N. Eilan, 43–69. Cambridge, MA: MIT Press.

Merleau-Ponty, Maurice. 1962. *Phenomenology of Perception.* Translated by Colin Smith. London: Routledge.

Merzenich, M. M., R. J. Nelson, J. H. Kaas, M. P. Stryker, W. M. Jenkins, J. M. Zook, M. S. Cynader, and A. Schoppmann. 1987. Variability in Hand Surface Representations in Areas 3b and 1 in Adult Owl and Squirrel Monkeys. *Journal of Comparative Neurology* 258, no. 2:281–96.

Millikan, R. G. 2000. *On Clear and Confused Ideas: An Essay on Substance Concepts.* Cambridge: Cambridge University Press.

Montgomery, J. W. 1993. Haptic Recognition of Children with Specific Language Impairment: Effects of Response Modality. *Journal of Speech and Hearing Research* 36, no. 1:98–104.

Morgan, R. 1980. Musical Time/Musical Space. *Critical Inquiry* 6:527–38.

Muller, B. Forthcoming. Metaphor, Environmental Receptivity, and Architectural Design. In *Symbolic Landscapes,* edited by G. Backhaus and J. Murungi. Lanham, MD: Lexington Books.

Narayanan, S. 1997a. *Embodiment in Language Understanding: Sensory-Motor Representations for Metaphoric Reasoning about Event Descriptions.* Ph.D. diss., Department of Computer Science, University of California, Berkeley.

———. 1997b. KARMA: Knowledge-Based Active Representations for Metaphor and Aspect. Master's thesis, University of California, Berkeley.

———. 1997c. Talking the Talk Is Like Walking the Walk: A Computational Model of Verbal Aspect. In *Proceedings of the Nineteenth Annual Conference of the Cognitive Science Society.*

Needham, A. 1998. Infants' Use of Featural Information in the Segregation of Stationary Objects. *Infant Behavior and Development* 21:47–75.

Newell, A., and H. Simon. 1976. Computer Science as Empirical Inquiry: Symbols and Search. *Communications of the ACM* 19:113–26.

Pederson, E., E. Danziger, S. Levinson, S. Kita, G. Senft, and D. Wilkins. 1998. Semantic Typology and Spatial Conceptualization. *Language* 74:557–89.

Pelto, W. 1994. An Alternative to Rule Memorization for Written Theory. Presentation to a special panel, Applying a Theory of Expressive Meaning in the Written- and Aural-Theory Classrooms, for the College Music Society.

Polanyi, M. 1969. *Knowing and Being.* Edited by M. Grene. Chicago: University of Chicago Press.

Putnam, H. 1981. *Reason, Truth, and History.* Cambridge: Cambridge University Press.

———. 1987. *The Many Faces of Realism.* LaSalle, IL: Open Court.

———. 1988. *Representation and Reality.* Cambridge, MA: MIT Press.

———. 1995. *Pragmatics: An Open Question.* Oxford: Basil Blackwell.

Quine, W. V. O. 1951. Two Dogmas of Empiricism. *Philosophical Review* 60:20–43.

Quirk, G. J., G. K. Russo, J. L. Barron, and K. Lebron. 2000. The Role of Ventromedial Prefrontal Cortex in the Recovery of Extinguished Fear. *Journal of Neuroscience* 20, no. 16:6225–31.

Regier, T. 1996. *The Human Semantic Potential Spatial Language and Constrained Connectionism.* Cambridge, MA: MIT Press.

Richards, I. A., and C. K. Ogden. 1923. *The Meaning of Meaning.* New York: Harcourt, Brace and Co.

Rizzolatti, G., and L. Craighero. 2004. The Mirror-Neuron System. *Annual Review of Neuroscience* 27:169–92.

Rizzolatti, G., L. Fogassi, and V. Gallese. 2000. Cortical Mechanisms Subserving Object Grasping and Action Recognition: A New View on the Cortical Motor Functions. In *The Cognitive Neurosciences,* 2nd ed., edited by M. S. Gazzaniga, 539–52. Cambridge, MA: MIT Press.

———. 2001. Neurophysiological Mechanisms Underlying the Understanding and Imitation of Action. *Nature Neuroscience Review* 2:661–70.

———. 2002. Motor and Cognitive Functions of the Ventral Premotor Cortex. *Current Opinion in Neurobiology* 12, no. 2:149–54.

Rizzolatti, G., and M. Gentilucci. 1988. Motor and Visual-Motor Functions of the Premotor Cortex. In *Neurobiology of Neocortex,* edited by P. Rakic and W. Singer, 269–84. Chichester, NY: Wiley.

Rochat, P. 1987. Mouthing and Grasping in Neonates: Evidence for the Early Detection of What Hard and Soft Substances Afford for Action. *Infant Behavior and Development* 10:435–49.

Rohrer, T. 2001a. Pragmatism, Ideology and Embodiment: William James and the Philosophical Foundations of Cognitive Linguistics. In *Language and Ideology: Cogni-*

tive Theoretic Approaches, vol. 1, edited by René Dirven, Bruce Hawkins, and Esra Sandikcioglu, 49–81. Amsterdam: John Benjamins.

———. 2001b. Understanding through the Body: fMRI and ERP Studies of Metaphoric and Literal Language. Paper presented at the Seventh International Cognitive Linguistics Association conference, Santa Barbara, CA, July.

———. 2005. Image Schemata in the Brain. In Hampe and Grady 2005, 165–96.

———. Forthcoming. Embodiment and Experientialism. In *The Oxford Handbook of Cognitive Linguistics,* edited by D. Geeraerts and Hubert Cuyckens. New York: Oxford University Press.

Rorty, R. 1989. The Contingency of Language. In *Contingency, Irony, and Solidarity,* 3–22. Cambridge: Cambridge University Press.

Saslaw, J. 1997–98. Life Forces: Conceptual Structures in Schenker's *Free Composition* and Schoenberg's *The Musical Idea. Theory and Practice* 22–23:17–34.

Savage-Rumbaugh, S., R. A. Sevcik, and W. D. Hopkins. 1988. Symbolic Cross-Modal Transfer in Two Species of Chimpanzees. *Child Development* 59, no. 3:617–25.

Schenker, H. 1932/1969. *Five Graphic Music Analyses.* Edited by F. Salzer. New York: Dover.

———. 1979. *Free Composition.* Translated by E. Oster. New York: Longman.

Schwoebel, J., C. B. Boronat, and H. B. Coslett. 2002. The Man Who Executed "Imagined" Movements: Evidence for Dissociable Components of the Body Schema. *Brain and Cognition* 50, no. 1:1–16.

Searle, J. 1969. *Speech Acts: An Essay in the Philosophy of Language.* Cambridge: Cambridge University Press.

———. 1979. Metaphor. In *Expression and Meaning: Studies in the Theory of Speech Acts,* 76–116. Cambridge: Cambridge University Press.

Sessions, R. 1941. The Composer and His Message. In *The Intent of the Artist,* edited by A. Centeno, 101–34. Princeton, NJ: Princeton University Press.

Sheets-Johnstone, M. 1999. *The Primacy of Movement.* Amsterdam: John Benjamins.

Shelton, J. R., E. Fouch, and A. Caramazza. 1998. The Selective Sparing of Body Part Knowledge: A Case Study. *Neurocase* 4:339–51.

Slater, A. M., and V. Morrison. 1985. Shape Constancy and Slant Perception at Birth. *Perception* 14:337–44.

Sperry, R. W. 1943. Effect of a 180-Degree Rotation of the Retinal Field on Visuomotor Coordination. *Journal of Experimental Zoology* 92:263–79.

Stawarska, B. 2003. Merleau-Ponty in Dialogue with the Cognitive Sciences in Light of Recent Imitation Research. *Philosophy Today, SPEP Supplement,* pp. 89–99.

Steen, G. 1997. *Metaphor in Literary Reception: A Theoretical and Empirical Study of Understanding Metaphor in Literary Discourse.* Amsterdam: Vrije Universiteit te Amsterdam.

Stern, D. 1985. *The Interpersonal World of the Infant: A View from Psychoanalysis and Developmental Psychology.* New York: Basic Books.

Stevenson, C. L. 1944. *Ethics and Language.* New Haven, CT: Yale University Press.

Strauss, Erwin. 1966. *Phenomenological Psychology.* New York: Basic Books.

Suzuki, K., A. Yamadori, and T. Fujii. 1997. Category Specific Comprehension Deficit Restricted to Body Parts. *Neurocase* 3:193–200.

Sweetser, E. 1990. *From Etymology to Pragmatics: Metaphorical and Cultural Aspects of Semantic Structure*. Cambridge: Cambridge University Press.

———. 1998. Regular Metaphoricity in Gesture: Bodily Based Models of Speech Interaction. In *Actes du 16ème Congrès International des Linguistes*. CD-ROM, Elsevier.

Talmy, Leonard. 1985. Force Dynamics in Thought and Language. *Chicago Linguistics Society* 21, pt 2, *Possession in Causatives and Agentivity,* 293–337.

Taub, S. 1997. *Language in the Body: Iconicity and Metaphor in American Sign Language*. Ph.D. diss., Department of Linguistics, University of California, Berkeley.

Tillich, P. 1957. *The Dynamics of Faith*. New York: Harper and Row.

Tomasello, M., S. Savage-Rumbaugh, and A. C. Kruger. 1993. Imitative Learning of Actions on Objects by Children, Chimpanzees, and Enculturated Chimpanzees. *Child Development* 64, no. 6:1688–1705.

Trevarthen, Colwyn. 1993. The Self Born of Intersubjectivity: The Psychology of an Infant Communicating. In *The Perceived Self: Ecological and Interpersonal Sources of Knowledge,* edited by U. Neisser, 121–73. Cambridge: Cambridge University Press.

Tucker, Don. Forthcoming. *Mind from Body: Experience from Neural Structure*. Oxford: Oxford University Press.

Turing, A. M. 1937. On Computable Numbers, with an Application to the Entscheidungsproblem. *Proceedings of London Mathematical Society,* 2nd. ser., 42:230–65.

———. 1950. Computing Machinery and Intelligence. *Mind* 59, no. 236:433–60.

Turner, M. 1991. *Reading Minds: The Study of English in the Age of Cognitive Science*. Princeton, NJ: Princeton University Press.

van Gelder, T. 1995. What Might Cognition Be, If Not Computation? *Journal of Philosophy* 92, no. 7:345–81.

Varela, F., E. Thompson, and E. Rosch. 1991. *The Embodied Mind: Cognitive Science and Human Experience*. Cambridge, MA: MIT Press.

Warrington, E. K., and T. Shallice. 1984. Category Specific Semantic Impairments. *Brain* 107:829–54.

Winner, E., M. Engel, and H. Gardner. 1980. Misunderstanding of Metaphor: What's the Problem. *Journal of Experimental Child Psychology* 30:22–32.

Winter, S. 2001. *A Clearing in the Forest: Law, Life, and Mind*. Chicago: University of Chicago Press.

Wright, H. G. 2002. *Means, Ends, and Medical Care*. Ph.D. diss., Department of Philosophy, University of Oregon.

Young, Iris Marion. 1980. "Throwing Like a Girl." *Human Studies* 3:141–59.

Zbikowski, L. 2002. *Conceptualizing Music: Cognitive Structure, Theory, and Analysis*. Oxford: Oxford University Press.

Zuckerkandl, V. 1969. *Sound and Symbol: Music and the External World*. Princeton, NJ: Princeton University Press.